Critical Essays on
W. B. Yeats

Critical Essays on
W. B. Yeats

Richard J. Finneran

G. K. Hall & Co. • Boston, Massachusetts

Library of Congress Cataloging-in-Publication Data
  Main entry under title:

Critical essays on W. B. Yeats.

  (Critical essays on modern British literature —
  Bibliography: p. 246
  Includes index.
  1. Yeats, W. B. (William Butler), 1865–1939 —
Criticism and interpretation — Addresses, essays, lectures. I. Finneran, Richard J.
II. Series.
PR5907.C75   1986   821'.8   85-30207

ISBN 0-8161-8758-4

This publication is printed on permanent/durable acid-free paper
MANUFACTURED IN THE UNITED STATES OF AMERICA

CRITICAL ESSAYS ON MODERN BRITISH LITERATURE

Richard J. Finneran's original collection of essays is unique in the sense that rather than choose among the more than 200 items that comprise the annual critical output of Yeats scholarship, he has sought out fourteen of the world's leading Yeats critics and asked them to choose their own most appropriate essays for inclusion in this volume. The result is a dazzling display by our most respected Yeats scholars, on the full range of subjects in Yeats criticism. Published chronologically in the order of their original appearance, the essays span the last three decades of scholarship. Finneran's introduction is a brief but comprehensive essay and descriptive bibliography of the history of Yeats criticism. Concentrating on book-length studies, Finneran emphasizes "studies of the poetry or books of broad general interest." He also appends to the volume a critical bibliography of previous collections of already published Yeats criticism. The current collection cannot help but be the standard anthology of Yeats scholarship of the last thirty years.

University of Delaware   ZACK BOWEN, GENERAL EDITOR

CONTENTS

INTRODUCTION

Among the earliest preserved manuscripts of W. B. Yeats is a draft of a letter to one Mary Cronan, an early friend of whom little is known. Sending her a poem, Yeats explained that "my peculiaritys . . . will never be done justice to until they have become classics and are set for examinations."[1] At the time he was probably no more than nineteen years old (if that), and he had yet to publish a single word. But what might have struck Miss Cronan as youthful hyperbole has in fact come to pass, at least in the main. Yeats is now the acknowledged master of poets writing in English in this century, and for many decades he has been the subject of examinations at all levels and in many countries. Whether his magnificent achievement has been done "justice to" — or whether it ever can be — is of course another question.

Yeats scholarship — the "Yeats industry," if you will — is a field unto itself. The first published commentary on Yeats, an 1887 review by his friend Katharine Tynan, prophesied that Yeats would "take high place among the world's future singers."[2] A bibliography of criticism that began with that notice and continued through 1971 listed almost 6,000 items, and it deliberately excluded certain materials, most notably the large body of work on Yeats in Japanese.[3] Nor are there any signs of a decline in scholarly output. The annual bibliographies of criticism that K. P. S. Jochum has been contributing to *Yeats: An Annual of Critical and Textual Studies* since 1983 have averaged about 200 items per year. What follows, then, is necessarily a highly selective sketch of Yeats criticism.[4]

By 1891 Yeats had already published a poetic drama (*Mosada*, 1886), a collection of poetry (*The Wanderings of Oisin and Other Poems*, 1889), and a novelette and short story (*John Sherman and Dhoya*, 1891) — thus foreshadowing the continuing variety of his oeuvre — but much of the critical attention he received in his early years was connected with his efforts to revive or, perhaps more accurately, to create a distinctive and cohesive Anglo-Irish literature. By 1894 this movement was sufficiently established as to require its own historian. Writing in *The Irish Literary Revival: Its History, Pioneers and Possibilities*, W. P. Ryan emphasized the dreamer in Yeats, warning him that he should develop "other characteris-

1

tics to the same degree as that already attained by his imaginative faculty and power of vision" and that "he must shake himself free from the passing craze of occultism and symbolism, and realise also that the universe is not tenanted solely by soulths and sheogues."[5]

By the end of the century Yeats was widely regarded as an important younger poet. In a study essentially completed in the autumn of 1899, the influential critic William Archer described Yeats as "the incarnation of the Irish Kelt" and praised his "astonishing union of primitive imagination and feeling with cultivated and consciously artistic expression."[6] Yeats's American lecture tour of 1903–4 resulted in the first separate study of his work, *William Butler Yeats and the Irish Literary Revival* by Horatio Sheafe Krans, though the volume offered little beyond summary and paraphrase and included what was by then the commonplace attack on Yeats's "recondite imagery."[7]

Yeats was now devoting much of his time and energy to the Abbey Theatre, and he published relatively little new verse. Indeed, some believed that the appearance of the sumptuous eight-volume *Collected Works in Verse and Prose* in 1908 signaled the end of a poetic career, a view that continued into the next decade. In what is arguably the best of the contemporary books on Yeats, *W. B. Yeats: A Critical Study* (1915), Forrest Reid suggested that Yeats's powers were fading:

> For that declination from the highest beauty to a lower beauty, in which skill and theory occupy a larger place and inspiration and emotion a smaller, seems to be the inevitable fate of every artist, once he has reached his own particular perfection; and to the poet, one knows not why, it seems to come sooner than to others.[8]

Still, this opinion was not universally accepted. In the very next year, 1916, Yeats was the subject of two full-length studies, a naive investigation of his sources by Patty Gurd (*The Early Poetry of William Butler Yeats*) and a survey of the canon by his future biographer, Joseph Hone (*William Butler Yeats: The Poet in Contemporary Ireland*). Yeats also figured prominently in Ernest Boyd's important *Ireland's Literary Renaissance* (1916; rev. 1922).

While these and other scholars and critics were interpreting his work and debating his achievement, Yeats was in the process of transforming himself from an important literary figure to one of the major writers of literature in English, a process that became evident in such volumes as *Responsibilities* (1914; rev. 1916), *The Wild Swans at Coole* (1917; rev. 1919), and *Michael Robartes and the Dancer* (1921). In 1923 his stature was confirmed when he became the first Irishman to be awarded the Nobel Prize for Literature. Other honors followed, and Yeats might well have been expected to settle into a comfortable if unproductive old age. Instead, his best work was yet to come. In 1928 he published *The Tower*, perhaps the finest single volume of lyric poetry in his career. This was followed by another masterpiece, *The Winding Stair and Other Poems* (1933). The canonical *Collected Poems* also appeared in 1933. As usual, he was also publishing important work in other genres — plays, essays, criticism, and that volume which defies a simple label, *A Vision* (1925, rev. 1937).

By the 1930s Yeats was such a fixture in modern poetry that negative evaluations by the younger generation were inevitable. In particular, Yeats was attacked for a lack of involvement in the "real" world, especially the world of politics. Representative is the discussion of Yeats by Stephen Spender in *The Destructive Element: A Study of Modern Writers and Beliefs*, where he suffers badly in comparison with W. H. Auden and T. S. Eliot: although Yeats "has much wisdom, he offers no philosophy of life," and his poetry is "devoid of any unifying moral subject."[9] Even J. H. Pollock, writing on Yeats in the "Noted Irish Lives" series, concluded that he was an artist of "exquisite technique, but limited appeal."[10] Not all the voices of the 1930s were negative, of course. In *Aspects of Modern Poetry*, for instance, Edith Sitwell described some of Yeats's recent poems as "undoubtedly the greatest lyrics of the last hundred years, because of their intense fusion of spirit and matter, because of their overwhelming fire and their strange old-world wisdom, sung in the voice of one who is impatient with 'the loveless dust.' "[11] For his part, Yeats continued to confound his critics by continuing to produce work of major significance, as in the lyrics collected in *New Poems* (1938) and *Last Poems and Two Plays* (1939).

Yeats died on 28 January 1939. Within a short time, two events occurred that securely established his critical reputation. The first was a lecture entitled "The Poetry of W. B. Yeats," presented at the Abbey Theatre in June 1940 by T. S. Eliot, after Yeats's death clearly the most important contemporary English writer. Although some of Eliot's earlier remarks on Yeats had not been consistently positive, by the second sentence of his talk he had described Yeats as "the greatest poet of our time — certainly the greatest in this language, and so far as I am able to judge, in any language." He concluded that Yeats

> was one of those few whose history is the history of their own time, who are a part of the consciousness of an age which cannot be understood without them. This is a very high position to assign to him, but I believe that it is one which is secure.[12]

The second event was the publication of the special Yeats issue of *The Southern Review* in the winter of 1941–42. This issue contained fifteen essays by some of the leading critics of the time; a large proportion of them have become seminal documents in the history of Yeats scholarship. One thinks, for example, of Austin Warren's sympathetic essay on Yeats's occult interests ("Religio Poetae") or of "Yeats's Romanticism: Notes and Suggestions" by Allen Tate, which concludes with the accurate prophecy that "the study of Yeats in the coming generation is likely to overdo the scholarly procedure, and the result will be the occultation of poetry which I believe is nearer the center of our main traditions of sensibility and thought than the poetry of Eliot or of Pound. Yeats's special qualities will instigate special studies of great ingenuity, but the more direct and difficult problem of the poetry itself will be delayed."[13]

The first decade of scholarship after Yeats's death was dominated by biographical criticism. An authorized biography by Joseph Hone, *W. B. Yeats: 1865–1939*, was published in 1943 (2d ed., 1962). Hone had virtually unlimited access to Yeats's manuscripts, but unfortunately he chose to paraphrase much of that material without so informing his readers. Still, until the publication of the new authorized biography by Roy Foster, Hone's work offers the most details on Yeats's life. Less valuable is *W. B. Yeats: Man and Poet* (1949, 2d ed., 1962) by A. Norman Jeffares, which likewise is long on paraphrase and quotation and short on analysis. By far the best biographical study — and perhaps the earliest book on Yeats that remains required reading for any serious student — is Richard Ellmann's *Yeats: The Man and the Masks* (1948; new ed., 1979). Ellmann concentrates on the sense of division that Yeats constantly felt and his equally constant search for unity. He offers an excellent account of Yeats's occult interests and of his relationship with his father, John Butler Yeats, a painter of some distinction. Other important books of this first decade are Louis MacNeice's *The Poetry of W. B. Yeats* (1941), a solid introductory study; Peter Ure's *Towards a Mythology: Studies in the Poetry of W. B. Yeats* (1946), a discussion of Yeats's use of myth with particular reference to *A Vision*; and Donald A. Stauffer's *The Golden Nightingale: Essays on Some Principles of Poetry in the Lyrics of William Butler Yeats* (1949), a demonstration of the overall unity of Yeats's work. Of less note is *The Development of William Butler Yeats* (1942; 2d ed., 1960) by V. K. Narayana Menon.

Yeats scholarship in the 1950s had an auspicious beginning with T. R. Henn's *The Lonely Tower: Studies in the Poetry of W. B. Yeats* (1950; 2d ed., 1965), a work that also discusses the plays and *A Vision*. Henn is particularly good on the Irish background to Yeats's work, and his chapter on "Painter and Poet" is a pioneering study of visual sources. An equally important volume is *W. B. Yeats, Self-Critic: A Study of His Early Verse* (1951) by Thomas Parkinson, a cogent account of the development of Yeats's style and of the intimate connection between style and content. Parkinson stresses the effect of Yeats's work in the theatre on his poetic style. The third major book of this decade was Richard Ellmann's *The Identity of Yeats* (1954; 2d ed., 1964), a study that treats a number of related topics and draws extensively on unpublished materials. Ellmann concludes that Yeats's art is characterized by "affirmative capability."[14] A volume of limited value is *W. B. Yeats: The Tragic Phase* (1951) by Vivienne Koch, which uses a New Critical approach on thirteen late lyrics. Virginia Moore's *The Unicorn: William Butler Yeats' Search for*

Reality (1954) is more important for the unpublished material it cites than for the analysis of its several topics.

The 1960s marks the highpoint of Yeats scholarship, with the various celebrations surrounding the 1965 centenary producing a flood of publication. Among the most important books of this period are Edward Engelberg's *The Vast Design: Patterns in W. B. Yeats's Aesthetic* (1964) and Thomas R. Whitaker's *Swan and Shadow: Yeats's Dialogue with History* (1964). Engelberg shows how Yeats's aesthetic is organized around various pairs of opposites and discusses his attempts to reconcile them. He argues that Yeats sought a "single image" that would be "an heroic image, one of the 'heraldic images' which it was his aim to restore to literature."[15] Whitaker suggests that Yeats sees history variously as "a bright reflection of the poet's self" (swan) or "a shadowy force opposed to that self" (shadow), and that the constant conflict between those views ultimately issues in Yeats's insistence on embracing the full self to achieve transcendence.[16] Also of particular interest is *Yeats and Georgian Ireland* (1966) by Donald T. Torchiana, an exhaustive account of Yeats's relationship with Anglo-Irish tradition.

The most important book on the poetry from this period is Thomas Parkinson's *W. B. Yeats: The Later Poetry*, which examines many topics related to the later poems and makes effective use of manuscript materials. The book includes a seminal chapter on Yeats's prosody and another on the value of Yeats to contemporary poets. Two volumes by Jon Stallworthy offer studies of the manuscripts of selected poems: *Between the Lines: Yeats's Poetry in the Making* (1963) and *Vision and Revision in Yeat's "Last Poems"* (1969). George T. Wright's *The Poet in the Poem: The Personae of Eliot, Yeats, and Pound* (1960) argues that Yeats's total vision is larger than that of his individual speakers. In *The Lyric of Tragedy* (1961) B. L. Reid offers some cogent explications of selected poems, though the comparison of lyric poetry with tragic drama is forced. More restricted in scope are Arra M. Garab's *Beyond Byzantium: The Last Phase of Yeats's Career* (1969), which offers relatively little that is new; and Allen R. Grossmann's *Poetic Knowledge in the Early Yeats: A Study of "The Wind Among the Reeds"* (1969), an interesting study of that 1899 volume, with much attention to Yeats's sources. Also concerned with sources are Giorgio Melchiori's important *The Whole Mystery of Art: Pattern into Poetry in the Work of W. B. Yeats* (1960), which concentrates on visual ones; and F. A. C. Wilson's *W. B. Yeats and Tradition* (1958) and *Yeats's Iconography* (1960), which discuss Yeats's indebtedness primarily to Neoplatonic tradition.

In the 1970s the specialization of Yeats studies that Allen Tate predicted was everywhere evident. Most of the books on the poetry considered only a selected segment of the canon: we are offered, for instance, two books on the early verse (Frank Hughes Murphy, *Yeats's Early Poetry*, 1975; Thomas L. Byrd, Jr., *The Early Poetry of W. B. Yeats:*

The Poetic Quest, 1978), and three on the later poetry (Shankar Mokashi-Punekar, *Interpretations of the Later Poems of W. B. Yeats*, 1973; Giacomo Cosentino, *Studies in Yeats's Later Poems*, 1974; Stanley Sultan, *Yeats at His Last*, 1975). Some critics chose to examine a particular kind of poetry, as in Robert Snukal's *High Talk: The Philosophical Poetry of W. B. Yeats* (1973) or Colin Meir's *The Ballads and Songs of W. B. Yeats: The Anglo-Irish Heritage in Subject and Style* (1974); or to employ a particular approach, as in Stuart Hirschberg's *At the Top of the Tower: Yeats's Poetry Explored through "A Vision"* (1979). Others simply chose the poems they wanted to discuss: Daniel Albright's *The Myth Against Myth: A Study of Yeats's Imagination in Old Age* (1972), for instance, is essentially a study of four poems, including one of Yeats's earliest. While all of those studies contained occasional insights, for most students they were less rewarding than the broader studies of the previous decades by such scholars as Ellmann, Henn, and Parkinson. Perhaps the single exception is Daniel A. Harris's *Yeats: Coole Park & Ballylee* (1974), which—although still on a limited selection of poems—combines careful research with original and provocative thought.

Of the general studies from this decade, two are of particular note.[17] In *The Mysteries of Identity: A Theme in Modern Literature* (1977), Robert Langbaum devotes two long chapters to Yeats, chronicling his search for a total identity. In *The Rhizome and the Flower: The Perennial Philosophy—Yeats and Jung* (1980), James Olney develops the extensive parallels between the two figures, tracing them to common sources in ancient philosophy. Olney demonstrates in great detail that

> the Yeatsian and Jungian blossoms that we now observe are of the present and of consciousness, but there is both an historical rhizome and a psychical rhizome from which they draw their life, for those two momentary flowers have their roots, alike and together, in ancient Greece and in the collective depths of the unconscious.[18]

The emphasis on specialized studies continues in the present decade. Recent books on the poetry, for instance, have included one that concentrates on three lines (James Lovic Allen, *Yeats's Epitaph: A Key to Symbolic Unity in His Life and Work*, 1982) and another that unsuccessfully attempts to locate a single persona throughout the canon (Gale C. Schricker, *A New Species of Man: The Poetic Persona of W. B. Yeats*, 1982). More interesting are the chapters on Yeats in *The Modern Poetic Sequence: The Genius of Modern Poetry* (1983) by M. L. Rosenthal and Sally M. Gall. General studies of note include *Yeats* (1983) by Douglas Archibald, though it is more a series of essays than a survey of the career; *A Colder Eye: The Modern Irish Writers* (1983) by Hugh Kenner, in which Yeats figures prominently; *The Last Courtly Lover: Yeats and the Idea of Woman* (1983) by Gloria C. Kline; and *Philosophy of the Literary Symbolic* (1983) by Hazard Adams, which offers two provocative chapters on Yeats. Adams argues that "Yeats's thought . . . glorifies its own radical creativity, but it leads us not to regard that creativity as everything."[19]

The present decade is also characterized by intensive editorial activity. John S. Kelly and a series of coeditors are bringing out *The Collected Letters*, a complete edition of which the first was published in in 1986. Richard J. Finneran and George Mills Harper are co-General Editors of a Collected Edition of the Works, of which *The Poems* has already been published.[20] Also in progress is the Cornell Yeats, a multivolume edition of Yeats's manuscripts. The first poetry volume in the series, George Bornstein's edition of *The Island of Statues* and *Mosada*, will be published in 1986. When all these projects are completed, as well as the authorized biographies of Yeats by Roy Foster and of Mrs. Yeats by Ann Saddlemyer, scholars and critics will have extensive new materials to examine. The value of the study of the manuscripts, for example, has already been well documented in David R. Clark's *Yeats at Songs and Choruses* (1983), a cogent commentary on seven poems written between 1926 and 1931.

In a valuable essay-review of 1979, Thomas Parkinson cautioned that Yeats may have been "so over-documented as to paralyze the will" and that "what is required is a freshness of perception that makes for humane responsiveness."[21] One cannot argue with that assessment, but I would add in commentary that not only will the forthcoming editorial work generate new critical studies, but also that the essential greatness of Yeats's achievement will always inspire new attempts to do "justice" to his work.

RICHARD J. FINNERAN

Newcomb College, Tulane University

Notes

1. *The Letters of W. B. Yeats*, ed. Allan Wade (London: Rupert Hart-Davis, 1954), 30. Spelling was never one of Yeats's strong points.

2. Katherine Tynan, "Three Young Poets," *Irish Monthly* 15, no. 165 (March 1887):166–68.

3. K. P. S. Jochum, *W. B. Yeats: A Classified Bibliography of Criticism* (Urbana, Chicago, and London: University of Illinois Press, 1978). Jochum also lists some items from 1972 and 1973.

4. In particular, I will emphasize either studies of the poetry or books of broad general interest. Vast areas of the scholarship will thus be neglected, including what has become an increasingly important body of work on Yeats's plays. The most comprehensive surveys of Yeats criticism are the chapters by Richard J. Finneran in *Anglo-Irish Literature: A Review of Research* (New York: Modern Language Association, 1976), 216–314, and *Recent Research on Anglo-Irish Writers: A Supplement to "Anglo-Irish Literature: A Review of Research"* (New York: Modern Language Association, 1983), 85–153. Those essays will be revised and updated in *Anglo-Irish Literature: A Guide to Research*, scheduled for publication by the Modern Language Association in 1988. See also the introductions to the several collections of criticism listed in the Bibliography at the end of this volume.

5. W. P. Ryan, *The Irish Literary Revival: Its History, Pioneers and Possibilities* (London: the author, 1894), 135.

6. William Archer, *Poets of the Younger Generation* (London and New York: John Lane, The Bodley Head, 1902), 532. Like Ryan, Archer cautioned Yeats against using a "petrified, fossilised symbolism" (556).

7. Horatio Sheafe Krans, *William Butler Yeats and the Irish Literary Revival* (New York: McClure, Phillips, 1904), 105.

8. Forrest Reid, *W. B. Yeats: A Critical Study* (London: Martin Secker, 1915), 243.

9. Stephen Spender, *The Destructive Element: A Study of Modern Writers and Beliefs* (London: Jonathan Cape, 1935), 128.

10. J. H. Pollock, *William Butler Yeats* (London: Duckworth; Dublin: Talbot Press, 1935), 112.

11. Edith Sitwell, *Aspects of Modern Poetry* (London: Duckworth, 1935), 89. The quotation is from Yeats's "From the 'Antigone.' "

12. James Hall and Martin Steinmann, eds. *The Permanence of Yeats* (New York: Macmillan, 1950), 296–307. Quotations from 296 and 307.

13. Allen Tate, "Yeats's Romanticism: Notes and Suggestions," *Southern Review* 7, no. 3 (Winter 1941): 600. The cover gives the date as "Winter 1942," the title page and copyright notice as 1941.

14. Richard Ellmann, *The Identity of Yeats*, 2d ed. (London: Faber and Faber, 1964), 238.

15. Edward Engleberg, *The Vast Design: Patterns in W. B. Yeats's Aesthetic* ([Toronto]: University of Toronto Press, 1964), 210.

16. Thomas R. Whitaker, *Swan and Shadow: Yeats's Dialogue with History* (Chapel Hill: University of North Carolina Press, 1964), 4.

17. Although its title suggests a general study, Harold Bloom's *Yeats* (New York: Oxford University Press, 1970) is in fact an idiosyncratic study of Yeats's relationship to the Romantics and an attempt to offer a particular theory of literary influence.

18. James Olney, *The Rhizome and the Flower: The Perennial Philosophy — Yeats and Jung* (Berkeley, Los Angeles, London: University of California Press, 1980), 13.

19. Hazard Adams, *The Philosophy of the Literary Symbolic* (Tallahassee: Florida State University Press / University Presses of Florida, 1983), 323.

20. *The Poems: A New Edition*, ed. Richard J. Finneran (New York: Macmillan, 1983; London: Macmillan, 1984).

21. Thomas Parkinson, "Some Recent Work on Yeats: From Great Modern Poet to Canonical Classic," *Southern Review* 15, no. 3 (July 1979):742–52. The quotation is from p. 752.

ARTICLES AND ESSAYS

The Sacred Book of the Arts   Hugh Kenner*

The way out is via the door, how is it no one will use this method?
— Confucius

1. Catechism

Q: In "Among School Children" we read of a "Ledaean body." Where are we to seek information about that?

A: Not from the mythological dictionary, but as everybody knows, from the poem "Leda and the Swan."

Q: And where is this poem to be discovered?

A: On the previous page.

Q: Very good. You are on the way to noticing something. Now consider the last stanza of "Among School Children." After an apostrophe to "self-born mockers of man's enterprise" we read:

> Labour is blossoming or dancing where
> The body is not bruised to pleasure soul,
> Nor beauty born out of its own despair,
> Nor blear-eyed wisdom out of midnight oil.
> O chestnut-tree, great-rooted blossomer,
> Are you the leaf, the blossom or the bole?
> O body swayed to music, O brightening glance,
> How can we know the dancer from the dance?

That "where" is by its placing in the line made very emphatic. Its gesture implies a place or a state intensely real to Yeats. Does he print lines elsewhere that might be taken as descriptive of that place or state?

A: He does; in "Colonus' Praise," after invoking "immortal ladies" who "tread the ground / Dizzy with harmonious sound" (which invocation of course we are meant to connect with "O body swayed to music"), he goes on,

> And yonder in the gymnasts' garden thrives
> The self-sown, self-begotten shape that gives
> Athenian intellect its mastery . . .

*From *Gnomon: Essays on Contemporary Literature* (New York: McDowell, Obolensky, 1958), 9–29.

the self-born no longer a mocker, body and intellect thriving in unison, neither bruised to pleasure the other; and the miraculous olive-tree that, as he goes on to tell us, symbolizes that perfection, is to be connected with the domestic "chestnut-tree, great-rooted blossomer" of the famous peroration.

Q: Excellent, excellent. And now tell me where, in relation to "Among School Children," this song in praise of Colonus is to be found?

A: On the following page.

Q: You are answering today with admirable point and economy. Now tell me: were the three poems you have mentioned as bearing upon one another written, as it were, simultaneously?

A: I find by the chronology at the back of Mr. Ellmann's *Identity of Yeats* that the first was written nearly four years before the last. I notice furthermore that the arrangement of the poems in the volume we are discussing, *The Tower*, is far from chronological. "Sailing to Byzantium" (Sept. 26, 1926), with which it begins, was written *after* "Among School Children" (June 14, 1926), which is located two-thirds of the way through the book. In between there are poems dating as far back as 1919, and the volume ends with "All Souls' Night," 1920.

Q: We should be lost without these American scholars. You would say, then, that the arrangement of poems within the volume was deliberate rather than casual or merely chronological.

A: I would indeed. But wait, I have just noticed something else. In "Sailing to Byzantium," at the beginning of the book, the speaker has abandoned the sensual land of "dying generations" and is asking the "sages standing in God's holy fire" to emerge from it and be his singing-masters. At the end, in "All Souls' Night," he announces that he has "mummy truths to tell" and would tell them to some mind that despite cannon-fire from every quarter of the world, can stay

> Wound in mind's pondering
> As mummies in the mummy-cloth are wound.

In the former poem he was calling forth sages to teach him; throughout "All Souls' Night" he is calling up ghosts to hear him. Pupil has become master.

Q: How often must I enjoin precision on you? It is the land of sensual *music* he has left: bird-song, love-songs. "All Souls' Night" opens, by contrast, with the formal tolling of "the great Christ Church Bell," like the "great cathedral gong" that dissipates "night walkers' song" in "Byzantium." Furthermore, there is a calling-up of ghosts near the beginning of the book too, in the poem called "The Tower," where he summons them not (as later) to instruct them but to ask a question. What else have you noticed?

A: Why, it gets more and more deliberate as one examines it. He began the volume by renouncing his body; he ends it in the possession of disembodied thought:

> Such thought—such thought have I that hold it tight
> Till meditation master all its parts . . .
> Such thought, that in it bound
> I need no other thing,

Wound in mind's wandering
As mummies in the mummy-cloth are wound.

Earlier he had expected to need the body of a jeweled bird. Through that volume, *The Tower*, runs a dramatic progression if I ever saw one. And the presence of such a progression, once it is discerned, modifies all the parts. Now I have a theory . . .

Q: Stop, you grow prolix. Write it out, write it out as an explanation that I may read at my leisure. And please refrain from putting in many footnotes that tire the eyes.

2. Explanation

"Among School Children," to begin with that again, is as centrifugal a major poem as exists in the language. Whoever encounters it out of the context Yeats carefully provided for it, for instance in an Anthology Appointed to be Taught in Colleges, will find himself after twenty minutes seeking out who Leda was and what Yeats made of her, and identifying the daughter of the swan with Maud Gonne (excursus on her biography, with anecdotes) and determining in what official capacity, through what accidents of a destiny sought and ironically accepted, the poet found himself doubling as school inspector. So true is this of the majority of his major poems, that the anthologists generally restrict themselves to his minor ones, his critics practice mostly a bastard mode of biography, and his exegetists a Pécuchet's industry of copying parallel passages from *A Vision* (first and second versions), from letters and diaries, from unpublished drafts, and occasionally from other poems. Even Dr. Leavis calls his poetry "little more than a marginal comment on the main activities of his life." Occasionally someone feels that Yeats' poems need to be reclaimed for the modern critic's gallery of self-sufficient objects, and rolling up his sleeves offers to explain "Two Songs from a Play" without benefit of *A Vision*. This requires several thousand words of quasi-paraphrase. The least gesture of unannounced originality on a poet's part suffices to baffle critical presupposition completely—and the two regnant presuppositions of the mid-twentieth century—the old one, that poems reflect lives and announce doctrines, the new one, that poems are self-contained or else imperfect—are rendered helpless by Yeats' most radical, most casual, and most characteristic maneuver: he was an architect, not a decorator; he didn't accumulate poems, he wrote books.

It would have been surprising if he had not, preoccupied as he was with sacred writings. When he functioned as a critic, as in his essay on Shelley or his useful generalizations on Shakespeare, it was the oeuvre, not the fragment, that held his attention.

The place to look for light on any poem is in the adjacent poems, which Yeats placed adjacent to it because they belonged there. And the unit in which to inspect and discuss his development is not the poem or sequence of poems but the volume, at least from *Responsibilities* (1914) to *A Full Moon in March* (1935).[1] This principle is sometimes obvious enough; anyone can see that the six songs following "The Three Bushes" belong in its entourage, or that "The Phases of the Moon" incorporates the half-dozen poems appended to it. Such obvious instances are, however, slightly misleading; one is apt to think of the main poem as not quite completed, raveling out into lyrical loose ends, or not quite definitive in scope, making shift to appropriate, like a handful of minnows, lesser foci of energy that ought to have been brought within its sphere at the time of composition. In the Age of Eliot, the poet is supposed to gather his interests and impulses and discharge them utterly in a supreme opus every so often, and evades this responsibility at the price of being not quite a major poet. Those weren't the terms in which Yeats was thinking; we misread him if we suppose either that the majority of the poems are casual or that in each he was trying for a definitive statement of all that, at the time of composition, he was.

"Men Improve with the Years" looks like an attempt of this kind; it cuts off, of course, too neatly. The poet was once young, and a lover; now he is a monument, and no lady will love him. The quality of the rhetoric is impeccable, but the poem, on some acquaintance, appears to reduce itself to its mere theme, and that theme so simple-minded as to invite biographical eking out. The unspoken premise of Yeats criticism is that we have to supply from elsewhere — from his life or his doctrines — a great deal that didn't properly get into the poems: not so much to explain the poems as to make them rich enough to sustain the reputation. It happens, however, that "Men Improve with the Years" has for context not Yeats' biography but two poems about a man who did not undergo that dubious improvement: at the climax of "In Memory of Major Robert Gregory" we read,

> Some burn damp faggots, others may consume
> The entire combustible world in one small room
> As though dried straw, and if we turn about
> The bare chimney is gone black out
> Because the work had finished in that flare.
> Soldier, scholar, horseman, he,
> As 'twere all life's epitome,
> What made us dream that he could comb grey hair? . . .

Dried straw, damp faggots; in "Men Improve with the Years" we discover a "burning youth" succeeded by water:

> A weather-worn, marble triton
> Among the streams.

Major Robert Gregory, "all life's epitome," concentrated all in an instantaneous conflagration; the speaker of "Men Improve with the Years" has advanced serially through phases one can enumerate to the condition of a statue. Statues, of course, have their immortality, their nobility of arrested gesture. Yeats isn't being picturesque in specifying the kind of statue; tritons blow their wreathèd horns, and a marble one would be puffing soundlessly at a marble trumpet, like an official Poet; not even in the open sea, but amid the fountains of Major Gregory's mother's garden. The poem isn't a small clearing in which Yeats sinks decoratively to rest, it is a counterrhetoric to the rhetorical memorial poem. It doesn't come quite on the heels of that poem, however; between the two we hear the dry tones of the Irish Airman ("soldier, scholar, horseman") himself:

> Those that I fight I do not hate,
> Those that I guard I do not love.

Midway between Yeats' contrasting rhetorics, Gregory ("An Irish Airman Foresees His Death") hasn't a rhetoric but a style. He wasn't exhilarated by the prospect of consuming "the entire combustible world"; "a lonely impulse of delight" redeems from calculation the decision born of an explicit disenchantment:

> I balanced all, brought all to mind,
> The years to come seemed waste of breath,
> A waste of breath the years behind
> In balance with this life, this death.

Those are the words from which we pass to these:

> I am worn out with dreams:
> A weather-worn, marble triton
> Among the streams.

— the traditional sonorities, the diction ("my burning youth!"), the conventional elegances of cadence evoking (while just evading) a "literary" tradition against which is poised the next poem in the volume: "The Collar-bone of a Hare."

> Would I could cast a sail on the water
> Where many a king has gone
> And many a king's daughter,
> And alight at the comely trees and the lawn,
> The playing upon pipes and the dancing,
> And learn that the best thing is
> To change my loves while dancing
> And pay but a kiss for a kiss.

This live rhythm quickens a remote, folkish idiom, unsonorous and wry. "Men Improve with the Years" seems in retrospect heavier than ever. In this pastoral kingdom not only are there no marble tritons (its tone has nothing in common with that of the Land of Heart's Desire where the Princess Edain was "busied with a dance"), but the newcomer's characteristic gesture is to look back through "the collar-bone of a hare" and laugh at "the old bitter world where they marry in churches" with a lunatic peasant slyness. The symbol of trivial death proffers a peephole or spyglass; it doesn't, as death is reputed to do, open vistas, You can squint with its aid at the old world, from fairyland. Yeats is trying out different arrangements of a poetic universe with the blunt fact of death in it. In the next poem he reverses the situation and rearranges the perspective. Stretched for nonchalant slumber "On great-grandfather's battered tomb," Beggar Billy sees the dancing-world: not

> The comely trees and the lawn,
> The playing upon pipes and the dancing,

but

>   a dream
> Of sun and moon that a good hour
> Bellowed and pranced in the round tower . . .
>
> That golden king and that wild lady
> Sang till stars began to fade,
> Hands gripped in hands, toes close together,
> Hair spread on the wind they made;
> That lady and that golden king
> Could like a brace of blackbirds sing.

This is the celebrated music of the spheres; and Beggar Billy decides that "great-grandfather's battered tomb" that educes such noisy and energetic visions is no place for him. So the book, having degraded its initial persona to beggardom (there are curious analogies with *Lear*) and preoccupied itself with themes and images of death until it has set the celestial boiler shop going, takes leave of this theme for a time and turns to quieter matters like the dead lovers Solomon and Sheba.

That initial persona now wants looking at. The volume we are examining, *The Wild Swans at Coole*, began not with the Gregory elegy — that is its second poem — but with "The Wild Swans at Coole" itself: an image of personal dejection ("And now my heart is sore") that uses the permanent glory of the swans to silhouette the transience attending human beings who must keep their feet on the ground and try to assimilate the "brilliant creatures" by counting them.

> All's changed since I, hearing at twilight
> The first time on this shore,
> The bell-beat of their wings above my head
> Trod with a lighter tread.
>
> Unwearied still, lover by lover,
> They clamber in the cold
> Companionable streams or climb the air;
> Their hearts have not grown old; . . .

"All's changed" is a mood, not a summary of presented facts; this initial poem confines itself to a wholly familiar *Angst*, a setting documented in a spare but traditional manner—

> The trees are in their autumn beauty,
> The woodland paths are dry—

a specified month and time of day, a poet who does and thinks and feels nothing unusual, verbs no more than inert copulas, and swans that are scarcely more than swans. We are in the presence of a mind reflecting nature and then reflecting Locke-wise upon what it reflects: tantalized— not teased, but undergoing the pangs of Tantalus—because it must undergo change while nature—the swans—remains other, "unwearied still." Though none of the great Romantics could have written it with such economy and directness, the poem remains within, say, the Coleridgean orbit of experience.

It is upon experience resignedly ordered in this plane that the brilliant death of Major Robert, the Irish Airman, impinges; he took wing like the swans; his heart has not grown old; he demonstrated that it lay within human capacity to

> consume
> The entire combustible world in one small room
> As though dried straw.

This death and the contemplation of the poet's impotent middle age ferment and interact throughout the volume, entoiling other materials, discovering unexpected resonances in the pastoral mode ("Shepherd and Goatherd") and in the lingering end of Mabel Beardsley ("Upon a Dying Lady"), never for long oblivious of the piercing hypothesis that maximum human intensity coincides with human extinction. What is arrived at is an extinction not of the person but of his natural context. At the end of the volume October water no more mirrors a natural sky:

> On the grey rock of Cashel the mind's eye
> Has called up the cold spirits that are born
> When the old moon has vanished from the sky
> And the new still hides her horn.

The mind's eye, no longer the Newtonian optic; and that moon isn't nature's moon. Nor does the mind's eye see swans that fly away, but calls up three arresting figures—one a sphinx—observed not in placidity but in active intensity:

> Mind moved but seemed to stop
> As 'twere a spinning-top.
>
> In contemplation had those three so wrought
> Upon a moment, and so stretched it out

> That they, time overthrown,
> Were dead yet flesh and bone.

The poem — and the volume — closes on a note of triumph; Yeats tells us he "arranged" — deliberate word — his vision in a song —

> Seeing that I, ignorant for so long
> Had been rewarded thus
> In Cormac's ruined house.

The poles of this volume are its first and last poems, "The Wild Swans at Coole" and "The Double Vision of Michael Robartes," as the poles of *The Tower* are "Sailing to Byzantium" and "All Souls' Night." Between the observation of the swans and the vision of the sphinx passes the action of the book. The crisis occurs when, in "Ego Dominus Tuus" (which immediately follows the account of the Dying Lady's heroic arrogance) "Ille"[2] determines to "set his chisel to the hardest stone" and forget about the kind of self-fulfillment envisaged by people who tell us that men improve with the years. Immediately a long poem devotes itself to the moon, the faded cliché of a thousand mewling nature poets; and examining it not as they do in the Irish sky but by way of the sort of diagram one discovers in a penny astrology book, sets the stage for the double vision of Michael Robartes.

The Wild Swans at Coole is a book about death and the will. A component poem like "Men Improve with the Years" will no more pull loose from it than the "foolish fond old man" speech will pull loose from *King Lear*. It is a radical mistake to think of Yeats as a casual or fragmentary poet whose writings float on a current discoverable only in his biographable life. How much time does he not spend telling us that he has carefully rendered the mere events of his life irrelevant!

3. Anti-Nature

Yeats' quarrel with nineteenth-century popular Romanticism encompassed more than its empty moons. He turned with increasing vehemence against a tradition that either laid streams of little poems like cod's eggs or secreted inchoate epics. Against the poet as force of nature he placed of course the poet as deliberate personality, and correspondingly against the usual "Collected Poems" (arranged in the order of composition) he placed the oeuvre, the deliberated artistic Testament, a division of that new Sacred Book of the Arts of which, Mr. Pound has recalled, he used to talk. It was as a process of fragmentation, into little people and little poems, that he viewed the history of European poetry, from the *Canterbury Tales* to the Collected Poems of, say, Lord Byron.

> If Chaucer's personages had disengaged themselves from Chaucer's crowd, forgot their common goal and shrine, and after sundry magnifications become each in turn the centre of some Elizabethan play, and

had after split into their elements and so given birth to romantic poetry, must I reverse the cinematograph?

The *Canterbury Tales*, it should be recalled, isn't a bloated descant on some epic idea but, like *The Divine Comedy* or *The Wild Swans at Coole* — or *The Cantos* — a unity made by architecture out of separate and ascertainable components. And the cinematograph seemed indeed reversible:

> . . . a nation or an individual with great emotional intensity might follow the pilgrims as it were to some unknown shrine, and give to all those separated elements and to all that abstract love and melancholy, a symbolical, a mythological coherence.

This unity isn't substituted for the existing traditions of poetry, it unites them. Ireland, furthermore, might well be the chosen nation:

> I had begun to hope, or to half hope, that we might be the first in Europe to seek unity as deliberately as it had been sought by theologian, poet, sculptor, architect, from the eleventh to the thirteenth century.

For Ireland had her autochthonous mythology, and "have not all races had their first unity from a mythology, that marries them to rock and hill?"[3]

It was natural that he should inspect the practice of any discoverable forerunners, and inevitable that he should see himself as standing in the same relation to Irish folklore as Wordsworth to the English folk ballads. One of his own false starts (seduced by this parallel) had been to write ballads; Wordsworth's unreconsidered false start, it must finally have seemed to Yeats, had been to marry only himself and not his race to "rock and hill." Wordsworth had undertaken his work with an insufficient sense of hieratic dedication; for him a poet was only "a man speaking to men" (though a more than usually conscious man), not the amanuensis of revelation. That is why old age overtook not only his body but his speech. *The Prelude* is a narrative of self-discovery, in which the lesson of life, muffled by the automatic grand style, is that knowledge and experience will not synchronize.

HIC: And I would find myself and not an image.
ILLE: That is our modern hope, and by its light
       We have lit upon the gentle, sensitive mind
       And lost the old nonchalance of the hand;
       Whether we have chosen chisel, pen or brush,
       We are but critics, or but half create,
       Timid, entangled, empty and abashed. . . .

That is the formula of Wordsworth's decline. As Yeats moved into middle age, the sole survivor of the Rhymers' Club's "Tragic Generation," the parallel between his destiny and Wordsworth's grew more insistent; had Wordsworth not in the same way survived for a quarter of a century Keats,

Shelley, and Byron, the other members of the last great wave of creative force? And had he not, assuming the laureateship, turned into a "sixty year old smiling public man," moving further and further from the only time in his life when he had been alive, and lamenting over the dead imaginative vigor of his boyhood? That is the context of the defiant opening of "The Tower":

> Never had I more
> Excited, passionate, fantastical
> Imagination, nor an ear and eye
> That more expected the impossible —
> No, not in boyhood when with rod and fly,
> Or the humbler worm, I climbed Ben Bulben's back
> And had the livelong summer day to spend.

"Or the humbler worm" is a tip to the reader; it isn't Yeatsian diction but a parody of Wordsworth's. Unlike Wordsworth, Yeats the poet has passed sixty undiminished and needs no man's indulgence.

Wordsworth had developed "naturally," moving on the stream of nature; and streams run downhill. For the natural man the moment of lowest vitality is the moment of death; in the mid-eighteenth century the image of an untroubled decline into the grave fastened itself upon the imagination of England, and "*Siste viator*" was carved on a thousand tombstones. "Pause, traveller, whoever thou art, and consider thy mortality; as I am, so wilt thou one day be." The traveler came on foot, examined the inscription, and went on his way pondering, his vitality still lower than before. This was one of the odd versions of pastoral sentiment that prepared the way for Wordsworth's career of brilliance and decline; Yeats turns powerfully against it in the Goatherd's song on Major Gregory (see "Shepherd and Goatherd"), more powerfully still in the epitaph he designed for himself. The last division of his Sacred Book closes with an apocalypse, superhuman forms riding the wintry dawn, Michelangelo electrifying travelers with his Creation of Adam, painters revealing heavens that opened. The directions for his own burial are introduced with a pulsation of drums:

> Un dé báre Bén Búl bén's héad
> In DRUMcliff churchyard . . .

The mise en scène is rural and eighteenth century — the churchyard, the ancestral rector, the local stonecutters; but the epitaph flies in the face of traditional invocations to passers-by:

> *Cast a cold eye*
> *On life, on death.*
> *Horseman, pass by.*

Much critical ingenuity has been expended on that horseman. He is simply the designated reader of the inscription, the heroic counterimage of the foot-weary wanderer who was invited to ponder a "*siste viator*";[4] the only reader Yeats can be bothered to address. And he is not to be weighed down by the realization of his own mortality; he is to defy it.

The life a counterlife, the book not a compendium of reflections but a dramatic revelation, the sentiments scrupulous inversions of received romantic sentiment; what more logical than that Yeats should have modeled the successive phases of his testament on the traditional collections of miscellaneous poems, and (as he always did when he touched a tradition) subverted the usual implications? He dreamed as a young man of creating some new *Prometheus Unbound.* One applauds his wisdom in not attempting that sort of *magnum opus*, but it was not likely that he should forget the idea of a work operating on a large scale. Each volume of his verse, in fact, *is* a large-scale work, like a book of the Bible. And as the Bible was once treated by exegetists as the self-sufficient divine book mirroring the other divine book, Nature, but possessing vitality independent of natural experience, so Yeats considered his Sacred Book as similar to "life" but radically separated from it, "mirror on mirror mirroring all the show." In "The Phases of the Moon," Aherne and Robartes stand on the bridge below the poet's tower, where the candle burns late, and in mockery of his hopeless toil expound, out of his earshot, the doctrine of the lunar wheel. It is clear that they know what he can never discover; they toy with the idea of ringing his bell and speaking

> Just truth enough to show that his whole life
> Will scarcely find for him a broken crust
> Of all those truths that are your daily bread.

It is an entrancing idea:

> He'd crack his wits
> Day after day, yet never find the meaning.

But it is late; Aherne determines to pass up this satisfaction.

> And then he laughed to think that what seemed hard
> Should be so simple — a bat rose from the hazels
> And circled round him with its squeaky cry,
> The light in the tower window was put out.

Why is it put out? Because Yeats has finished writing the poem! Aherne, Robartes, the doctrine of the phases, the baffled student, all of them, we are meant suddenly to realize, are components in a book, and so is the man who is supposed to be writing the book. What we see in this mirror, the page, is reflected from that one, "life"; but the parallel mirrors face each other, and in an infinite series of interreflections life has been acquiring its images from the book only that the book may reflect them again. The book, then, is (by a Yeatsian irony) self-contained, like the Great Smaragdine Tablet that said, "Things below are copies," and was itself one of the things below; a sacred book like the Apocalypse of St.

John, not like most poetry a marginal commentary on the world to be read with one eye on the pragmatical pig of a text.

"Day after day," Yeats wrote at the end of *A Vision*, "I have sat in my chair turning a symbol over in my mind, exploring all its details, defining and again defining its elements, testing my convictions and those of others by its unity. . . . It seems as if I should know all if I could but banish such memories and find everything in the symbol." On that occasion nothing came; the symbol was perhaps too limited. But the conviction remains with Yeats that a book, if not a symbol, can supplant the world; if not supplant it, perpetually interchange life with it. Nothing, finally, is more characteristic than his dryly wistful account of the perfected sage for whom the radiance attending the supernatural copulation of dead lovers serves but as a reading light:

> Though somewhat broken by the leaves, that light
> Lies in a circle on the grass; therein
> I turn the pages of my holy book.

Notes

1. In *Editing Yeats's Poems* (London: Macmillan; New York: St. Martin's, 1983), p. 65, Richard J. Finneran has offered conclusive evidence supporting Curtis Bradford's conjecture that Yeats was not responsible for the contents or order of *Last Poems & Plays* (1940).

2. "Willy," commented Ezra Pound.

3. Above quotations from *The Trembling of the Veil*, Book I, Ch. 23–24.

4. Though Swift wrote, "*Abi, Viator, et imitare si poteris. . . .*" which Yeats paraphrased as "Imitate him if you dare, / World-besotted traveller."

The Passionate Syntax   Thomas Parkinson*

The Stress of Song

The prosodic possibilities available to Yeats as a poet writing in English were four in number. He could conceive of the line as written in feet, chiefly iambic, and he could attempt to maintain a set number of feet per line, as in the standard iambic pentameter. He could count syllables and keep a fixed syllable count of six, eight, ten, any given number, to a line. Or he could ignore syllable count or the concept of the foot and simply maintain a relatively fixed number of heavy stresses per line, with wide range of syllable count. Or he could ignore any fixed count

*From *W. B. Yeats: The Later Poetry* (Berkeley and Los Angeles: University of California Press, 1964), 203–31. This excerpt is preceded by a sketch of Yeats's prosody.

of foot, stress, or syllable and write in free verse, using breath and phrase as prosodic units. It has always seemed to me peculiarly fruitless to exert on Yeats's verse the norms of foot meter, and to be quite frank I am extremely skeptical of the value of scanning most English verse by breaking it down into patterns of syllables that form something called feet. I find no positive evidence that Yeats thought in terms of feet, and my own persuasion is that he combined a syllabic and a stress prosody. In such a prosody a five-stress line is the equivalent of a ten-syllable line, and the two are interchangeable. The ten-syllable line may have in it well over five stresses; the five-stress line may have more or less than ten syllables; but they are equivalent. Any given poem may be in one or the other measure predominantly, and in Yeats's prosody there tends to be a correlation between the kind of poem and the kind of line used. His more formal, commemorative, and meditative poems tend to be in decasyllabic lines that give them their air of philosophic weight and contemplative grasp. His brief intense lyrics, on the other hand, are written in lines that are best understood as being divisible into a fixed number of stresses, with a wide range of syllable count.

One fine example of a poem written in a three-stress line is "Mohini Chatterjee," which has often been compared with a very early Yeats poem, "Kanva on Himself." Although I am not here primarily concerned with Yeats's development from his early work, "Kanva" is so illuminating a contrast and suggests so clearly the vigor of his later prosody that it seems useful to reprint it:

> Now wherefore hast thou tears innumerous?
> Hast thou not known all sorrow and delight
> Wandering of yore in forests rumorous,
> Beneath the flaming eyeballs of the night.
>
> And as a slave been wakeful in the halls
> Of Rajas and Mahrajas beyond number?
> Hast thou not ruled among the gilded walls?
> Hast thou not known a Raja's dreamless slumber?
>
> Hast thou not sat of yore upon the knees
> Of myriads of beloveds, and on thine
> Have not a myriad swayed below strange trees
> In other lives? Hast thou not quaffed old wine
>
> By tables that were fallen into dust
> Ere yonder palm commenced his thousand years?
> Is not thy body but the garnered rust
> Of ancient passions and of ancient fears?
>
> Then wherefore fear the usury of Time,
> Or Death that cometh with the next life-key?

> Nay, rise and flatter her with golden rhyme,
> For as things were so shall things ever be.

Many young poetic aspirants are pleased by this poem, for, if Yeats once wrote so badly, the Nobel Prize may not be past their reach. The padded lines, the funny images, the unspeakable statements ("Or Death that cometh with the next life-key"), the closing platitude, the weary archaisms, the twisted syntax — it is a perfect compendium of faults. In the early drafts of the second part of "Mohini Chatteriee," some of these characteristics were carried over, and the excision of them was one of his major motives. The first section began easily, following a prose draft:

> What prayers should I pray? Do not pray, said the Brahmin but say
> I have been man and woman, king and slave, myriad of beloveds have
> sat on my knees, I have sat on a myriad knees and shudder thinking that
> soon I must change again always as insect in the roots of the grass.

He then wrote a draft, underpunctuated but close to the final version:

> I asked if I should pray
> But the Brahmin said
> "Pray for nothing, say
> Every night in bed
> 'I have been a king
> I have been a slave
> Nor is there anything
>
> a. Any fool, rascal, knave
> b. Fool, rascal, knave
>
> a. I have not been
> b. That I have not been
>
> And yet upon my breast
> A myriad heads have lain.' "

It is characteristic of Yeats's manuscripts that the original versions of poems should be underpunctuated, for he evidently felt no need to indicate syntactic pauses at the close of lines: the ending of a line automatically indicated a pause. The revision of line 8 shows Yeats excising a redundant word, diminishing the number of syllables in the line and exerting heavier stress on individual words, and it is a vivid example of the way that he manipulated lines, relying on the uniformity of stress pattern to justify the variation of syllables. The problems posed by the second part of the poem, however, did not involve filing and heightening but choosing situation, icon, and moral judgment.

What he had settled in the first section of "Mohini Chatterjee" was its rhythmic norm, and this controlled whatever suggestions came to his mind for incorporating judgments fundamentally similar to those in "Kanva on Himself." Having made the utterance, he sought to identify the speaker:

> A stranger with strange eyes
> Murmured in my youth
> These or words like these
> And add then to that
> All that has been shall be

He was trying to find a three-stress equivalent to "And as things are so shall they ever be." He gave up trying to characterize his speaker after another false try ("Mohini Chatterjee / A young handsome man / Spoke these or words like these"), and concentrated on the meaning of the statement:

> I heard those words in youth

> a. And never have I found
> b. And much have thought thereon
> a. A more majestic truth
> b. But found no better truth

> So wherefore groan and moan
> About old wrong (?)
> Seeing there's time for all

Not satisfied with the abstract statement, and certainly not satisfied with the "wherefore" of "Kanva on Himself," so inappropriate to this new utterance, he sought out more concrete data and fixed on the image of the lovers:

> Feet that once were light
>
> Eyes that once were bright
>
> Feet
>
> Eyes
>
> Eyes remembered bright
>
> Feet in old days light shall
>
> Shall once
>
> Once more be light and bright
>
> Once more be bright or light

> A Foot
>
> All
>
> All that

> a. Lovers or companions
> b. All old companions

> a. Living and dying side
> b. Live side by side
> c. Be once more side by side

> The starry circuit run
>
> a. Till they be satisfied
>
> b. That they be satisfied

Of all these efforts, only the very last ("That they be satisfied") won a place in the final version. The rest were put aside, the feet and eyes because too literally "abstract" from the meanings and figures intended, although the "feet" would reappear in the final version and be integrated with the figure of repeated design suggested by the "starry circuit." But the eyes and feet that, these notes suggest, were to be rekindled and reanimated were assimilated into the lovers who, in the final version, would gain in the whole pattern of time what they were not granted in their single segment. These notes were conceptual statements: lovers will not be eternally separated because the larger designs of the universe favor their fulfillment.

The facing page of the notebook establishes yet another concern of the poem while reinforcing the concept of the circuit, which is here seen as "human" or "mortal" rather than "starry," though it is still a dominant force: "The circuit sets the pace." The fresh concern, which balances love, is war:

> Old soldiers face to face
>
> a. And every fight fought (?) out
> b. Every fight fought out
> c. All old fights fought out
>
> The circuit sets the pace
> For strategic thought

Both lover and warrior live within the "circuit" that sets the tempo of experience. Trying to bring the two together, he was driven to an exclamation: "Aye life oh life." And trying to see war and love as one unit, he saw them first as expressions of emotion — love — versus reason — war ("Whether in thought or desire") — but then altered the phrasing to fix both love and war as the expressions of passions, "Whether from hate or desire." He could then see the two as part of a large design of death and birth:

> By a myriad of births
> By a myriad of deaths
>
> Then by a myriad births
> A myriad graves appear
>
> A myriad of births
> A myriad of graves

So end the preliminaries to the ultimate composing of the poem. What we have witnessed, so far as the manuscripts and my imagination can take us, is the refinement of a subject suggested by the original "Kanva on Himself," beginning with a prose redaction of the occasion that gave rise to the early poem, followed by a versification of Chatterjee's speech. This versification established a norm of three stresses for the poem, and within that norm Yeats was committed to work. His rejection of the "feet" and "eyes" of these notes may in part have come from the impossibility of accommodating them to the three-stress line:

Eyes remembered bright

Feet in old days light shall

Shall once

Once more be light and bright

The modal "shall" presented a prosodic problem not worth working on, and that fact combined with the abstractness of statement to let him jettison "eyes" and "feet."

Out of this process emerged the completed poem, and that process was lifelong, both in technical development and in the scrutiny of obsessive pattern. The design of the dance, the faith in a cosmos of continuing life, the prideful assertion of self, the sense of circularity, the admiring emphasis on the irrational — these are familiar elements in the body of Yeats's work. The prosody, at once so simple and so adaptable, so free and so structured, makes vocalic and immediate these motives. In spite of the Brahmin's advice against praying, the poem is prayerful in the sense that it invokes powers resident in the person but latent unless brought into existence by language. The commentary is a declaration that willfully creates the conditions it describes and identifies the poet with the Brahmin and the sages, makes him a sayer as well as seer:

I asked if I should pray,
But the Brahmin said,
"Pray for nothing, say
Every night in bed,
I have been a king,
I have been a slave,
Nor is there anything,
Fool, rascal, knave,
That I have not been,
And yet upon my breast
A myriad heads have lain.

That he might set at rest
A boy's turbulent days
Mohini Chatterjee
Spoke these, or words like these.
I add in commentary,
"Old lovers yet may have

> All that time denied —
> Grave is heaped on grave
> That they be satisfied —
> Over the blackened earth
> The old troops parade,
> Birth is heaped on birth
> That such cannonade
> May thunder time away,
> Birth-hour and death-hour meet,
> Or, as great sages say,
> Men dance on deathless feet."

The syllable count ranges from four ("Fool, rascal, knave") to seven ("A myriad heads have lain"), but most of the lines have three major stresses. The certain exceptions are the last two lines, each of which has four stresses:

> Or, as gréat ságes sáy,
> Mén dançe on deáthless feét.

But these two lines and the preceding one ("Birth-hour and death-hour meet"), which might also be construed as having four major stresses, have six syllables only. This substitution of a six-syllable line for a three-stress line is so common a practice in Yeats's later verse that we might think of it as a convention of the poetry. The principle of linear substitution grants his work extraordinary flexibility.

In some of his lyrics the complications of this prosody are extraordinary, and one high point is "Crazy Jane and Jack the Journeyman." I have already discussed one account of the poem's origins in Yeats's visionary experience. In the context of "Words for Music Perhaps," part of the poem's impact comes from its dramatization of the anti-Christian Black Mass of Eden that underlies that series and in which Jane and Jack are primary embodiments of Yeats's argument for a religion of ignorance. The poem is so deliberately committed to bodily earthly life that it even denies the paganism of the Neo-Platonist. But the poem began with rather different motives. It was at first part of the long argument between man and woman that Yeats found an obsessive subject, Jack declaring the immortality of his love, Jane skeptically (and ruefully) giving him the lie.

> Wild Jack when he was drunk
> Said love could never die
>
> Half drunk he cried that such a love
> Outlived moon and sun;
> I stamped my foot and cried in rage
> Easy got and gone

The argument was then phrased in dialogue form:

> She
> "The more I leave the door unlatched
> The sooner love is gone"
> He
> What matter though a look can make
> Me tremble in my bone

This implied argument with its suggestive sexual overtones forms the base of the final poem, which acts as an aftermath to a prior quarrel. The crystallizing element in the poem's construction was the phrase "the door unlatched," and its peculiarly haunting rhythm, echoed at first by "look can make" and later more effectively by "when looks meet." The key phrase was at first not leading and dominant:

> Half drunk he cried that such a love
> Outlived moon and sun

But when he turned to concentrated composing he noted his key rhythmic phrase first:

> The more I leave the door unlatched
> The sooner love is gone
> Although a look can make

Attacking the opening once again he worked toward shaping a line that would parallel his guiding rhythm:

> I know although this eye can make
> Me tremble to the bone
>
> I know although this eye can make
> Of life mockery
>
> I know although when look meet look
> I tremble to the bone

And finally, with the underpunctuation so typical of early drafts:

> I know although when looks meet
> I tremble to the bone
> The more I leave the door unlatched
> The sooner love is gone

The design of the poem was then established: an opening line of four major stresses, with two of those stresses closely juxtaposed at the close of the line, this line followed by a three-stress line close to the conventional rising pattern. The even lines rhyme, the odd lines do not, and the syntax makes each pair of lines a unit of meaning, so that the effect is of a single line broken. There are, then, units within units, pairs of lines within the stanza, lines within pairs, and the stanza identical with the period. Within the longer lines, the divisions are further intensified by the use of internal rhyme:

> I know although . . .
> The more I leave the door . . .

And within these units there are further interweavings of sound, partly through end-rhyme, partly through simple echo:

> I know, although when looks meet
> I tremble to the bone,
> The more I leave the door unlatched
> The sooner lover is gone[,]
> For love is but a skein unwound
> Between the dark and dawn[.]

This stanza established the rhythmic pattern for the poem, and from that point the problem of composition diminished. Each stanza followed the same basic pattern, and the fifth line of the first and second stanzas interlocked in rhyme with the (otherwise unrhyming) third lines of the second and third stanzas. His only difficulties came with the opening line of the second stanza, where he tried "soul" at first before choosing the primitive and in part depreciative "ghost," and with the concluding stanza's form of address.

> A lonely ghost the ghost is
> That to God shall come;
> I — love's skein upon the ground,
> My body in the tomb —
> Shall leap into the light lost
> In my mother's womb.
> But were I left to lie alone
> In an empty bed,
> The skein so bound us ghost to ghost
> When he turned his head
> Passing on the road that night,
> Mine must walk when dead.

The difficulty with the concluding stanza grew in part from the remains of the original dialogue form of the poem, for even in the early printed versions the last stanza addressed Jack as "you," in spite of the poem's attempt to separate the living from the dead. In the completed context of the Crazy Jane series, intimate address was replaced by the dominant tone of public confession and outrage. The deliberate turning from the light to the dark community of sexual and earthly love is a declaration of commitment to death.

   This poem, which I have always thought one of Yeats's greatest triumphs, is hardly exhausted by consideration of its prosody. But there seems to me no doubt that its impact as well as its evolution are conditioned by the most careful rhythmic discriminations that in a large sense controlled the poem's shaping. The rhythmic design is a major one in Yeats's later work, granting him the deep primitive simplicity of ballad meter ("Words for Music Perhaps") and the force of deliberate conscious shaping, so that the most simple and most sophisticated find common ground. Like Blake and Lawrence, Yeats had the capacity to think in designs that cut through the incrustations of modern life to those permanent realities that center and support our experience. His prosody was one major force that drove him to realities that other modern poets never genuinely reached. The pattern of "Crazy Jane and Jack the Journeyman" is in detail the pattern used in many of the poems in "A Man Young and Old" and *Last Poems*, but the basic stress prosody that underlies this poem and "Mohini Chatterjee" is a dominant mode in the verse that grants him access to a life at once strong and accurate, simple and sophisticated, passionate and intellectually magnificent.

The Articulation of Syllables

Yeats's verse, taken as a dramatic whole, moves "between extremities" always. The integrative aim figured by the centaur urged him toward projecting a total sense of possibility in prosody as in dramaturgy and iconography. His prosody allowed him to present through his stress lines the simple emotive expression of personified passions, the longer lines fixed mainly by syllabic count expressing the meditation of the civilized intellect.

In his syllabic as in his stress prosody, the guiding motives were the passionate syntax of the sentence, which was in turn qualified by stanzaic pattern and his tendency toward making stanza and period coincide. The same compensations already noted in his stress prosody operated in lines governed mainly by syllable count. Just as in the last three lines of "Mohini Chatterjee" he substituted lines of six syllables and four stresses for the normal three-stress line, he would in writing a poem in decasyllables feel free to substitute a five-stress line when the emergencies of syntax required it. For his poems, the concept of the iambic line with variable feet is ugly and redundant, and, since simple hypotheses are most elegant and most useful, the best prosodic hypothesis for poems like "Sailing to Byzantium" and "Among School Children" is that he wrote them in lines of ten syllables. What minor deviations occur can be accommodated by assuming that he often slurred (elided) a weakly stressed syllable and sometimes substituted a five-stress for a ten-syllable line.

In composing, Yeats at first wrote his decasyllables in a loose form, often merely filling out a line to satisfy the prescribed rhyme scheme so that he could maintain his momentum. He then reduced syllabic redundancy as much as possible until he had so concentrated a line that each syllable was carrying weight and the line was normally reduced to ten syllables. I have already cited above the alteration in "Among School Children" that causes some syntactic confusion:

> And that must sleep or struggle to escape
>
> And that must sleep, shriek, struggle to escape

Here the addition of *shriek* is not necessary for propriety if one is merely concerned with the norm of the foot, but it is needed by the criterion of reducing redundancy and giving each syllable as much semantic weight as it can carry. The difference between the first draft and the final version of a single ottava rima stanza — and a reasonably characteristic one — shows how his mind worked over and altered flaccid lines:

> We too had many pretty toys when young:
> A law indifferent to blame or praise,
> A speedy remedy to obvious wrong
> No swaggering soldier on the public ways
> Who weighed a man's life lighter than a song;
> A general confidence in future days
> In some great thing to come, because we thought
> That the worst rogues and rascals had died out.

Of these lines (in "Nineteen Hundred and Nineteen"), only the first two and the last would survive. Some lines he reshaped in order to develop concepts relevant to the preceding stanza; from others he excised certain figures because, as matters developed, they would fit more properly in following stanzas. But generally, he changed in order to get the densest possible semantic arrangement within a decasyllabic line:

> We too had many pretty toys when young:
> A law indifferent to blame or praise,
> To bribe or threat; habits that made old wrong
> Melt down, as it were wax in the sun's rays,
> Public opinion ripening for so long
> We thought it would outlive all future days.
> O what fine thought we had because we thought
> That the worst rogues and rascals had died out.

In part the changes were warranted by changes in the first stanza, for the third line of the first stanza had at one point noted the "insolence of the sun"; but when the poem had progressed to the point of the second stanza, the sun could be removed from the first stanza and appear here in the function that Yeats more systematically endowed it with: that of representative of the rational faculty. The line that gave him this opening was the extremely flaccid "A speedy remedy to obvious wrong," for, even if we take the line to be ironic, why should we expend irony on such flabbiness? The objects of Yeats's contempt have at least to be worthy of it. The swaggering soldier could also be put off, as his proper function in succeeding stanzas was revealed. Hence the second stanza could serve the role of balancing against the "ingenious lovely things" that seemed "sheer miracle" to the Grecian populace the habits and laws that with public opinion were supposed equally to work miracles for the European world before 1914. The statement, at once sympathetic and mocking, makes the abstractions of law, habit, and public opinion equivalent to the concretions of Athena's image, the ivories of Phidias, and the golden grasshoppers and bees, both object and abstraction being defenseless against the circle of the moon and the whirling dust of history. To make the stanza an appropriate contrast, he had to identify himself with the aspirations of pre-war Europe while making clear their futility.

The motivation for change was, then, not simply prosodic but conditioned by the metaphorical structure of the entire poem and by Yeats's sense of his special position as spokesman — participant and articulator. What resulted was a stanza of decasyllabic lines in which a deliberate voice evaluated precisely and economically a wide context of experience. The difference between original and final lines demonstrates the forceful economy of his control of the line:

a. A spéedy rémedy to obvious wróng
b. To bribe or thréat; hábits that mádc old wróng

a. No swággering sóldier on the públic wáys
b. Melt dówn, as it were wáx in the sún's ráys

a. A geńeral cónfidence in fúture dáys
b. We thoúght it wóuld outlive all fúture dáys

a. In some gréat thing to comé, becaúse we thóught
b. O what fiñe thought we hád becaúse we thóught

The lines were thus established, basically decasyllabic, with as many major stresses as the syntax would bear.

One more stanza, the famous stanza on the divided tree in "Vacillation," is so indicative of his habits of composition that it will serve as conclusion to this section. In this stanza, which I take as a microcosm of his habits, we can see Yeats's mind contemplating numerous possibilities, rejecting, seeking further, shaping the icon to suit the special definitive motives of the poem. We can see also the evolution of the stanza from inchoate potentiality to ultimate ordered prosodic shape. The stanza shows with remarkable clarity the kind of considerations he made.

"Vacillation" as a whole is composed of disparate yet central elements in Yeats's experience. Two sections of the poem — I and IV — come from earlier experience, stanza IV developing an experience of special intensity over fifteen years in the past, stanza I evidently coming out of an earlier period in his style and probably written some years before. In spite of the earlier origins of these sections of the poem, my own belief is that the occasion for the composition of the poem rose from his contemplation of the icon of the divided tree.

The sources of the icon are several, but the motive for its use is single. The tree is one of the most celebrated and most often remarked of Yeats's icons, and he used it frequently and throughout his career. Its importance is evident in the drafts of "Among School Children," where the briefly appearing hawthorn tree is asked whether it is all or the creator of all. The tree is a godlike force, and whether hawthorn, chestnut, or hazel, it has supernatural weight. Like birds, trees participated in a dual nature, rooted in earth, feeding on air, organic and fluent, between heaven and earth, self-complete. From his studies in Blake and in the cabala he learned of the dual trees of life and knowledge, and in the Mabinogion he learned of Peredur's divided tree and cited it in his essay (1897) on "The Celtic Element in Literature." He contemplated the tree in various forms throughout his lyrics, and he read of the tree of Attis in *The Golden Bough, Hastings' Encyclopedia of Religion and Ethics*, and Julian's hymn to the Great Mother of the Gods. The tree of Peredur was composed of two great opposites, moisture and fire, and, although in the Mabinogion it merely took its place as one more odd item in the landscape, Yeats by integrating it in his total understanding of the generic icon endowed it with rich connotations. The tree that eventually appeared in his poem was original in the sense that it was a new complex of elements, the pine tree of the priests of Gallus, the trees of life and of knowledge, Peredur's tree, and the organic form of the Romantic imagination. Several cultures were thus folded together into the special form required by Yeats's imagination.

His imagination in this poem was operating in a syncretic fashion similar to that already analyzed in "Lines Written in Dejection." For "Vacillation" is one of those synoptic poems that Yeats occasionally wrote to bring himself to momentary definition. Like the "Dialogue of Self and Soul," it considered the extremities of human experience and chose, in a deliberately good-humored manner, the extreme of commitment to unregenerated life. The fabled tree of this stanza becomes a center for opposed forces that live in a constant process of mutual feeding that can be transcended only by the interposition of the image of Attis. Hence the poem treats once again the puzzle that grows from the artist's necessity at once to transcend and to accept the limits of the generated soul.

His first notes on the tree are vague and inconclusive, although the initial line is settled:

> And And From its broad roots T its cry let out
> There is a tree that from its topmost bough
>   the other
> Is half flame, and one all one half a rusty flame,
>   leaf
>   leaf
>   the other
> Is half all flame and half all abound all
>   and half abounding leaf
> And half green
> That is for ever nourished with the dew
> The tree of knowledge mounts

In succeeding versions, several of these elements are conserved: the sense of abundance in the foliage, the presence of dew, the basic idea of the tree as divided equally into moisture and flame. The tree of knowledge, however, he saw to be not an adequate connotation for his inclusive intention. In conception the meaning of this central icon had not been established, and he had as yet no stanza form. The one relatively firm line — "There is a tree that from its topmost bough" — established the dominant form as decasyllabic, and it is possible that the obscure line concerned with the roots was tentatively placed as a possible rhyme of "out" and "bough." But the tree's roots would have no place in the final version.

On the page that contains his succeeding effort, a list of rhymes appears

> bough
> leaf   green
> dew
> chief   scene
> anew
> belief
> grief

What he evidently did was to take first the original draft and note the two lines that were close to acceptable form, ending respectively in "bough" and "leaf." He then filled out a general stanza scheme as a working design and started to write to it:

> There is a tree from that from its topmost bough
>   all
> Is half all flame, and half all leafy green
>   the other leafy green
>
>   with
> That is for ever chilly in the dew
>
>   So The

The substitution of "green" for the rhyme word "leaf" compelled him to the revision of rhyme scheme, and as he continued the poem even the new set of rhymes was not appropriate. He still, in an unassimilated line, tried to fill out a line to the rhyme word "scene." With the beginning line established, he turned to a new attack:

> Is one half glittering flame, the other green
> Abounding foliage moistened with the dew
>   They that
> And some let Attys image hang between
> Consuming flame and lush abounding leaf
> Know not what they know but know not grief.

With the beginning line, he had six completed lines, but as he observed the shape of the stanza it moved toward ottava rima, and he considered his second "B" line, using the rhyme word "scene" that his sketch of rhyme scheme had suggested:

> The tree of knowledge and of life and
> scene.

The tree was now more inclusive, not merely the tree of knowledge but also the tree of life. Hence he corrected his earlier notation, and in filling out the line to maintain his momentum and consider the possibilities implied by "scene," he learned what his tree would be. Knowledge and life, flame and dew—these were set, and in his drafts and in his noted rhyme scheme he had the following possibilities for pattern:

> bough
> green
> dew
> scene
> anew
> leaf
> grief

Thus he had established the ottava rima form, and the further development of the stanza was checked by this rhyme scheme:

> A tree there is and from the topmost bough
> One half is glittering flame, the other dewy green
> Abounding foliage moistened with the dew
> a. Knowledge and life made one for in the scene
> b. Wisdom displays all death but in the scene
> c. Wisdom has summoned death but in the scene
> What it destroys the foliage must renew
>   He that
> And some like let Attys ancient image hang between
> They know not what they know but know not
> a. Consuming flame and the lush dewy leaf
> b. That staring fury and the blind lush leaf
> May know not what he knows but knows not grief

The evolution from the first notes growing from his various sources to the ultimate ottava rima stanza was by this point practically complete, and his main concern now was to clarify the relation between the staring fury and the blind lush leaf:

> A tree there is that from its topmost bough
> Is half all glittering flame and half all green
> Abounding foliage moistened with the dew;
> a. And half is half and yet is all the scene
> b. For ignorance and knowledge fill the scene
> c. But no not half for each is all the scene

    a. What one consumes the other can renew
    b. And half and half consume what they renew
    c. And what they most consume they most renew

    And he that Attys image hangs between
    That staring fury and the blind lush leaf
    not know not
    May mind now what he knows but knows no grief

He could then shape the first printed version:

    A tree there is that from its topmost bough
    Is half all glittering flame and half all green
    Abounding foliage moistened with the dew;
    And half is half and yet is all the scene;
    And half and half consume what they renew,
    And he that Attis' image hangs between
    That staring fury and the blind lush leaf
    May know not what he knows, but knows not grief.

    What the evolution of this stanza shows is reasonably representative
of the procedures that Yeats followed in establishing his highly formalized
stanzaic patterns. Here he began with an icon of rich suggestiveness that
expressed many of his basic preoccupations. He presented it to his
imagination and contemplated it with fixed attention until he had
formulated a linear statement that limited the possible rhythmic pattern to
the decasyllabic form ("There is a tree that from its topmost bough").
With the primary conceptual statement made, so that the divided tree of
Peredur became the physical reality of the stanza, he then sought out the
implied stanzaic pattern, writing a list of rhyme words, and writing one
line of nonsense in order to maintain the composing energy that both icon
and prosody released. Within that stanza he was limited by rhyme scheme
and the numerical limit of lines, and his problem was, accepting those
limits, to implicate in the lines the greatest possible range of meaning.
Hence his heavy abstraction in early drafts, the stress on wisdom, death,
ignorance, knowledge, life, the attempt to gain inclusiveness by generality.
The suppression of those overt concepts left the final version deliberately
evasive and strangely mocking, even playful. The interchange of moisture
and flame takes on the character of fluid dance, with equality set by the
intervention of Attis' image, and the two extremities depreciated. In
Yeats's several sources there is no reference to any "staring fury," and this is
his way of identifying flame, death, and knowledge, each a destructive
peril. And the blind lush leaf of ignorant life is seen as equally menacing to
those who seek revelation beyond grief.
    The lines, balanced in their movement, check and qualify the
extremity of statement, so that the ultimate effect is tantalizing and
haunting. His sources are thus reduced and arranged to a new shape. This
is a tree that has been taken from Peredur and Attis so that it is no longer

theirs, nor is it simply to be identified with the exemplary organic form that the Romantics—and Yeats in certain moods—took trees to be. The tree that he so certainly asserts to exist is ancient, dual, widely distributed in the folk religious imagination, associated with ritual practices, so inclusive as to subsume the twin trees of the cabala, and made up of both mere stupid persistent life and the all-revealing flame of deathful knowledge. The stanza has a wide and deliberately suppressed context. The deliberateness is shown in the substrata of thought present in the several rejected lines. The poet may tell all; but the stanza will not permit him to, for it forces compressions and omissions upon his merely personal will. The collision between the personal intent and the impersonal form generates a fresh tension.

The stanza is typical of Yeats's method of composing his decasyllabic lines. The stanza and the period coincide; the rhymes are guides to composition, and one pair is strikingly imperfect; the only lines that appear to have extra syllables are easily justified if one considers the natural elisions that take place in reading the lines aloud ("glittering" and "foliage" would easily slur to form two syllables each). "Vacillation" taken as a whole indicates the range of Yeats's prosody from the tight sparse stress lines of part I through the ottava rima of parts II and III, with their decasyllabic lines, and the stress lines of IV, V, and VI to the decasyllables of VII and thence to the rough fourteener of VIII. The inclusiveness that we have seen in his construction of the icon of the tree is exhibited throughout the poem, in the dramaturgy, the iconography, and the prosody. In its extraordinary ease and density, its sensitively varied texture, the poem represents one of Yeats's most revealing and rewarding works. He saw its theme as central to his view of experience, and his treatment of the icon of the tree, both in his sense of its connotations and in his disciplined ordering of the stanza, is indicative of the supreme integration of diverse materials and techniques that distinguished this poem and his entire career.

Anomalies

If we assume that Yeats used a dual prosody in which lines were justifiable by either stress or syllable count, and if we assume further that his concern with vocalic pressure and passionate syntax led him to minor violations of the decasyllabic line that can be accommodated by elision ("glittering," "foliage," "memory," "bodily"), then the anomalies in his lyric verse are remarkably few. The principle of linear substitution accounts for the peculiar prosodic structure of a poem like "Lapis Lazuli," where the eight-syllable and four-stress line have equal value and where he wins some of his most free and jubilant prosodic triumphs. There are, however, lines that violate even the wide range of expectations that my phrasing of his prosody allows. These lines occur with greater frequency in *Last Poems* than in *The Tower*, and there are two possible explanations. First, one might assume that the poems of his last years were not subjected to the same involved process of rewriting that gave many of his later poems that special quality of finish, even patina, that distinguishes his work. But this seems to me, in view of the extremely elaborate rewriting that underlay the printed versions of *Last Poems*, not a reasonable assumption. The second possibility, which seems to me more probable, is that the prosody of the poems after *The Winding Stair* displays the same effort toward liberation that I have already discussed in relation to his iconography. His growing recklessness, his increasing indifference to social judgment, is apparent in the dramaturgy and iconography of these final declarations, and the prosody exhibits the same motives. A line in one of his most celebrated poems shows his prosodic freedom. In "The Statues," after asserting that Pythogoras planned the statues and that there was then no reason for surprise or even for being attracted by the systematized forms of Greek statuary, he continued to talk in favor of an art of passion (personality) rather than of individualized character. These carefully engineered statues evoked responses that went deeper than any merely individual identity. And yet the statues presented a reality greater than any that Pythagoras could have construed, for all his intellectual brilliance:

> No! Greater than Pythagoras, for the men
> That with a mallet or a chisel modelled these
> Calculations that look but casual flesh, put down
> All Asiatic vague immensities,
> And not the banks of oars that swam upon
> The many-headed foam at Salamis. . . .

The first two lines can be reasonably justified as having five major stresses, and the last three are decasyllabic. The one really anomalous line is "Calculations that look but casual flesh," and even if we assume that Yeats looked on "calculations" as having only one major stress (a line in the fourth stanza of the poem confirms this), the line is too heavily loaded to be justified even by Yeats's very flexible prosody. One has to say either that the line has five major loci of stress and is justifiable only by a foot prosody, or one has to say that here Yeats's prosody breaks down under the demands of his syntax. What happened is, I think, an amalgamation of these two possibilities. The phrase "Calculations that look but casual flesh" has the weight and balance of a Yeatsean line as well as the exact phrasing of one of his obsessive aims. The phrase "put down" is by this very fact given an extraordinary emphasis that is further stressed by the suspended syntax. A passion that cannot be balked overpowers the formal requirement and establishes another norm (that of the casual flesh?) that distorts the expected shape. It can be justified prosodically but largely, I think, because we want to justify it, because of its cogency and the articulation of the stanza, rather than because of the norms of any prosody.

The anomalies merely dramatize the special qualities of Yeats's prosody, for the simplicity and range of his linear sense come directly from his concern with immediacy and permanence. In the minute discriminations of the line he sought the same reconciliation of opposites that he reached toward in his quest for a dramaturgy that would accept the peculiarities of his experience and the generality of his passions and for an iconography that would move with equal ease in the pageantry of cosmic process and the unreliable events of a fallen world. His syntax and prosody are the essential agents of his work, for it is in the pace and rhythm of language that poetry makes its most incisive effects. Each man has a prosody and syntax that limit the permissible relations of his language and thus condition his accessibility to experience. It is possible to change the dramatic or symbolic content of a mind and leave that mind essentially unchanged if no corresponding alteration of syntactic and rhythmic habits has been effected. The mind can always find equivalents to the exorcised symbols and remain as impervious as before. The mind's defenses are shrewd. Poetry, however, imposes a rhythm that impels the opening of new nervous channels, and it is the combination of syntax and prosody that ultimately liberates. The range of human possibility is limited by kinesthetic habit, and part of the resistance to poetry comes from a deep and justified conviction that it will make an exorbitant claim, will ask that we change our lives or, with overwhelmingly dangerous intimacy, force us to move in designs that until then we had neither entertained nor imagined. Yeats, moving within the main prosodic tradition of English, brought to it his highly charged and demanding apprehension of the fragmented mind in which we all participate, and he offered a troubling and suffering integrity to heal our inner divisions. The integrity of the prosody is the emblem of the wholeness and inclusiveness of his art, and of its insistence that we know ourselves and our condition afresh.

[On "Meditations in Time of Civil War"]
Thomas R. Whitaker*

The dialogue between self and shadows — whether antiselves or projections of the self — produced in "Meditations in Time of Civil War" a rich orchestration of personal and historical conflicts. The poem is a complex act of creation and self-judgment in the realm of the spiritualized soil.

*From Swan and Shadow: Yeats's Dialogue with History (Chapel Hill: University of North Carolina Press, 1964), 171–87.

"Surely . . ." The dialogue enters with that stress on the very first word, as the speaker yearningly considers "Ancestral Houses." Already the opening sentence contains the seeds of its own negation:

> Surely among a rich man's flowering lawns,
> Amid the rustle of his planted hills,
> Life overflows without ambitious pains . . .

Gradually the image of the fountain emerges, establishing the correspondence of spirit and soil which underlies the entire poem. But the pale abstractness of the setting, in which the fountain alone "rains down life," already calls into question the reality of that social ideal. The retort is deserved: "Mere dreams, mere dreams!" But a surprising counterassertion follows:

> Yet Homer had not sung
> Had he not found it certain beyond dreams
> That out of life's own self-delight had sprung
> The abounding glittering jet . . .

It is the intuition of a radical self-sufficiency and vitality, which has been too hastily projected into the inadequate landscape of ancestral houses. The allusion to Homer suggests the reason for the inadequacy: sweetness must come from strength. Life cannot merely overflow "without ambitious pains"; the "abounding glittering jet" results from a pent-up force that can surmount obstacles. The dream must be revised: it is precisely the ambitious pains of violent and bitter men that

> might rear in stone
> The sweetness that all longed for night and day,
> The gentleness none there had ever known . . .

Instead of an effortless fountain, a monumental synthesis of opposites: but though "in stone," such a synthesis is momentary, a historical climax which bears the seeds of its own destruction. The eighteenth-century elegance, mimed in the verse itself, renders ambitious pains unnecessary and dries up the fountain:

> O what if levelled lawns and gravelled ways
> Where slippered Contemplation finds his ease
> And Childhood a delight for every sense,
> But take our greatness with our violence?

Where then may the speaker himself seek the transfiguration of the fallen world? He turns from the world dreamed of to the world possessed, from "Ancestral Houses" to "My House." At the time he was writing this sequence, 1921–22, Yeats was relating the "sense of possession" he had felt in Sligo to his concept of "Unity of Being": "All that moves us is related to our possible Unity; we lose interest in the abstract and concrete alike; only when we have said, 'My fire,' and so distinguished it from 'the fire' and 'a fire,' does the fire seem bright. Every emotion begins to be related, as musical notes are related, to every other."[1] In "My House" we see a measure of historical continuity, but also strength and even violence:

> An ancient bridge, and a more ancient tower,
> A farmhouse that is sheltered by its wall,
> An acre of stony ground,
> Where the symbolic rose can break in flower,
> Old ragged elms, old thorns innumerable,
> The sound of the rain or sound
> Of every wind that blows . . .

Isaiah had prophesied the spiritualization of a soil very like this stony ground: "The wilderness and the solitary place shall be glad for them; and the desert shall rejoice, and blossom as the rose." Blake had envisioned in such a place the marriage of Heaven and Hell:

> Roses are planted where thorns grow,
> And on the barren heath
> Sing the honey bees[2]

But in the harsh Yeatsian landscape even the symbolic rose must *break* in flower.

Here the speaker does not inherit the glory of the rich; he re-enacts the founding of a house:

> Two men have founded here. A man-at-arms
> Gathered a score of horse and spent his days
> In this tumultuous spot,
> Where through long wars and sudden night alarms
> His dwindling score and he seemed castaways
> Forgetting and forgot;
> And I, that after me
> My bodily heirs may find
> To exalt a lonely mind,
> Befitting emblems of adversity.

The isolated modern poet's need to forge his own tradition may itself be a condition of great achievement: his spiritual inheritance is that of adversity, with its attendant opportunities. Yet the comparison of founders ominously reduces the man-at-arms to the speaker's own proud and introverted isolation. Such was not the condition of those violent, bitter men who could rear in stone the sweetness and gentleness that all had longed for. In a wilderness where art is divorced from power and communion, the symbolic rose threatens to be more dream than reality.

That lurking conflict is already evident in the first stanza of "My House." This is a poem of interior landscapes, one in which "familiar woods and rivers . . . fade into symbol." The speaker might say with Wordsworth,

> bodily eyes
> Were utterly forgotten, and what I saw
> Appeared like something in myself, a dream,
> A prospect in the mind

— or feel with Coleridge that the object of Nature is "the dim awaking of a forgotten or hidden truth of my inner nature."[3] Hence, as we move from "Old ragged elms, old thorns innumerable," to

> The stilted water-hen
> Crossing stream again
> Scared by the splashing of a dozen cows . . .

we should suspect an ironic self-image, as yet unexplored. The second stanza takes up that stilted isolation, presenting as another spiritual ancestor Milton's Platonist, atop his winding stair, in his "chamber arched with stone," withdrawn from the crude traffic of the world:

> Benighted travellers
> From markets and from fairs
> Have seen his midnight candle glimmering.

The ironic parallels are as yet but implicit; the speaker has not allowed himself to examine his proud isolation in full daylight.

Asking why such blindness is possible, we note a further implication in the Platonist who, the speaker imagines,

> toiled on
> In some like chamber, shadowing forth
> How the daemonic rage
> Imagined everything

Both he and his spiritual heir, though lonely creators of emblems, castaways from the world of markets and fairs, are yet at home in a lighted chamber, communing with the world soul, while others are "benighted." But they do not commune with the "holy calm" that overspread Wordsworth's soul and caused him to see the landscape as a prospect in the mind. The demiurgic power as this speaker experiences it is a "daemonic rage," the transcendental corollary of his own bitter violence and of the "long wars and sudden night alarms" that isolate him as they once isolated the first founder in this spot. Again the poem's complex theme modulates from reassuring unity to division and fragmentation. But the conflicts in "My House" are submerged, apparent only because the speaker is shadowing forth more complete emblems of his own condition than he yet admits.

He turns now to another possession, the table whereon he shadows forth that daemonic rage. Into his world of adversity, isolation, and cyclical change comes "Sato's gift, a changeless sword," placed by pen and paper

> That it may moralise
> My days out of their aimlessness.

But for a poet aware of the virtues of change as well as its dangers, that is a vexing symbol:

> In Sato's house,
> Curved like new moon, moon-luminous,
> It lay five hundred years.
> Yet if no change appears
> No moon; only an aching heart
> Conceives a changeless work of art.

Though a world of tortured change needs an image of the changeless, does not that image itself imply a fallacious ideal, a static culture, empty and unproductive?[4] No, the speaker surmounts his objection by imagining in the East an unchanging tradition maintained by centuries of mental alertness, inspired by transcendental longings:

> Soul's beauty being most adored,
> Men and their business took
> The soul's unchanging look;
> For the most rich inheritor,
> Knowing that none could pass Heaven's door
> That loved inferior art,
> Had such an aching heart
> That he, although a country's talk
> For silken clothes and stately walk,
> Had waking wits; it seemed
> Juno's peacock screamed.

There, in contrast to the milieu of "Ancestral Houses," the grandson was no "mouse," the "inherited glory of the rich" was not an empty shell, the peacock did not merely stray "with delicate feet upon old terraces" while Juno was ignored by the "garden deities."

But is that peacock scream, that apocalyptic annunciation,[5] more than another illusion? Whether dream or past reality — and it is slightly distanced by the ironic diction of this section — it can now do no more than stimulate this speaker's aching heart. Is that not function enough? An ambiguous answer emerges in the next section, "My Descendants." Returning to the cyclical world of the West, to the lunar inheritance which for better or worse he must enjoy and transmit, the speaker presents himself as one who "must nourish dreams" — but is he obligated or condemned to do so? And are they unsubstantial fantasies or symbolic roses, evasion or transfiguration of life?

> Having inherited a vigorous mind
> From my old fathers, I must nourish dreams
> And leave a woman and a man behind
> As vigorous of mind, and yet it seems

> Life scarce can cast a fragrance on the wind,
> Scarce spread a glory to the morning beams,
> But the torn petals strew the garden plot;
> And there's but common greenness after that.

But if his descendants should lose that ambiguous flower, he would, enraged, hasten the very cyclical destruction that haunts him:

> May this laborious stair and this stark tower
> Become a roofless ruin that the owl
> May build in the cracked masonry and cry
> Her desolation to the desolate sky.

No longer dare he hope that his "bodily heirs" may find, to their advantage, "Befitting emblems of adversity." He may be both founder and last inheritor —

> The Primum Mobile that fashioned us
> Has made the very owls in circles move

— and he will therefore take consolation only in the goods of the moment:

> And I, that count myself most prosperous,
> Seeing that love and friendship are enough,
> For an old neighbor's friendship chose the house
> And decked and altered it for a girl's love . . .

Though still unable to refrain from adding another phrase which contemplates at least some bare monument to the present —

> And know whatever flourish and decline
> These stones remain their monument and mine

— in his minimal optimism he has now abandoned even the immortality of the "changeless work of art." Surely here at least the speaker may find the self-sufficiency for which he longs: no mere dream, but the reality of "life's own self-delight."

Yet in glimpsing the depths of his isolation, he has begun to reach outward: "Seeing that love and friendship are enough." That evocation of a sweetness and gentleness not "in stone," as in ancestral houses, but memorialized by these "stones," translates the entire problem to a different plane. The isolation itself called into question, the speaker turns from house and descendants to "The Road at My Door."

> An affable Irregular,
> A heavily-built Falstaffian man,
> Comes cracking jokes of civil war
> As though to die by gunshot were
> The finest play under the sun.

He turns from lunar tragedy to solar comedy, from lofty poetic isolation to the gay cameraderie of a modern man-at-arms — or (in terms of what Yeats called Shakespeare's dominant myth, and was one of his own) from that porcelain vessel, Richard II, saluting his native soil with ostentatious sentiment and telling sad stories of the death of kings, to those vessels of clay, Falstaff and Prince Hal, with their rough humor and affection.[6] Adversity and violence need not imply isolation, nor can the poet dismiss this comedy as trivial:

> A brown Lieutenant and his men,
> Half dressed in national uniform,
> Stand at my door, and I complain
> Of the foul weather, hail and rain,
> A pear tree broken by the storm.

It is not a symbolic rose that has broken, and the contrast of persons recalls the unacknowledged difference in "My House" between the introverted speaker and the first founder in that tumultuous spot. By night the Platonist in his tower had seemed romantically superior to the travellers; by day the retiring and complaining poet becomes a half-comic, half-pathetic pastoral foil to the new military hero.[7] He is, in fact, like that "shadow" noted earlier, the stilted waterhen "Scared by the splashing of a dozen cows."

> I count those feathered balls of soot
> The moor-hen guides upon the stream,
> To silence the envy in my thought;
> And turn towards my chamber, caught
> In the cold snows of a dream.

What dream has been nourished? In this solitary place what narcissus has broken in flower? The implied answer is developed in "The Stare's Nest by My Window," and it will lead, in "I See Phantoms. . . ," beyond the humility of perception to a new reconciliation: an ironic acceptance of the poet's vocation.

> The bees build in the crevices
> Of loosening masonry, and there
> The mother birds bring grubs and flies.
> My wall is loosening; honey-bees,
> Come build in the empty house of the stare.

He no longer imagines a sweetness that bitter men might rear in stone, nor does he hope defiantly for the destruction of his tower and for owls to "build in the cracked masonry." He now sees that sweetness may reside in the very loss he had feared—the very loosening of his wall. This is an inevitable discovery—or rather, rediscovery, for the breaking of protective walls, the nakedness before the winds of heaven, had long been known to Yeats as a prerequisite of poetic vision. Although the invoked honey bees recall those in Porphyry's cave of the nymphs—souls who are "eminently just and sober" and who, "after having performed such things as are acceptable to the gods," will reascend from the world of generation[8] — they also, and perhaps more importantly, recall those which Blake imagined as singing on the barren heath, on the desert that blossoms as the rose. Yeats had once read that prophecy thus: "Freedom shows beauty like roses, and sweetness like that given by the honey of bees, in the road where morality had only revealed a desert or a heath."[9] Given Blake's understanding of negative and restrictive morality (a disguise for the impulse to tyrannize, to wall others in or out), the sweetness which comes with the abandonment of such morality is not opposed to that ("both cathartic and preservative"[10]) produced by Porphyry's bees. For the speaker of this poem such sweetness can come only with freedom from his own self-confinement. Though able, in Shelley's symbolic language, to imagine his tower as contrary in meaning to a dark cave,[11] he now sees that the cloistered permanence of his "chamber arched with stone" is what it always was, the cavern of the mind of which Blake had written: "For man has closed himself up, till he sees all things thro' narrow chinks of his cavern."[12] As this speaker states it, now fusing visions of himself and of society:

> We are closed in, and the key is turned
> On our uncertainty; somewhere
> A man is killed, or a house burned,
> Yet no clear fact to be discerned:
> Come build in the empty house of the stare.

He shares Eliot's waste land —

> We think of the key, each in his prison
> Thinking of the key, each confirms a prison
> Only at nightfall, aethereal rumours
> Revive for a moment a broken Coriolanus

— and the waste land of Claudel's Coufontaine:

> Là-bas on dit qu'il y a eu je sais quoi,
> Les villes de bois qui brûlent, une victoire vaguement
> gagnée. L'Europe est vide et personne ne parle sur la terre.[13]

But the besieged dynastic house or prison is not, from this speaker's humbled position, the abbey of Coufontaine or even "some marvellous empty sea-shell"; it is an empty starling's nest.

Not through coincidence or mere rhetorical artifice does he fuse here the isolation and vastation sprung from his own mind and those imposed by violence from without. He has moved from a romantic parallel between poet and man-at-arms to a humiliating acknowledgment of their differences, and now to an agonized perception of their moral identity:

> A barricade of stone or of wood;
> Some fourteen days of civil war;
> Last night they trundled down the road

> That dead young soldier in his blood:
> Come build in the empty house of the stare.
>
> We had fed the heart on fantasies,
> The heart's grown brutal from the fare;
> More substance in our enmities
> Than in our love; O honey-bees,
> Come build in the empty house of the stare.

The poet's barricade of self-sufficiency and his consequent self-brutaliza-
tion are, in his introverted realm, equivalent to the nationalist-inspired
civil war that rages about him. "Was not a nation . . . bound together by
this interchange among streams or shadows . . . ?" His fantasies that
bitterness and violence might bring sweetness, his glorying in adversity,
and his rage against his descendants have earned his indictment. But the
indictment itself is a partial release from the prison: hence the initial
statement, in the first person singular, "My wall is loosening," leads to
community in isolation, "We are closed in," and then to a perception of
shared guilt, a moral identification of self and those beyond all barricades,
"We had fed the heart on fantasies . . ." In the final cry to the honeybees
the arrogant dream of self-sufficiency is transcended; the perception that
"love and friendship are enough" has flowered, purged of its complacency.

The poet can now climb his winding stair, not to a chamber arched
with stone, but to the top of a *broken* tower, where he is possessed by a
vision:

> I climb to the tower-top and lean upon broken stone,
> A mist that is like blown snow is sweeping over all,
> Valley, river, and elms, under the light of a moon
> That seems unlike itself, that seems unchangeable,
> A glittering sword out of the east. A puff of wind
> And those white glimmering fragments of the mist sweep by.
> Frenzies bewilder, reveries perturb the mind;
> Monstrous familiar images swim to the mind's eye.

Every "Space that a Man views around his dwelling-place / Standing on
his own roof . . . is his Universe." But as the animating wind makes clear,
this universe is no longer a confining mental chamber. The speaker is
naked to the winds of heaven. He leans upon the very ruin of self-
sufficiency; sweeping over the landscape are the "cold snows of a dream"
shared by those beyond the broken barricades. Though he sees by a light
whose ominously unchangeable source is a bizarre transmutation of his
own earlier ideal, "A glittering sword out of the east," and though the
"monstrous" images that come are also damningly "familiar," this is no
private fantasy but a vision based upon his own complicity in the
engulfing horror.

The first group of phantoms objectifies the brutality and hatred he
has just recognized:

"Vengeance upon the murderers," the cry goes up,
"Vengeance for Jacques Molay." In cloud-pale rags, or in lace,
The rage-driven, rage-tormented, and rage-hungry troop,
Trooper belabouring trooper, biting at arm or at face,
Plunges towards nothing, arms and fingers spreading wide
For the embrace of nothing . . .

But he is no longer a lofty Platonist, shadowing forth the "daemonic rage";
he glimpses the abyss within himself:

and I, my wits astray
Because of all that senseless tumult, all but cried
For vengeance on the murderers of Jacques Molay.

The next group, phantoms of the "heart's fullness," provides an emotional
antithesis:

Their legs long, delicate and slender, aquamarine their eyes,
Magical unicorns bear ladies on their backs.
The ladies close their musing eyes. No prophecies,
Remembered out of Babylonian almanacs,
Have closed the ladies' eyes, their minds are but a pool
Where even longing drowns under its own excess;
Nothing but stillness can remain when hearts are full
Of their own sweetness, bodies of their loveliness.

But this is not an ethical antithesis: these apparitions are not the invoked
honeybees. Here one aspect of the self-sufficiency and self-delight which
the speaker first projected into the fountain of "Ancestral Houses" achieves
final definition: not a fountain but a pool, not an abounding jet of life but
an eternal stillness of self-contemplation. However beautiful, it is the
deathly goal of Narcissus. For the living speaker these ladies and unicorns
can image not a solution but one term of a predicament.

Indeed, they are strangely similar to their antitheses, the rage-driven
troop: "even longing drowns under its own excess." Because the vision has
moved from one blindness to another, from the ravenous imperception of
Breughel's blindmen careening into the abyss to the closed eyes of Moreau's
narcissistic women and unicorns,[14] it can now move easily, through an
inversion of details further stressing that affinity, to a harshly empty
synthesis:

The cloud-pale unicorns, the eyes of aquamarine,
The quivering half-closed eyelids, the rags of cloud or of lace,
Or eyes that rage has brightened, arms it has made lean,
Give place to an indifferent multitude, give place
To brazen hawks.

Predatory rage and static self-satisfaction merge in a yet more terrible
blindness:

> Nor self-delighting reverie,
> Nor hate of what's to come, nor pity for what's gone,
> Nothing but grip of claw, and the eye's complacency,
> The innumerable clanging wings that have put out the moon.

Such is the consummation the speaker envisions in modern history, such the consummation of his own ethical dialectic. Yet, though inescapably of his time, he is partly freed by the vision itself. He does not fully yield to the rage of the avenging troop, and he cannot now adopt the transcendent narcissism of aquamarine or closed eyes. The poem renders a precarious solution: not the imagined escape from the prison of self through freedom in love, but the open-eyed self-recognition of the half-trapped poet.

> I turn away and shut the door, and on the stair
> Wonder how many times I could have proved my worth
> In something that all others understand or share;
> But O! ambitious heart, had such a proof drawn forth
> A company of friends, a conscience set at ease,
> It had but made us pine the more.

The "ambitious pains" which vexed him at the beginning of the poem cannot be escaped. The dialogical movement here as throughout the meditation — "But O! ambitious heart" — renders the speaker's alertness to the continual temptations to self-containment. It renders, therefore, his actual if momentary freedom from such self-containment. Because all images of fulfilment carry their own irony, he must accept the problematic human state, with its attendant guilt and dissatisfaction. And if life cannot in any facile way be self-delighting —

> The abstract joy,
> The half-read wisdom of daemonic images,
> Suffice the ageing man as once the growing boy.

The irony of "suffice," which has led critics to comment upon Yeats's vacillation between action and contemplation or upon his "unfortunate" dabbling in the occult, can be fully weighed only in the context of this rich meditation on what may and what may not suffice the heart. That irony implies no dismissal of the poetic task as "mere dreams." Nor is the speaker now Shelley's "visionary prince" priding himself, through romantic irony, on "mysterious wisdom won by toil."[15] He is rather the fortunate victim of the "daemonic images" we have just seen, which are for him the burden of self-knowledge. He no longer strives for the goal of action or that of fantasy — a substitute for action.

> The rhetorician would deceive his neighbours,
> The sentimentalist himself; while art
> Is but a vision of reality.[16]

The complex irony in that "but," as in the "suffice" of this poem, partly answers any objection that "Meditations in Time of Civil War" does not move to a clear ethical transcendence of the speaker's problem, as glimpsed in "The Stare's Nest at My Window." A willed vision of what the honeybees might bring would be factitious; the poet can realize only what he is. The rest may come of its own accord when, through being perceived, the psychic walls begin to crumble. Ribh would say, "He holds him from desire" — and, indeed, the final section of this poem has rendered just such a "symbolical revelation received after the suspension of desire" as "What Magic Drum?" describes. "Does not all art come," Yeats wrote, "when a nature, that never ceases to judge itself, exhausts personal emotion in action or desire so completely that something impersonal . . . starts into its place, something which is as unforeseen, as completely organised, even as unique, as the images that pass before the mind between sleeping and waking?"[17] Such are the "daemonic images" of this last section; such, in a larger sense, is the entire poem.

Despite Yeats's frequently quoted remarks about virtue as dramatic, the wearing of a mask,[18] this poem renders his understanding of the fact that attention is the mother of virtue as it is of art. Though the speaker wears various masks of poetic or moral ambition, engages in the deceits of rhetorician and sentimentalist, he closely watches the self that does so. From that watching, that attention, spring both the ethical development of the speaker and the poem itself. For the poem, the "vision of reality," is of that mask-wearing self, and it is therefore, like the poems of Villon, finally "without fear or moral ambition" though decidedly ethical in its substance. In 1905, arguing against didactic art, art composed with the intent to persuade, Yeats had said:

> If we understand our own minds, and the things that are striving to utter themselves through our minds, we move others, not because we have understood or thought about those others, but because all life has the same root. Coventry Patmore has said, "The end of art is peace," and the following of art is little different from the following of religion in the intense preoccupation that it demands. Somebody has said, "God asks nothing of the highest soul except attention", and so necessary is attention to mastery in any art, that there are moments when we think that nothing else is necessary, and nothing else so difficult.[19]

Yeats clearly understood another of Patmore's statements: "Attention to realities, rather than the fear of God, is 'the beginning of wisdom'. . ." Given the bold prophetic note sounded by his art, we can see that he also might say with Patmore: "Indeed, it is difficult to say how far an absolute moral courage in acknowledging intuitions may not be of the very nature of genius and whether it might not be described as a sort of interior sanctity which dares to see and confess to itself that it sees, though its vision should place it in a minority of one."[20]

In "Meditations in Time of Civil War," as in the apocalyptic romances of the nineties, a partial yielding to the daemonic voice enables the poet to perceive and judge those powers within him which, unconsciously obeyed, would lead and have led to historical catastrophe. But this poem of dramatic experience shows more clearly the complex interior dialogue through which suffering moves toward illumination, as the daemonic is incorporated into the precarious equilibrium of personality — and so transformed. The last sentence of the poem, ironically echoing Wordsworth's "Ode on Intimations of Immortality,"[21] reinforces this conclusion. Wordsworth had said:

> Shades of the prison-house begin to close
> Upon the growing Boy,
> But He beholds the light, and whence it flows,
> He sees it in his joy . . .

And in compensation for the complete loss of that light, Wordsworth had found "soothing thoughts that spring / Out of human suffering," a "faith that looks through death," a "philosophic mind." But the Yeatsian speaker, aware of the Wordsworthian atrophy so rationalized, ironically affirms in his own life a lack of change, and so points to a more genuinely continuing growth:

> The abstract joy,
> The half-read wisdom of daemonic images,
> Suffice the ageing man as once the growing boy.

Though his continuing joy is "abstract," an inevitable limitation arising from his turning inward to the source of daemonic images, the light shining through those images has led him to perceive the existence of his own prisonhouse, his chamber arched with stone, and to prevent it from closing upon him irrevocably. It has led him also to see that the "philosophic mind," with *its* "eye's complacency" is another form of the spiritual atrophy that tempts through every image that asks to be taken as a final truth, another phantom illustrating the multiform blindness which he precariously escapes. Perception must "suffice," and full perception warns that our wisdom is momentary and but "half-read."

The symbolic rose, which here *breaks* in flower so diversely, cannot be forced. It must bloom in the midst of civil war: a unity of being that maintains the abounding jet of life must arise from the perception of disunity. No individual may complacently possess that fountain of life's self-delight. He may know it only through continuing openness, continuing vulnerability. Yeats had recognized as much, in a passage of 1917 which foreshadowed this poem:

> A poet, when he is growing old, will ask himself if he cannot keep his mask and his vision without new bitterness, new disappointment . . .
> Surely, he may think, now that I have found vision and mask I need not suffer any longer. He will buy perhaps some small old house, where like Ariosoto, he can dig his garden, and think that in the return of birds and leaves, or moon and sun, and in the evening flight of the rooks he

may discover rhythm and pattern like those in sleep and so never awake out of vision. Then he will remember Wordsworth withering into eighty years, honoured and empty-witted, and climb to some waste room and find, forgotten there by youth, some bitter crust.[22]

And the speaker of "Meditations in Time of Civil War" had guessed as much, near the beginning of the poem: "Homer had not sung . . ." The *Iliad* offers no Goethean assurance of the eternal harmony of existence; indeed, Homer taught Goethe that in our life on earth we have, properly speaking, to enact Hell. The rose, finally, is the meditation itself, the spiritualization of that tragic soil, the vision of that state. For both the poet and the man, Yeats was discovering, the "peace" of that vision is the paradoxically active means of transfiguring the wheel of destiny.

Notes

1. *V-A*, p. 61.

2. Isaiah 35:1; Blake, *Complete Writings*, p. 148.

3. William Wordsworth, *The Prelude*, Bk. 2, lines 349 ff.; Samuel Taylor Coleridge, *Anima Poetae* (Boston, 1895), 115.

4. For an earlier description of Eastern traditionalism ("the painting of Japan, not having our European Moon to churn its wits . . .") see *E&I*, p.225 (1916).

5. Cf. *V-B*, p. 268.

6. See *E&I*, pp. 103–9 (1901). There, as in this poem, Yeats has an eye for the tragic ironies in both porcelain and clay. A simpler use of the metaphor appeared in *The Countess Cathleen* (*CPlays*, p. 29).

7. Yeats's use of such a foil comes, of course, from literary tradition as well as from personal experience. He used it more simply for romantic pathos in *The Countess Cathleen*, as Cathleen says of the gardener (*Poems* [London, 1895], p. 98):

> Pruning time,
> And the slow ripening of his pears and apples,
> For him is a long, heart-moving history.

In *L'Otage* (p. 14), amidst the breaking of nations, occurs this dialogue:

> Coufontaine: Il était temps de nous mettre a l'abri.
> Je reconnais le vent de mon pays.
> Sygne: Quel dommage! Les pommiers étaient si beaux!
> Il ne restera pas un pépin sur l'arbre.

8. Quoted in *E&I*, p. 84 (1900); see *Selected Works of Porphyry*, tr. Thomas Taylor (London, 1823), p. 185.

9. *E&Y*, 61.

10. *Select Works of Porphyry*, p. 181.

11. CF. *E&I*, p. 87 (1900).

12. Blake, *Complete Writings*, p. 154.

13. Claudel, *L'Otage*, p. 54.

14. For a more explicit image of the blindmen, see "A Dialogue of Self and Soul," *CP*,

p. 232, or "On a Political Prisoner," *CP*, p. 181; for Yeats's possession of Moreau's "Women and Unicorns," see *The Letters of W. B. Yeats*, ed. Allan Wade (New York, 1955), p. 865.

    15. "The Phases of the Moon," *CP*, p. 161.

    16. "Ego Dominus Tuus," *CP*, p. 159.

    17. *Au*, p. 200.

    18. *Au*, p. 285.

    19. *P&C*, p. 161.

    20. Coventry Patmore, *Principle in Art, and Religio Poetae* (one-vol. ed.; London, 1913), pp. 244, 290.

    21. As Richard Ellmann has suggested, *The Identity of Yeats* (New York, 1954), p. 223.

    22. *Mythologies* (New York, 1959), p. 342.

Some Yeatsian Versions of Comedy

Hazard Adams[*]

> Joy and woe are woven fine.
>   — Blake

    In this centenary year, as we pause to salute a great achievement, it is well to remind ourselves that Yeats wrote not only poems and plays but also two of the most remarkable books of his time — the *Autobiographies* and *A Vision*. Perhaps because we are still staggered by Yeats's poetic accomplishments we are inclined to overlook the fact that these works are, so to speak, books in themselves. Of course, we have read them with care, but usually as if they were mines of interpretation situated somewhere underneath the poetry. Because they have been so very helpful to us as mines, the qualities which they possess in themselves are not often remarked. One of their most absorbing qualities is the comic. Nevertheless, in a recent excellent study, *The Irish Comic Tradition*, Professor Vivian Mercier has disregarded both books; indeed Yeats has usually been considered an essentially tragic writer. There is nothing fundamentally wrong with such an assessment: all of us know that the tragic and the comic, rather than being incompatible, are necessary contraries. But the scales of Yeats criticism have long been tipped rather too far in the direction of high seriousness. The result is that without fail we have tended to discover behind Yeats's poetic ironies a brooding solemnity, and we have tended to treat it as more fundamental than the gesture of the language itself. Although I accept the essential tragedy in many of Yeats's poems, I must insist that when we examine *Autobiographies* and *A Vision* it will positively not do to pass through Yeats's outward gesture too rapidly. *Autobiographies* and *A Vision* are serious books, but their seriousness

*From *In Excited Reverie: A Centenary Tribute to William Butler Yeats, 1865–1939*, ed. A. Norman Jeffares and K. G. W. Cross (London: Macmillan; New York: St. Martin's, 1965), 152–70.

comes to us in a very complicated way and is perhaps more the act of coming than what comes. The books *are* gestures. That this is so should not surprise us when we consider the emphasis which Yeats himself put upon drama and gesture not only in art but in life as well.

The comic in *Autobiographies* and *A Vision* is more than casually related to Yeats's strong but peculiar sense of fate. Fatality is, of course, the source or vehicle of much tragedy. To couple it with comedy may call for explanation. Fatality in Yeats is curiously different from that irrepressible cosmic force in, say, Hardy. Yeats's vision is at all time dialectical, and one finds his idea of fatality inevitably attached to a curious freedom. Although Yeats refers to exterior fate in a prose passage I am about to quote, generally we can say that Yeatsian fate flows outward from within the individual; it is not primarily an outer force pressing down on the hero but something generated out of his human nature and even his own individuality.[1] Furthermore, the idea of fate has ultimately no meaning for Yeats without the contrary existence of the will. Yeats writes in *The Trembling of the Veil:*

> Among subjective men (in all those, that is, who must spin a web out of their own bowels) the victory is an intellectual daily recreation of all that exterior fate snatches away, and so that fate's antithesis; while what I have called "the Mask" is an emotional antithesis to all that comes out of their internal nature. We begin to live when we have conceived life as tragedy. (p. 116)[2]

We have here the dialectic of the gyres. The last sentence tips the balance for tragedy just as critics of Yeats have so often done, but we must remember that much of Yeats's writing takes up where this quotation ends: what does one do after one makes such a formulation of experience? What does one do after one has begun to live? One must take a stance before tragic truth. One must make one's laughter *contain* the tragic perception, rather than allowing tragedy to smother one's will:

> Their eyes mid many wrinkles, their eyes,
> Their ancient, glittering eyes, are gay.
> ("Lapis Lazuli")

Is it not important to remember, then, the following passage from *Estrangement?*

> Tragedy is passion alone, and rejecting character, it gets form from motives, from the wandering of passion; while comedy is the clash of character. Eliminate character from comedy and you get farce. Farce is bound together by incident alone. In practice most works are mixed: Shakespeare being tragi-comedy. Comedy is joyous because all assumption of a part, of a personal mask, whether of the individualised face of comedy or of the grotesque face of farce, is a display of energy, and all energy is joyous. (p. 286)

The remark about farce here is interesting, particularly with respect to *A Vision*, and I shall return to it. But I am more concerned with the implied interweaving of comedy and tragedy and with Yeats's association of the comic with the mask.[3] In examining *Reveries over Childhood and Youth* we might well note that the Yeats of that book is well masked, indeed twice masked. He is masked first by the "confessional" nature of the work, which invites us by its own inner form to neglect judging it on the basis of biographical veracity and to remember as we read that the speaker himself is part of the construction. In this case he is a character thinking, and the book as a whole is the familiar romantic monologue of a created voice. But because the character is speaking of his past there is a further removal. The character recreated by the monologist is in turn the child, the young man, and the dramatist of about 1900. All of these, it is well to remember, are creations *from a point of view*. We might call the whole thing an intimate distancing, in which romantic expressiveness is balanced by what T. S. Eliot characterized as the necessary extinguishing of the personality. The whole book might be called an excellent example of Keats's "negative capability" exhibited in autobiographical circumstances. Yeats's flowers come not upon the highway to be doted upon.

The source of Yeats's comedy is similar to that of fatalistic tragedy. It lies in the relation of the individual to fate; but rather than Hardy's brooding cosmic or natural force, Yeats's fate seems to be generated out of self.

> I know now that revelation is from the self, but from that age-long memoried self, that shapes the elaborate shell of the mollusc and the child in the womb, that teaches the birds to make their nest; and that genius is a crisis that joins that buried self for certain moments to our trivial daily mind. There are, indeed, personifying spirits that we had best call but Gates and Gate-keepers, because through their dramatic power they bring our souls to crisis, to Mask and Image, caring not a straw whether we be Juliet going to her wedding, or Cleopatra to her death; for in their eyes nothing has weight but passion. We have dreamed a foolish dream those many centuries in thinking that they value a life of contemplation, for they scorn that more than any possible life, unless it be but a name for the worst crisis of all. They have but one purpose, to bring their chosen man to the greatest obstacle he may confront without despair. (pp. 164–5)

We must always remember that we ourselves contain the gates and gate-keepers here mentioned. We look through gates much as, according to Kant, we wear involuntarily the spectacles of time and space. Because he acknowledges this undesired wilfulness in us, Yeats often sees us fool-like and doltish in ridiculous conflict not only with our time and place ("body of fate") but also with the fate we ourselves apparently and mysteriously generate. Yeats's versions of comedy lie in his sense of the fundamental irrationality of life, glimpsed from a position as rational as we partly irrational creatures can make it. Unfortunately under the circumstances no position is ever either irrational or rational enough. Therefore, the speaker of Yeats's books becomes involved in farce as both observer and object of comedy, and the comedy is ironic.

In *Reveries Over Childhood and Youth* the Yeats recalled is a child, the Yeats speaking an adult. As the speaker views the child he generates an ironic distance not unusual in reminiscences of youth. There is something conventionally comic in observing childish activities from an adult point of view or observing adult life from the point of view of childhood. But it is clear that this manipulation of point of view in *Reveries*, which is apparently conventional, becomes less so in the later books, where the author watches the young man Yeats observing not adults from childhood but other adults. Finally in *A Vision* the author's curious treatment of himself as a character in the book controls the work's whole drama. The result of this sort of distance is not primarily tragic but curiously humorous. Indeed, if we look back at *Reveries* after reading the whole of *Autobiographies* we sense that the humour there is not quite the sentimental humour we conventionally thought it to be, that the author means more by the distance established in the discussion of childhood because he maintains it in the later books.

We must now examine what he does mean. In *Reveries* observations of the child lend considerable humour, and this fact is particularly interesting in the light of an assertion made in *The Trembling of the Veil* about "imaginative men who must always, I think, find youth bitter" (p. 225) and an even more personal statement early in *Reveries*:

> Indeed I remember little of childhood but its pain. I have grown happier with every year of life as though gradually conquering something in myself, for certainly my miseries were not made by others but were a part of my own mind. (p. 7)

Bitterness is not, however, the tone of *Reveries*. Rather the child is shown confused by the irrationalities of his intercourse with adults. The speaker's tone is that of a wondering, searching contemplation of human nature. The child himself is the comic victim of rapid shifts of attitude, sometimes his own:

> . . . having prayed for several days that I might die, I began to be afraid that I was dying and prayed that I might live. (p. 3)

This childish changeability does not, as we might expect, disappear in the later books. Instead it seems to be characteristic even of adulthood. Nor is the child's inconsistency the only peculiarity of life. The world itself is strange:

> . . . everybody had told me that English people ate skates and even dog-fish, and I myself had only just arrived in England when I saw an old man put marmalade in his porridge. (p. 21)

So all that had been told him of the English was true! And more! But then his grandfather, though Irish, spoke approvingly of the eating of skates. How strange! Perhaps the child is asking too much of the world. Perhaps he takes things too much at their face value:

> . . . because my grandfather had said the English were in the right to eat skates, I carried a large skate all the six miles or so from Rosses Point, but my grandfather did not eat it. (p. 31)

Is the moral here that words do not lead to deeds and that causality is complex? Does the child discover anything quite so precise as all that? He discovers certainly that his grandfather did not eat the skate. Does he conclude, too, that the world is irrational?

In an unexpectedly irrational world, perhaps it is the naïvely rational creature who is its victim or dolt because he is out of step with experience. Certainly adults misunderstand the child as much as the child misunderstands them:

> Several of my uncles and aunts had tried to teach me to read, and because they could not, and because I was much older than children who read easily, had come to think, as I have learned since, that I had not all my faculties. (p. 14)

The speaker often remembers his childish incapacities:

> My father was still at Sligo when I came back from my first lesson and asked me what I had been taught. I said I had been taught to sing, and he said, "Sing then" and I sang
>
> > Little drops of water,
> > Little grains of sand,
> > Make the mighty ocean,
> > And the pleasant land.
>
> high up in my head. So my father wrote to the old woman that I was never to be taught to sing again. (p. 15)

In the face of these peculiar adult acts it is no wonder that thought becomes unmanageable for the child. But there is also something working within the child himself that is responsible:

> My thoughts were a great excitement, but when I tried to do anything with them, it was like trying to pack a balloon into a shed in a high wind. (p. 25)

Indeed, the irrationality of the "real" world of adulthood seems to become even for the older narrator its central form, and the experience of it in childhood seems permanently to have affected his adult attitudes towards people and the supernatural. There is no doubt that, as he looks back, the speaker of *Autobiographies* relishes the remembrance of what seems to be wild eccentricity in others. He likes to think of this wildness as characteristically Irish. His remembrance of people has a mythical quality beginning as early as the appearance of an Irish schoolmaster in his English school:

> There was but one interruption of our quiet habits, the brief engagement of an Irish master, a fine Greek scholar and vehement teacher, but of fantastic speech. He would open the class by saying, "There he goes, there he goes," or some like words as the headmaster passed by at the end of the hall. (p. 25)

Wild eccentricity Yeats associates with freedom, but because Yeats also believes in a fate generated from within, he sees that freedom must be positively asserted against some other aspect of the self. Therefore he detects in the people he mythicizes and most admires a certain theatricality. He recalls in various episodes the theatricality of his Pollexfen grandfather and several of the Yeatses, including his father. The Middletons, on the other hand, lacked "the instinctive playing before themselves that belongs to those who strike the popular imagination" (p. 10), and Yeats's reverie seldom includes them. The theatrical sense is what separates Yeats's comic heroes from those unconsciously heroic and world-defying grandparents, uncles, and aunts of James Thurber.

In the many reminiscences of his studies in and experience of the occult, this love of the great character is combined with that comic self-disparagement recognizable in the treatment of his own youth. In the midst of a serious description of a seance there appears the following comment:

> I was now struggling vainly with this force which compelled me to movements I had not willed, and my movements became so violent that the table was broken. I tried to pray, and because I could not remember a prayer, repeated in a loud voice—
>
>> "Of Man's first disobedience and the fruit
>> Of that forbidden tree whose mortal taste
>> Brought death into the world and all our woe . . .
>> Sing, Heavenly Muse." (p. 64)

The ridiculousness here plays off Yeats's upbringing against conventional life, but in the most unexpected way, making his incapacity not pathetic but comical and in some curious way even possibly admirable. There is no pose implied by Yeats's quoting Milton in his excitement. Rather there is quite the opposite—an unwilled gesture—a sort of desperation in his recognition that *something* must be said. The speaker sees, alas, no theatricality in these early past selves. He would like to see it, but the world and himself get in the way. Or, to put it another way, he has been rudely thrust out upon the stage without a proper part. A little different are incidents and thoughts described in *The Trembling of the Veil*:

> I had various women friends on whom I would call towards five
> o'clock mainly to discuss my thoughts that I could not bring to a man
> without meeting some competing thought, but partly because their tea
> and toast saved my pennies for the 'bus ride home; but with women,
> apart from their intimate exchanges of thought, I was timid and
> abashed. I was sitting on a seat in front of the British Museum feeding
> pigeons when a couple of girls sat near and began enticing my pigeons
> away, laughing and whispering to one another, and I looked straight in
> front of me, very indignant, and presently went into the Museum
> without turning my head towards them. Since then I have often
> wondered if they were pretty or merely very young. Sometimes I told
> myself very adventurous love-stories with myself for hero, and at other
> times I planned out a life of lonely austerity, and at other times mixed
> the ideals and planned a life of lonely austerity mitigated by periodical
> lapses. (pp. 93–4)

Here the young man either fails to "act" or locks his theatricality in his
own fantasy, finds no mask. Behind this story we must remember the voice
of its teller, the dramatic masked Yeats, a speaker with the requisite stage
presence, consumed by his part. The actor must be able to communicate
his maskedness. As Dr. Johnson long ago pointed out, we never assume the
play to be "real." Indeed we want to know that the players are players so
that we may admire them, escaping out of the sense of the disagreeable or
agreeable into a sense of the beautiful. For Yeats aesthetic distance is a
state of mind relevant to the contemplation not merely of works of art but
of all life itself.

The young Yeats described is present in *Autobiographies* partly in
order to allow the speaking actor to blow off dramatic steam. The point is
not merely that egoistic masking is necessary to us all but that the mask is a
sort of ideal. (Therefore, when in *A Vision* Mary Bell holds up the egg
which will hatch the great rough beast of the new era, Denise de l'Isle
Adam [a pseudonym] comments, "She has done very well, but Robartes
should have asked me to hold it, for I am taller, and my training as a
model would have helped." [p. 53]) Behind this sort of gesture, often
farcical, as above, lies a very serious conception enunciated most clearly in
Estrangement:

> There is a relation between discipline and the theatrical sense. If
> we cannot imagine ourselves as different from what we are are and
> assume that second self, we cannot impose a discipline upon ourselves,
> though we may accept one from others. Active virtue as distinguished
> from the passive acceptance of a current code is therefore theatrical,
> consciously dramatic, the wearing of a mask. (p. 285)

Romantic imaginative creativity is here given a curious twist. In
order truly to create, the individual must seek a mask, an opposite perhaps
impossible to attain, and thus freedom is "fated" in so far as our natures
are not freely chosen. All such activity defies the logic of society as well as

of language: "Style, personality—deliberately adopted and therefore a mask—is the only escape from the hot-faced bargainers and the money changers" (p. 279). Indeed, logic is the villain. "Logic is a machine, one can leave it to itself; unhelped it will force those present to exhaust the subject, the fool is as likely as the sage to speak the appropriate answer" (p. 279).

When Yeats describes others in the *Autobiographies* it is a similar theatricality expressed with some strange irrational *élan* that he most admires. Of Madame Blavatsky Yeats remembers that Henley said to him, "Of course she gets up fraudulent miracles, but a person of genius has to do something" (p. 107). Yeats's meeting with her emphasizes her eccentricity, not the crazy heroism of Thurber's grandfather, insisting upon *his* own world and brandishing his sword against the Sciota River or breaking the spirit of his electric car, but that of a great lady on a stage:

> . . . I was kept a long time kicking my heels. Presently I was admitted and found an old woman in a plain loose dark dress : a sort of old Irish peasant woman with an air of humour and audacious power. I was still kept waiting, for she was deep in conversation with a woman visitor. I strayed through folding doors into the next room and stood, in sheer idleness of mind, looking at a cuckoo clock. It was certainly stopped, for the weights were off and lying upon the ground, and yet, as I stood there the cuckoo came out and cuckooed at me. I interrupted Madame Blavatsky to say, "Your clock has hooted me." "It often hoots at a stranger," she replied. "Is there a spirit in it?" I said. "I do not know," she said, "I should have to be alone to know what is in it." I went back to the clock and began examining it and heard her say, "Do not break my clock." (pp. 106–7)

The reminiscing Yeats admires nothing more than a person about whom a good story can be told. A good story seems to be one which contains a grain of comic irrationality or at least something unsuspected by logic. Madame Blavatsky provided that sort of story:

> When I first began to frequent her house, as I soon did very constantly, I noticed a handsome clever woman of the world there, who seemed certainly very much out of place, penitent though she thought herself. Presently there was much scandal and gossip for the penitent was plainly entangled with two young men, who were expected to grow into ascetic sages. The scandal was so great that Madame Blavatsky had to call the penitent before her and to speak after this fashion, "We think that it is necessary to crush the animal nature; you should live in chastity in act and thought. Initiation is granted only to those who are entirely chaste," but after some minutes in that vehement style, the penitent standing crushed and shamed before her, she had wound up, "I cannot permit you more than one." (p. 109)

The turnabout spoken in the grand style Yeats inevitably recalls. He also always remembers the paradoxical quip, true beyond apparent logic. So he quotes with great admiration Wilde's words about Shaw: "Mr. Bernard Shaw has no enemies but is intensely disliked by all his friends." He follows Wilde's lead himself in a letter of 1911 to T. Sturge Moore: "When a man is so outrageously in the wrong as Shaw he is indispensable, if it were for no other purpose than to fight people like Hewlett, who corrupt the truth by believing in it."[4]

He remembers also Madame Blavatsky saying that people sell their souls to the devil "to have somebody on their side." He delights in her description of religions:

> "That is the Greek church, a triangle like all true religion," I recall her saying, as she chalked out a triangle on the green baize, and then as she made it disappear in meaningless scribbles, "It spread out and became a bramble bush like the Church of Rome." Then rubbing it all out except one straight line, "Now they have lopped off the branches and turned it into a broomstick and that is protestantism." (p. 110)

Precisely what kind of theatricality is characteristic of the great "actors" Yeats observes? It is difficult to say, because Yeats, the actor in his book, quite consciously and for the sake of drama obfuscates the issue. The heroic, almost mythical figures of *Autobiographies* have a sort of discipline, but how it is achieved remains a mystery to the speaker. Yeats describes his own search for it:

> Discovering that I was only self-possessed with people I knew intimately, I would often go to a strange house where I knew I would spend a wretched hour for schooling sake. I did not discover that Hamlet had his self-possession from no schooling but from indifference and passion-conquering sweetness, and that less heroic minds can but hope it from old age. (p. 57)

We can agree that the speaker of these words has schooled himself in theatrical discipline. Much of *Reveries* is therefore composed of (1) a great actor's recollections of his own past fumblings for the mask of nonchalance and (2) remembrance of those in his life who lived their theatricality with glorious abandon, whether willed or fated. Such a gesture is apparently necessary to creative life, and it is essentially comic.

By the time that Yeats came to write *A Vision* he seems to have raised the idea of heroic theatricality and cosmic irrationality to principles of human existence. These ideas actually control the form of the work. In 1928 he was involved in the now well-known exchange of letters on epistemology, or more specifically John Ruskin's cat, with T. Sturge Moore. In one of these letters he wrote:

> If Kant is right the antinomy is in our method of reasoning; but if the Platonists are right may one not think that the antinomy is itself "constitutive," that the consciousness by which we know ourselves and exist is itself irrational? I do not yet put this forward as certainly the

thought of my instructors, but at present it seems the natural interpretation of their symbols.[5]

This sort of statement needs a great deal of qualification and perhaps some correction if it is to become philosophically responsible. Nevertheless it is quite helpful to us as we look at *A Vision* and its comedy. The comedy of *A Vision* arises constantly out of the idea that we cannot adequately know all things by logic or indeed by means of any symbolic system available to us.[6] The comedy is often farcical in Yeats's sense; that is, it is comedy with character eliminated and full of grotesquerie.

A *Vision* is not a discursive work with the aim of communicating a philosophical or pseudo-scientific system of thought. Its so-called "system" must be abstracted up and out of it with the greatest care, for the book as a whole has a dramatic shape and a recognizable, though complicated, gesture. Taken in this way the introductory material of the book must be considered as intimately related to the more technical parts. In *A Vision*, as in *Autobiographies*, the speaker is contained by the total form of the book, and his gesture is a fictional one. Within this form, Yeats the speaker reminisces about Yeats the questor for mysterious cosmic knowledge. At the same time Yeats the speaker creates fabulous farcical stories about the discovery of the system of thought he is about to expound. These stories seem to reflect in life what the system puts to us more abstractly, the idea that the "antinomies cannot be solved."[7] The characters in the stories about Michael Robartes and the preparation of the cosmic egg to hatch the new cultural cycle are characterless characters. They are, in fact, nearly allegories representing aspects of their author's being. The world they inhabit is irrational, the author's treatment of them ridiculous, though at bottom the issues raised are quite serious. All the characters are driven, in the Yeatsian sense, towards mask and image.

There is not enough space here to make a long analysis of the introductory sections of *A Vision*, and one example of what Yeats is doing must therefore suffice.[8] In *Stories of Michael Robartes and his Friends* a man named John Bond tells a very strange story of falling in love with Mary Bell, wed to an elderly man who early in their marriage decided to devote his life to some philanthropic endeavour, namely teaching cuckoos to make nests. This virtually mad, certainly hopeless effort everyone in the story seems to take seriously enough, and indeed there is in the end a sort of Don Quixotish heroism about the old gentleman. John Bond and Mary Bell between them make him believe on his deathbed that one of his more intelligent students has at last succeeded in weaving a nest. The absurdity of the ideal and the seriousness of it from the old man's point of view emphasize the strangeness of those many human efforts we all know about which are perhaps only a little less absurd. John Bond and Mary Bell are names taken from William Blake's "William Bond" and "Long John Brown & Little Mary Bell," the latter of which is one of Blake's most raucous poems about sexual relations and their failure when the "selfhood" triumphs over the desire to annihilate the self in love. There is much giving of the self in John Bond's story. It does not result in a closer apprehension of reality on the part of any of the characters, but it does result in a limited sort of satisfaction. The old man dies content. Mary Bell has helped him to contentment through her efforts to produce a cuckoo's nest from her own hands and therefore she is to a degree content herself, and John Bond, an expert on birds, has been of service to both.

But more important even than these things is the epistemological problem of inner fate implied by the whole matter of teaching, or trying to coax cuckoos, who do not naturally build nests, to an unnatural effort. This matter is, in fact, taken up in *Autobiographies*:

> When Locke's French translator Coste asked him how, if there were no "innate ideas," he could explain the skill shown by a bird in making its nest, Locke replied, "I did not write to explain the actions of dumb creatures," and his translator thought the answer "very good, seeing that he had named his book *A Philosophical Essay upon Human Understanding*." Henry More, upon the other hand, considered that the bird's instinct proved the existence of the Anima Mundi, with its ideas and memories. Did modern enlightenment think with Coste that Locke had the better logic, because it was not free to think otherwise? (p. 160)

A few pages later, Yeats tells us that he himself keeps canaries and at one time provided them with an artificial nest, "a hollow vessel like a saucer," so that they were not in need of the wild bird's skill. The canaries would twist stems of grass around the nest. Yeats observed the mother and father birds taking care of the young, and he has observed his own children, concluding:

> When a man writes any work of genius, or invents some creative action, is it not because some knowledge or power has come into his mind from beyond his mind? It is called up by an image, as I think . . . but our images must be given to us, we cannot choose them deliberately. (p. 164)

We cannot, like the cuckoos, get very interested in nestmaking if we are not nest-making creatures. But we are poem-makers, perhaps—or at least some of us are—and Yeats seems here to express a romantic individualistic version of that old idea called possession by the Muse. In any case, revelation is "from the self," but from an "age-long memoried self." In the farcical story of *A Vision* in which Yeats recounts his experience with the mysterious instructors, he casts himself much as he remembers himself in *Autobiographies*, incapacitated by an irrational reality in which the whole direction of modern society with its logical education refuses to believe. The instructors come to him from within and yet from some strange "other" world as well. They are some part of himself, and yet he cannot control them or even communicate adequately with them. The results are farcical events—his wife falls into a trance in a restaurant because the instructors think them to be in a garden, the instructors complain about Yeats's slowness and literalness of mind, Yeats tries to drive away his wife's dream that she is a cat by barking like a dog. These events are very funny, verging sometimes upon the slapstick. The result is quite similar to that of the comedy in *Autobiographies*. It emphasizes the limits of man's control over himself and the naïvté of man's faith in simple "reality." It suggests that man inhabits a world where he will always look a bit foolish and will always confront something beyond his powers to understand. As a result, the gesture that man makes towards his situation is his most important function. Yeats recommends a fine balance of tragic irony and ironic comedy, the laughing lip praised by the red man in *The Green Helmet*,[9] the glittering eyes of the Chinese sages in "Lapis Lazuli," gay joy in the contemplation of theatrical eccentricity, willing acceptance of the joke upon oneself, even when that joke is a cosmic one. All of these stances imply the necessity of discovering what dignity one can salvage from cosmic farce:

> I think that the true poetic moment of our time is towards some heroic discipline . . . When there is despair, public or private, when settled order seems lost, people look for strength within or without. Auden, Spender, all that seem the new movement, *look* for strength in Marxian Socialism, or in Major Douglas; they want marching feet. The lasting expression of our time is not this obvious choice but in a sense of something steel-like and cold within the will, something passionate and cold.[10]

At first glance steel-like coldness seems antithetical to the comic, but perhaps if we study comedy carefully we shall see that it is not. In any case, the comedy which Yeats offers us is ironic comedy, laughter emanating from a mask of cold ideality. It leads oddly enough to a great sense of humanity which is nowhere better shown than in the ironic conclusion of *A Vision*. There, the absurd relationship between himself and his instructors having been set forth, Yeats admits to the limitations of his powers to interpret the instructors' message. Indeed does the message contain knowledge at all? Sitting in his chair, meditating upon the symbols of gyre and cone, he discovers, like Faust, that ultimate knowledge will not be his. For a moment he grieves, but

> Then I understand. I have already said all that can be said. The particulars are the work of the *thirteenth sphere* or cycle which is in every man and called by every man his freedom. Doubtless, for it can do all things and knows all things, it knows what it will do with its own freedom but it has kept the secret. (p. 302)

Yeats seems almost to exult in this conclusion. It does after all represent the achievement of a kind of knowledge—though ironic like that in which

Kant takes pleasure — but more important it completes a total gesture and concludes the ironic comedy of which it is a part.

Reveries over Childhood and Youth ends with a statement not unrelated to it:

> For some months now I have lived with my own youth and childhood, not always writing indeed but thinking of it almost every day, and I am sorrowful and disturbed. It is not that I have accomplished too few of my plans, for I am not ambitious, but when I think of all the books I have read, and of the wise words I have heard spoken, and of the anxiety I have given to parents and grandparents, and of the hopes that I have had, all life weighed in the scales of my own life seems to me a preparation for something that never happens. (p. 65)

Indeed this passage appears very much the antithesis of comedy, but by a sort of negative appraisal one can see, I think, that the statement is meant to reveal that there is a possible contrary to its speaker: a masked figure who cares not a fig for "preparation" or for some great day, a figure who believes in the "now" of things, in momentary gay gesture and in drama, a figure who believes that there are things more important than all that is laboriously achieved by material effort or consumed by the mill of the mind. In *Autobiographies* this contrary figure, a perhaps coarse and indecorous artist, insists on a considerable substance of comedy, serious as it may be, some of it satirizing the too-solemn, insufficiently masked young man remembered by the speaker, much of it remembering with affectionate awe great comedians among old acquaintances and their momentary acts.

> Beautiful lofty things: O'Leary's noble head;
> My father upon the Abbey stage, before him a raging crowd:
> "This Land of Saints," and then as the applause died out,
> "Of plaster Saints"; his beautiful mischievous head thrown back.
> ("Beautiful Lofty Things")

The comic is a necessary aspect of Yeats's art that should not be neglected. Its apprehension is necessary to any tragic perception we discover in Yeats's work. On the great poet's tombstone famous words advise the passing horseman to "Cast a cold eye / On life, on death." Let us remember that the warm eye laments and overflows. It is the cold eye, high on the mountain or on horseback, that, seeing abroad, glitters.

Notes

1. I am not referring here to what Yeats calls in *A Vision* the "body of fate," which *is* the outer world and its events, but am using the word "fate" to stand for something never directly named in his work except perhaps at the end of *A Vision*, where it is called peculiarly "freedom."

2. All quotations from Yeats's autobiographical writings are taken from *The Autobiog-*

raphy of William Butler Yeats, New York, 1953, published in England as *Autobiographies*, London, 1955. Page numbers following quotations refer to the New York edition.

3. It is important to remember that Yeats means nothing derogatory by his use of the word "mask." We associate masks perhaps with criminals and Hallowe'en hobgoblins, or a puritanism within us associates it with the impropriety of mimesis in the theatre, a sort of deception. But Yeats's aesthetic stance makes the tools of drama the avenue not to magical delusion but to ideal reality.

4. *W. B. Yeats and T. Sturge Moore: Their Correspondence, 1901–1937*, London, 1953, p. 19.

5. *W. B. Yeats and T. Sturge Moore: Their Correspondence, 1901–1937*, London, 1953, p. 131.

6. I have discussed this matter in "Symbolism and Yeats's *A Vision*," *Journal of Aesthetics and Art Criticism*, xxii, 4 (Summer, 1964), pp. 425–436.

7. Quoted from Yeats's "Genealogical Tree of Revolution," in A. N. Jeffares, *W. B. Yeats: Man and Poet*, London, 1962, p. 351.

8. For a longer discussion see my *Blake and Yeats: The Contrary Vision*, Ithaca, 1955, pp. 162–99.

9. The relevant lines are:

> . . . And I choose the laughing lip
> That shall not turn from laughing, whatever rise or fall;
> The heart that grows no bitterer although betrayed by all;
> The hand that loves to scatter; the life like a gambler's throw.

10. *The Letters of W. B. Yeats*, ed. Allan Wade, London, 1954, pp. 836–7.

"He Too Was in Arcadia": Yeats and the Paradox of the Fortunate Fall

Edward Engelberg*

I . . . believe that there [exists] in Ireland . . . an energy of thought about life itself, a vivid sensitiveness as to the reality of things, powerful enough to overcome all those phantoms of the night. Everything calls up its contrary, unreality calls up reality . . .
— W. B. Yeats, "First Principles" (1904)

" 'I want to see this Yeats thing . . .' She was awake now, and urgent." The awake and urgent lady so eager to see "this Yeats thing" is Carol Kennicott, heroine of Sinclair Lewis's *Main Street*. Place: Gopher Prairie, Minnesota; time: shortly before the first Great War; and the name of the "Yeats thing": *The Land of Heart's Desire* (1894). Carol persuades her husband and they go to see the play (followed by one of Dunsany's!), but

*From *In Excited Reverie: A Centenary Tribute to William Butler Yeats, 1865*-1939, ed. A. Norman Jeffares and K. G. W. Cross (London: Macmillan; New York: St. Martin's, 1965), 69–92.

only momentarily is Carol able to enter into the make-believe which she desperately seeks as escape from a dull life. Briefly she is "transported" to the world of thatched cottages and "green dimness," "caressing linden branches," "twilight women" and "ancient gods." How romantic! How different! How appropriate to hear her counterpart, Mary, also doomed to the drudgery of the kitchen, saying:

> Come, faeries, take me out of this dull house!
> Let me have all the freedom I have lost;
> Work when I will and idle when I will!
> Faeries, come take me out of this dull world . . .

Though Edmund Wilson saw "nothing sinister about the Sidhe in themselves"[1] in Yeats's early work, Mary gets a good deal more than she bargained for in her encounter with the Sidhe: at the end of the play she lies dead on the stage. Against all the advice of those who knew the dangers of tampering with that "other" world, Mary progressively succumbs to the lure of the faeries — until she pays with her life. Carol could not have salvaged much promise from the end of this play: perhaps that is why she finally decides not to leave Main Street.

Her first attempt to bring Yeats into her life occurs shortly after her marriage: she is sitting on a couch, "her chin in her hands, a volume of Yeats on her knees," from which she is reading to a pair of unwilling ears. "Instantly she was released from the homely comfort of a prairie town": linnets, gulls, Aengus, kings, and a "woeful incessant chanting" flood her imagination. "Heh-cha-cha!" coughed Dr. Kennicott: the cough breaks the magic spell and one is naturally sorry for Carol (and for Yeats); and the yawning husband deserves to be called the country yokel that he is. Yet the poor doctor's cough had perhaps performed an unintentional service, for was Carol being drawn into that ambiguous twilight world which had claimed the life of Mary?

I

The Island of Statues is juvenilia, and Yeats's decision to omit it from his canon is perfectly sound. But, mindful of Yeats's warning —

> Accursed who brings to light of day
> The writings I have cast away!

I think this early "Arcadian Faery Tale," published when Yeats was twenty, is worth the risk even of a Yeatsian curse. Aside from the intrinsic curiosity which all juvenilia of a major poet in time arouse, the play is important for two reasons: it anticipates a view of Arcadia as a fallen Eden, and this carries important implications into the later poetry; and it presents us with an early insight by a young poet into a crucial distinction — that between a state of "happiness" and a state of "peace." Happiness, Yeats concludes in this play, is a condition of fallen man and of mortality; peace is the absence of conflict, and only those beyond mortality (faeries, gods, enchantresses) can possess it. Finally, *The Island of Statues* makes it very clear that when supernatural creatures intrude into — or are intruded upon by — the mortal world, the result is disastrous — depending, of course, on your point of view. Death comes to both mortals and non-mortals in this play, but for mortals death, he shows, already in this early play, is part of the price that "living man" must pay for the laughter and joy of life.

There were, it is fair to say, moments when peace seemed possible as a human goal, as an escape from human misery: I am thinking of the late 'eighties when Yeats came to London and certainly found his peace disturbed by that cosmopolitan city as it had not been by the quieter Dublin where he wrote *The Island of Statues* (and surely not by the Sligo of childhood). Such hope seems devoutly wished for at least in "The Lake Isle of Innisfree" — "And I shall have some peace there, for peace comes dropping slow." But a touch of irony colours the anecdote he later told to a B.B.C. audience on the origin of that poem. It seems that while walking down the Strand on a very hot day, he caught sight of a rotating ball on top of a jet of water in a shop window, and that reminded him, he said, of lake water lapping. Apparently it was an advertisement for a cooling drink. Everything calls up its contrary: and, indeed, sometimes reality called up unreality.

But such hope for peace was only passing. Soon Yeats returned to his earlier distinctions: "happiness" was, by and large, the best a man could achieve in this life, even if all that happiness is paled by the perfection of faery land, as the man who "dreams" of it discovers. Yeats's realization that happiness was neither peace nor perfection does not at first seem profound; but it was perhaps the most significant insight of his youth. By 1900 he had strengthened his youthful insight with conviction, for by now he had made a choice between two views of life and death, both of which were well known to him — and attractive. One was embodied in Pater's *The Renaissance*, especially in the essay on Winckelmann and in its "Conclusion"; the other in Symons's "Conclusion" to *The Symbolist Movement in Literature*. Although Yeats made no unqualified choice, he emerged far closer to Pater than to Symons.

Since both books are often seen as a continuum to which the "early" Yeats was a climax, it is salutary to see that the two "Conclusions" are far more interesting for their extraordinary differences than for their similarities. Each book, though both deal with a "school" of writers, is really an attempt to define the "modern spirit." Coming some thirty years after Pater's, Symons's "Conclusion" points in quite another direction (Pater's "Conclusion" is dated 1868). Indeed, there is no better way to gauge the striking difference between Pater's modern Hellenism and Symons's "doctrine of Mysticism" and *fin-de-siècle* than a reading of these two books. Symons, a shrewd and perceptive critic, realized this himself when he introduced the American Modern Library edition of *The Renaissance*: he emphasizes Pater's devotion to "earthly beauty . . . made by men" but adds, speaking more for himself than for others, "It is a world into which we can only look, not enter, for none of us have his secret."

At the risk of simplifying: Pater saw art as the best that life could offer while Symons saw death as the worst that life promised; Pater saw art as a fulfilment of a life otherwise lacking in richness, while Symons recognized art as the only possible escape from life; Pater asked us to open our senses as generously as we dared—and to engage in the modern world with fully opened eyes, while Symons pleaded, eloquently, that salvation lay in closing our senses, deadening them to reality. "Our only chance," writes Symons in the "Conclusion" to *The Symbolist Movement*, "in this world, of a complete happiness, lies in the measure of our success in shutting the eyes of the mind, and deadening its sense of hearing, and dulling the keenness of its apprehension of the unknown." As for Pater, the present is, for Symons, quick and fleeting; but to become conscious of reality, to its "blinding light," is to die in terror: "it is with a kind of terror that we wake up":

> Till human voices wake us and we drown.

The great "conspiracy" is to "forget death": consciousness is threatening, and only in dreams can we escape the "sterile, annihilating reality" of life, the dreams transfixed by art and religion.[2]

For Symons happiness was the safety of a shadowed darkness; for Pater it was the joy of light. The chief image of *The Symbolist Movement* is darkness; the chief image of *The Renaissance* is light, the clarity which Pater celebrated as the greatest achievement of Hellenism and its reincarnation in the Renaissance. It is altogether fitting that light should be the dominant image of a book which closes by extolling the example of Goethe, among whose dying words, it is reported, were: "Mehr Licht."

More light is what Pater wants in order to illuminate modern life and thus save us both from the darkness of what he over-anxiously feared as a medieval *contemptus mundi* as well as the darkness he saw lurking in the modern habit of too much "speculation." The last essay preceding the "Conclusion" to *The Renaissance*, "Wincklemann," is in date the earliest, but the essay is ultimately about Goethe and the modern spirit, bridging past glory and future promise: it is about those soul-searching questions which Pater, with remarkable vision, already saw looming large at the end of the sixties. In the eighties and nineties these same questions tore violently into the lives of many who would end the century with something less than triumph. Pater's last essay thus dovetails neatly into his "Conclusion," where the spirit of Hellenic light in "Winckelmann"—its "sharp edge of light"—kindles into the "gemlike flame."

The most obsessive question in "Winckelmann" is: can the light be passed on to the modern age? The Hellenic torch, so steadfast in its original clarity and sureness, had already been disturbed: nearly extinguished in the early Middle Ages, it had become a flame all aflutter, nervous and tenuous in Michelangelo, a little too intensely melancholy in Leonardo, in danger of too much shadow in Giorgione, dampened in the eighteenth century. But Goethe had given it new strength, had steadied it and lent it the fire of a modern sensibility. Could we now retain its power and its wisdom, or would an indifferent beak of a modern age drop us into another darkness?

"Et ego in Arcadia fui": thus the epigraph to "Winckelmann," just as a similar epigraph had opened Goethe's *Italiänische Reise.* How does Pater mean us to take this Latin phrase, already a famous shibboleth of the elegiac tradition? Is this nostalgia for an Arcadia once perfect, now irrecoverable? The substance of "Winckelmann" indicates the contrary: Arcadia *is* mortality, and we must not bewail elegiacally an irrecoverable loss but, rather, we must continue to celebrate the liveable — the possible — Arcadia, for all its fallen state.

And so Yeats means us to take his Arcadia in *The Island of Statues,* his "Arcadian Faery Tale," for both Pater and Yeats refuse to acknowledge Death as a destroyer of a life not worth a *conscious* living. Death, for Yeats, was indeed the "great enemy" who was often discourteous; but he was never a *memento mori* from which he shrank in terror. In this he stands on the threshold of the kind of "modernity" we now associate with the name of Freud, for whom, ultimately, an unchallenged "death wish" became untenable, and who in later life elevated Eros and the urge to live and set them bravely against all the terrors of the abyss into which no one had looked more deeply than he. Yeats and Pater both emphasized man's instinctual resistance to death and his corresponding urgency to cling to life despite the spectacle of its brevity and its sadness. In all religions, even in Christianity, Pater saw a "pagan sentiment," which "measures the sadness" of man when he thinks of death descending upon him from the "irresistible natural powers." Yet such fear was also "the secret . . . of his fortune," for it made him cling to life all the more: "It is with a rush of home-sickness that the thought of death presents itself. [Pagan man] would remain at home for ever on the earth if he could."[3] Yeats too saw all ancient people possessed by a "melancholy," a trait which made them "delight in tales that end in death and parting," not because they wished themselves to die, but because death seemed after all so final: "Life was so weighed down by the emptiness of the great forests . . . by the loneliness of much beauty; and seemed so little and so fragile and so brief, that nothing could be more sweet in the memory than a tale that ended in death" — of others. As Yeats makes clear, men did not set to mourning for what the Fates had either bestowed or deprived, for "such mourning believes that life might be happy were it different, and is therefore the less mourning." Men mourned "because they had been born and must die with their great thirst unslaked."[4]

Yeats feared the loss of this "old simple celebration of life tuned to the highest pitch" with the coming of the "dangerous" revolution which might "establish the scientific complement of certain philosophies that in all ancient countries sustained heroic art".[5] It is only the *un*fulfilled man who can die heroically, the man who would stay on earth forever if he could: hence Yeats's own almost arrogant claim to his "soldier's right" to "live it all again," even the "crime of death and birth." The pagan yearning for life and earth, the resistance to death with its accompanying melancholy — these Yeats recognized as essential elements of the Celtic temper. And just as Pater knew that the primitive was eventually modified by Doric vigour and ascetic Christian discipline, so Yeats came to see that Celtic sorrow needed to be leavened by Greek "proportions" and that melancholy must give way to "tragic joy."

Pater saw all of Europe balanced by the marriage of Faust and Helena, modern Europe and Hellenic Greece, the "Romantic spirit" with its "profound subjectivity of soul" wedded to "transparency . . . rationality . . . desire of beauty. . . ." The matchmaker was, of course, Goethe: but would the marriage last? "Can we bring down that [Hellenic] ideal into the gaudy, perplexed light of modern life?" asked Pater, and the image remains that of light. As any young man fresh from a reading of Kant and Hegel, and no doubt flushed to the cheeks with "historical" self-awareness, Pater admitted that the Greeks had an easier world in which to attain unity, blitheness, repose. None the less, more than ever, he urged, we demand "completeness" and "centrality," and "Goethe . . . ready to be lost in the perplexed currents of modern thought . . . defines, in clearest outline, the eternal problem of culture — balance, unity with one's self. . . ."[6]

It was Yeats's Unity of Being, but he knew that man runs his course "between extremities," that "vacillation" was the necessary condition of attaining balance. For Pater as for Yeats, Time is the ultimate measure of one side of reality — and of all mortality. Reality is neither a mystical union with God nor the terrible confrontation of alienation — it is both. It is for Yeats also the tumult of life under the semblance of order:

> Civilization is hooped together, brought
> Under a rule, under the semblance of peace
> By manifold illusion; but man's life is thought
> And he, despite his terror, cannot cease
> Ravening through century after century,
> Ravening, raging, and uprooting that he may come
> Into the desolation of reality: . . . ("Meru")

The numinous, never denied, leads to the phenomenal "[There are] certain abstract thinkers, whose measurements and classifications continually bring me back to concrete reality. . . ." This in Yeats's *Diary* of 1930. And further: "An abstract thinker when he has this relation to concrete reality passes on both the thought and the passion; who has not remains in the classroom." He saw his whole life as a "drama" in which he struggled "to exalt and overcome concrete realities perceived not with mind only but as with the roots of my hair."[7] He would be Sancho Panza to his own Don Quixote, ravening and raging through "manifold illusion" into the "desolation of reality" where acceptance became finally possible.

Like Pater, Yeats had to locate meaning in the life of "perpetual motion," in the drama that both exalts and overcomes reality, Pater's challenge to modern times, voiced at the end of "Winckelmann," was clear enough: can the artist deal with the "conditions of modern life?" Modern art, "in the service of culture," must "rearrange the details of modern life, so to reflect it, that it may satisfy the spirit".[8] Spirit is reached through the sensible world. Here again is Yeats in his *Diary:* "Through the particular we approach the Divine Ideas."[9] To withstand modern life, said Pater, the spirit needs a "sense of freedom," but gone forever was the "naïve" freedom checked by the ultimate power of a superior force. If one looks carefully at Pater there is always a little of Darwin: "The chief factor in the thoughts of the modern mind concerning itself is the intricacy, the universality of natural law, even in the moral order." Yeats could never have said that, nor could he have agreed with Pater's philosophical cosmopolitanism: "For us, necessity is not, as of old, a sort of mythological personage without us" — but he would have assented to what followed, namely that modern man lived in a kind of "magic web woven through and through us . . . penetrating us with a network . . . bearing in it the central forces of the world." This being so, "Can art represent men and women in these bewildering toils so as to give the spirit at least an equivalent for the sense of freedom?" An audacious question for a young Englishman to be asking in 1867, but Pater was under no illusions about modern life: it was neither to be avoided as ugly nor to be distorted by making it beautiful. It was what it was: "this entanglement, this network of law . . . the tragic situation, in which certain groups of noble men and women work out for themselves a supreme *dénouement*." Like Yeats, then, Pater saw life as a drama with its "tragic situation," for we know Yeats's famous aphorism that we begin to live only when we have conceived of life as tragedy. And Pater's "tragic situation" is never bemoaned. "Who," he asks in the final and eloquent sentence of "Wincklemann," "if he saw through all, would fret against the chain of circumstance which endows one at the end with those great experiences?"[10]

"Experience": it is the key word of Pater's famous "Conclusion." Only by refining experiences can man comprehend their seemingly meaningless, random and ceaseless assaults upon our senses. Death allows Pater to plead for life: "this sense of the splendour of our experience and . . . its awful brevity" is what makes sense out of the "one desperate effort to see and touch. . . ." If, as Pater quotes, from Hugo, *"les hommes sont tous condamnés à mort avec des sursis indéfinis,"* we have at least the "interval" of light, and our "one chance" is to brighten it, by "expanding that interval. . . ."[11] It is an echo of Faust's magnificent, hopeless — because all too human — cry to the moment, the *Augenblick*: "Verweile doch, du bist so schön!" — a cry which he defiantly attempts to resist.

Yeats must have light, for "the greater the passion the more clear the perception, for the light is perception," as he writes in his *Diary*. Conflict is a price we must pay: "Passion is conflict, consciousness is conflict." Like Pater's "network" and "tragic situation," it is a consciousness and conflict we dare not refuse. Symons's comfort lies in darkness, and his sense of freedom is neither Pater's nor Yeats's: it is the "freedom of . . . sweet captivity" in the bosom of Beauty, and that is, warns Symons, a very perilous freedom indeed.[12] To release men from immobile captivity into the freedom of a world of risks is perhaps the major theme of Yeats's early play.

II

Set in Arcadia, *The Island of Statues* has, properly enough, a *dramatis personae* of shepherds and shepherdesses and the appropriate setting of woods and fields. Somehow Yeats also manages to place an island within his Arcadia, which is ruled by an Enchantress who has been busy for centuries turning to stone various individuals who have come to pluck a certain flower of magical properties but have failed to choose the correct one. The play opens as two crude shepherds quarrel over the fair Naschina who, of course, scorns both and is secretly in love with an Adonis named Almintor. In order to test his courage, Naschina eventually sends Almintor to the magic island, but he, as have all others in the past, fails the crucial test, chooses the wrong flower, and is summarily turned to stone. Only Naschina, we later learn, can save him, for she is fated to have the knowledge of the correct choice — though unconscious of that knowledge herself. Naschina hurries to the island disguised as a page and the Enchantress falls in love with her, a mistake that will cost her the power of rule. However, before plucking the correct flower, Naschina needs a human sacrifice, which she gets; once having overcome that last barrier, she undisguises herself, plucks the right flower, inherits the powers of the Enchantress — who must now die — and liberates all the statues on the island, turning them back into mortals. This, in brief, is the "plot" of the play.

Yet it is the ending which is intriguing and one may work backwards through the play to glimpse Yeats's intention. As the play closes, the grateful humans, restored from their stony sleep, elect as their royal couple Naschina and Almintor. The final stage direction reads:

> The rising moon casts the shadows of Almintor and the Sleepers far across the grass. Close by Almintor's side, Naschina is standing, shadowless.

The shadowless Naschina has replaced the Enchantress — this much we know; she is no longer purely a mortal and perhaps was never intended to be, since she was "fated" to rule by the pronouncements of some timeless prophecy or oracle.

Yeats is intent on emphasizing that his Arcadia is not timeless but a place in history: it has experienced Clytemnestra, the "fires of Troia," and Dido. A second essential idea, planted early in the play, is that "Joy's brother, Fear, dwells ever in each breast": it is Naschina who says this and it is also what prompts her to send Almintor on his dangerous quest for the flower. But, for all his courage, Almintor is a discouraged knight-errant, a melancholy youth for whom "The whole world's sadly talking to itself." Though such *Weltschmerz* is common to youthful lovers in Arcadian circumstances, the point seems more insistent: Almintor's melancholy is that of a fallen Adam aware that he will disturb the ultimate Paradise. When he is about to arrive on the enchanted island a "Voice," just before sensing the approach of some "un-faery thing," tells us that it recalls "When the tree was o'er-appled / For Mother Eve's winning / [I] was at her sinning." This Arcadia is as old as Creation: it is a place not only of history but one in which history repeats itself in the obvious parallels of Almintor's and later Naschina's flower-picking and Eve's apple-plucking. A fallen Arcadia is not the conventional land of literature.

In his brilliant essay, "Poussin and the Elegiac Tradition," Erwin Panofsky tells us that there have been traditionally two views of "natural man": "One view, termed 'soft' primitivism . . . conceives of primitive life as a golden age of plenty, innocence and happiness . . . civilized life purged of its vices. The other, 'hard' . . . conceives of primitive life as an almost subhuman existence full of terrible hardships . . . stripped of its virtues." Arcadia has traditionally been associated with the "soft" view — "golden-age primitivism" — but Yeats's view of "natural man" is really neither "soft" nor "hard." The best we can safely say about the Arcadia of Almintor and Naschina is that it rather resembles the world itself, and that life here is accordingly also very much more the risky business we would expect outside Arcadia, not within it.

Panofsky's essay traces the origins and meanings, particularly in iconography, of the Latin phrase "Et in Arcadia ego," a variant, we recall, of Pater's epigraph for "Winckelmann." Panofsky explains that the phrase meant both "I, too, was born, or lived, in Arcady" and "Even in Arcady, there am I" — the latter "I" being Death, as in Poussin's two famous paintings. The second version is further divisible: either a "thinly veiled moralism" which warns of Death's ubiquitousness, or as part of the "elegiac sentiment," "quiet, reminiscent meditation." The later Poussin painting shows the Arcadians coming upon a tomb neither shocked nor surprised at discovering Death (as they were in the earlier painting) but rather "immersed in mellow meditation on a beautiful past." It is this latter attitude which Panofsky calls "elegiac" and which, he claims, held sway, especially in England, where melancholia has been a consistently attractive and indulgent source for the arts. Again Yeats does not clearly fall into either subdivision—*memento mori* or elegiac—though quite possibly he knew of Poussin's paintings or some of their English imitations.[13]

Here is Naschina's speech to Almintor's page, just prior to leaving for her rescue mission to the island of statues:

> Antonio, if I return no more,
> Then bid them raise my statue on the shore . . .
> . . . and no name gild;
> A white, dumb thing of tears, here let it stand . . .
> And when the summer's deep, then to this spot
> The Arcadians bring, and bid the stone be raised
> As I am standing now . . .
> And once a-year let the Arcadians come,
> And 'neath it sit, and of the woven sum
> Of human sorrow let them moralize;
> And let them tell sad histories, till their eyes
> All swim with tears . . .
> And let the tale be mournful each one tells.

Naschina's orders for her tomb are almost a poetic gloss on Poussin's later painting, "Et in Arcadia ego," where the Arcadians, in melancholy attitudes, gather round the tomb and elegiacally contemplate Death. However, such a tomb will be unnecessary, for Naschina triumphs in a world that operates under something less than elegiacally Arcadian rules: instead of tombs being raised for her she raises the "dead" to life. Ironically, it is precisely with her magical act of animating the statues, that the now supra-mortal Naschina violates the last island where reality had not prevailed. It is with magic that she destroys magic: what she will do with her powers henceforth no one knows.

This violation occurs immediately on Naschina's arrival at the island. The Guardians of the flowers, hitherto innocent of "grief or care," are filled with "sudden melancholy": it is they who sit in mournful repose, singing baleful words in anticipation of some vague disaster. While awaiting the human sacrifice which must be made for Naschina before she can successfully choose the right flower, the Enchantress and the disguised Naschina converse about the central issue of the play: what is happiness?

Still duped by Naschina's disguise, the Enchantress snatches Naschina's laughter, cherishing this as a great conquest, for "e'en the fay that trips / At morn, and with her feet each cobweb rends, / Laughs not. / It [laughter] dwells alone on mortal lips . . ." Laughter, then, is a human privilege denied even to the "happiness" of faeries. Or *are* faeries "happy?" The Enchantress makes the distinction:

> Thou'lt teach me laughing, and I'll teach thee peace . .
> For peace and laughter have been seldom friends.

To the insistent questions put to her by Naschina—is she "happy?"—the Enchantress answers only: "Youth, I am at peace." And peace, it is clear, is a condition no mortal can know: it is hearing "Mid bubbling leaves a wandering song-rapt bird / Going the forest through," or seeing "with visage meek, / A hoary hunter leaning on his bow." Peace is an experience "deeper than men know." Those vignettes of "peace" which the Enchantress describes are, like the "Cold Pastoral" of Keats's urn, Attic shapes in "Fair attitude! with brede / Of marble men and maidens overwrought"— indeed like the Sleepers on the island, themselves turned from humans into "attitudes" of stone.

Such peace then is also the source of the Enchantress's power; and to break the spell of that peace, and with it the power, Naschina must now pluck the magic flower. The results will be no less far-reaching than Eve's plucking of the apple, for Sin and Death now enter the last sanctuary on Arcadia—the island itself. On the verge of death, the Enchantress prophesies a not altogether promising future for Naschina: she shall "outlive" her own "amorous happy time" and be witness to the death of her lover; she shall be committed to "dream*less* truth," and her soul, "pitiless and bright," shall, like her beauty, "fail . . . day and night / Beneath the burthen of the infinite, / In those far years."

Burdened with immortality, Naschina inherits ceaseless life but a failing soul, no longer human. When Naschina beholds only the traces of a dead green frog where once the powerful Enchantress ruled she exclaims:

> O Arcady, O Arcady, this day
> A deal of evil and of change hath crossed
> Thy peace . . .

Realizing that the "fall" has truly come to pass, Naschina now prepares to make the best of things: her first act is to awaken the Sleepers on the island. Again we are reminded how old this Arcadia is, for the Sleepers ask about Finn and Troy, Arthur and Pan, and for each the answer is the same: "He is long dead," or "Nay, he is gone. Wake! wake!" And awake they do, not into an immortal world of peace but into a mortal world of happiness—and death. In that state of "happiness" Almintor and Naschina are chosen as their royal couple "Until we die"—for they know that die they now must, in the natural course of time. But Naschina must know that she will outlive their happiness, that she will be soon without a husband and without laughter, for the sun fails to throw its light, and hence her shadow, on the grass. The price of happiness and laughter is mortality; the price of mortality is Death. The fall of man is therefore—as we have been told from the perspective of theology—"fortunate" in the context of Yeats's Arcadian play.

III

The opening poem of Yeats's *Collected Poems*, "The Song of the Happy Shepherd," was originally the Epilogue to *The Island of Statues* and to another work of his youth, *The Seeker*. As the Epilogue, it was called "Song of the Last Arcadian," and that the "last Arcadian" should be singing a "happy" song, whose opening words are "The woods of Arcady are dead," is in itself suggestive. Far from being a lament for a lost Arcady, the poem is, rather, an attempt to come to terms with that loss. What the shepherd tells us is that, indeed, Arcady is dead, the old order is gone, and the world now feeds on "Grey Truth" in place of "dreams." The only remedy appears to be to tell one's tale to a seashell which, in turn transmuting that tale into "melodious guile," will retell it. So in a sense Yeats at twenty envisions the seashell as his symbol or mediator between artistic impulse and articulation. Since Arcady is now dead, the only recourse for the poet is to keep it alive through poetry: "Words alone are certain good . . . / The kings of the old time are dead." Indeed, the whole world may be merely a "sudden flaming word" — a view of a self-generating and world-creating Imagination which Yeats never entirely abandoned as at least one half of an antinomy of his vision of reality. The final injunction of the shepherd is to dream, for both dreaming and singing are not elegiac requiems for a dead past but stratagems of art for preserving a once enviable world. It is true that Yeats would learn, in time, to rely less on the sovereignty of both words and dreams: in both, he would discover, begin responsibilities.

Yet the poem is very close to Pater's "Winckelmann" and his "Conclusion," to Pater's recognition that Greek serenity is gone forever, that the modern world is feverish and disturbing, but that our only salvation lies in creating an art which at once celebrates the past while fixing its vision on the future, an art written *in* the present. The shepherd in the first poem of Yeats's work is happy in the certainty that art alone is "good"; Yeats then wrote a parallel poem, "The Sad Shepherd," in which a self-pitying creature, a friend to Sorrow, bewails his state to an audience he can nowhere find. Stars, dew-drops, and seashell, each in turn, refuse to hear his "heavy story." His only aim is to send sadness through his listeners, and such simplistic attempts to find a listener in order that one's "burden may depart" through a kind of art-as-therapy Yeats does not allow. Indeed the seashell changes the shepherd's tale of sorrow — "Changed all he sang to inarticulate moan / Among her wildering whirls, forgetting him." No warning could be clearer: the poet must not succumb to mere self-pity; he must not write simply to rid himself of sorrow, lest his tale be doomed to dissolve into "inarticulate moan." In no way does the happy shepherd advise that we ignore reality; and his happiness comes in part from confronting the reality of its loss and finding his defences in "words": he is dedicated to self-trust, but not to self-pity, not to a wasteful regret for a vanished past.

To "dream" is not to forget: as Richard Ellmann recently suggested, the word is extraordinarily important and difficult in Yeats's poetry.[14] We would expect to find the word "dream" frequently in Yeats's early poetry and so we do. Though it disappears almost entirely from *Responsibilities* (1914), it reappears in *The Wild Swans at Coole* (1919) and thereafter contributes to major lines of major poems: "I dream of a Ledaean body," "there is no deformity / But saves us from a dream," "When sleepers wake and yet still dream," "Man makes a superhuman / Mirror-resembling dream," "Phidias / Gave women dreams and dreams their lookingglass." In two poems, especially, the word functions rather dramatically and gives some indication of the subtlety with which Yeats used such words.

In "The Fisherman" Yeats repudiates the audiences that have scorned him (and Synge) and creates in his imagination "A man who does not exist, / A man who is but a dream." To take "dream" here as wish-fulfillment or escape from realities that are unpleasant to confront is a misreading. For Yeats the dreamer is also the creator: we "Dream and so *create* / Translunar Paradise." So in "The Fisherman" Yeats recognizes that what does not exist must be created, by "God-appointed Berkeley" or by the poet. As in the later poem, "The Statues," Yeats envisions the creations of types that, ideally, a culture can emulate: if fishermen do not exist he must "dream" them — that is, create them. The entire *dramatis personae* of the later poetry function as so many rubrics of the master builder who rearranges with his "mythy mind" — to borrow a phrase from Wallace Stevens — the fictive world become real.

Why "*Broken* Dreams?" This beautiful love poem in which the poet dreams of his beloved whom he shall meet again in "the first loveliness of womanhood" is Yeats's clearest poetic embodiment of what was surely one of his main beliefs: that the "correspondence" of heaven must never distort, through perfection, the realities lived on earth. Though beautiful, the beloved had a flaw: the "small hands were not beautiful." The line hurts as it withers into the truth, and the image following is almost surrealistic and grotesque: "And I am afraid that you will run / And paddle to the wrist / In that mysterious, always brimming lake," where there *are* perfect beings. A plea concludes the poem that she "Leave unchanged / The hands that [he has] kissed, / For old sake's sake," the possessive "sake" implying "cause" or even "crime" (else the phrase makes no sense). For the sake of preserving the violation of perfection keep your imperfection in Paradise, keep your dream broken.

The insistence in "The Fisherman" that dreams create a reality and in "Broken Dreams" that a broken reality must remain broken even in dreams suggests something of the difficulties of the word in Yeats's poetry: we must be always on guard when we call him a "dreamer." No doubt that the dream — word and experience — undergoes transformations from youth to age; but the later poetry is again an attempt to "create" new dreams, in that special sense in which the dreaming sleepers of *The Island of Statues* are awakened into the dream of reality:

> Resemble forms that are or seem
> When sleepers wake and yet still dream,
> ("Under Ben Bulben")

As dreams became realized, or defeated, Yeats searched anew: though he knew that "The painter's brush consumes his dreams" — and so the poet's must consume *his*? — the heart remains a "resinous . . . foul rag-and-bone shop." Like the awakened sleepers in Yeats's juvenile Arcadian fantasy, Yeats's poetry progressively moves towards a certainty: living dreams and dreaming life are part of a single and indivisible process. So the final line of Yeats's opening poem, "Dream, dream, for this is also sooth," remains consistent. When dreams have gone he must create new ones and rededicate his imagination: to escape from the ghetto of a dreamless imagination into an "acre of green grass"; to redeem the soul from the pawnshop of exhausted dreams and in exchange purchase something from the heart; to prove once more that "He that sings a lasting song / Thinks in a marrow-bone." Yeats was a consistent economizer: one feels he held many dreams in escrow, and they would have begotten many more still had life granted him not only an old man's frenzy but more time.

Yeats's dreams were, initially, dreams of "islands." "I am haunted by numberless islands . . . / Where Time would surely forget us, and Sorrow come near us no more," cries the lover in "The White Birds," an early poem. The early Yeats was indeed haunted by islands: besides *The Island of Statues* there was Oisin's odyssey to the three islands and islands in many poems, all traditionally used as places out of Time where Yeats, conventionally, located his faeryland. But just as Yeats needed to sail the seas — literally and metaphorically — from his own island to other continents, so islands began to disappear from his poetry, and in "The Circus Animals' Desertion," "sea-rider Oisin" is recalled as having been "led by the nose / Through three enchanted islands, allegorical dreams . . ." All the islands were humanly unendurable: "Vain gaiety, vain battle, vain repose." Vain because, as also in the *Odyssey*, Time is also Memory which brings men back to what they have abandoned: country, soil, wife, child — joy and sorrow. Eternal peace is for Oisin, as for Odysseus, the promise of uncertain happiness, and it is indeed Sorrow which beckons Oisin to return to the real world, and to abandon the "dreams of the islands. . . ."

In *The Island of Statues* Yeats, in violating that special refuge within Arcadia with human happiness, and hence with sorrow, had already destroyed his "islands" though he was not then aware of it. When Pater said that the arts of the future are no longer sculpture and painting but music and poetry, he meant that the former arts had expressed, to perfection, a repose that was no longer suited to the motions of modern life. It is certainly interesting that Yeats should so early have envisioned an island of statues which quite literally comes to life. In "The Statues" those Grecian forms "moved or seemed to move / In marble or in bronze": they are not humans turned to stone but the artifacts that humans may kiss, thus joining life and art, animation and repose, without the aid of an intercessory magician. Perhaps this tells the parable of Yeats's journey from islands, statues, and magicians to art within history, and to "living man" alone. From that point of view his poetic journey reverses Shakespeare's, and — from a naïver perspective, of course — Prospero and Perdita begin, rather than end, his creative life.

IV

We must not be too harsh with Carol Kennicott for misreading some of Yeats's early poetry in Gopher Prairie, Minnesota. In an essay written more than twenty years ago, Allen Tate was convinced that Yeats's poetry was "nearer the centre of our main traditions of sensibility of thought than the poetry of Eliot or Pound," but he foresaw — correctly — that there would be some delay in such a valuation of Yeats. He also prophesied, again accurately, that ". . . Yeats's romanticism will be created by his critics."[15] Of course one must always be cautious with Yeats, and to rid him of all "romanticism" in his early verse by reshaping him into the suave and sophisticated Villon of thirty that undoubtedly he wished to be at twenty-five is as perverse as to make him purely a poet of the *symboliste* movement or a major figure of the English nineties. Clearly we must also not overstress the "toughness" of the "point of view" in the early verse as if that were an effective cover for its obvious "vapour" of language or as if, in re-examining the totality of a great poet, we are now anxious to find aspects of his work admirable which we had hitherto regarded more critically. That way lies bardolatry and we should have none of that now. But Mr. Tate's warnings were real enough: Yeats simply never was the total romantic or aesthete that provides critics with a label for his "early period." In a recent phrase by David Daiches Yeats was, from the first, a kind of "practical visionary."[16]

The major emphasis here has been to show this by illuminating his earliest distinction between "happiness" and "peace," a separation that permanently influenced all the subsequent work. I have already mentioned Freud's increasingly emphatic conclusion that man must cast his lot with life against death, with Eros against the imposing enemies ranged against him. Freud, no more than Yeats, could imagine conscious man at "peace"; but happiness was not impossible. The possibilities of achieving happiness are the central theme of *Civilization and its Discontents*, as it is of much of Yeats's poetry. Freud and Yeats, each clear-sighted men, put enormous faith in Eros, though neither flinched from the world of violence, death and aggression. Each was in his way an exile; each died away from home in the same year; and both suffered much and endured it with dignity, and with a faith in life.

"Civilized man," said Freud, "has exchanged a portion of his possibilities of happiness for a portion of security" — the security of becoming, and remaining, a "community." Yeats placed a high premium on the proper sort of "community": it is difficult to imagine that he would have found anything to disagree with in this sentence of Freud's book: "civilization is a process in the service of Eros, whose purpose is to combine single human individuals, and after that families, then races, peoples and nations, into one great unity, the unity of mankind."[17] Such an ideal is increasingly made possible, according to Freud, as man rids himself of "guilt" and "remorse," acts of self-acceptance and self-forgiveness which allow Eros to take the measure of Death: ". . . Measure the lot; forgive myself the lot! / When such as I cast out remorse / So great a sweetness flows into the breast / We must laugh and we must sing . . ."[18]

"Words alone are certain good" and "We must laugh and we must sing"; still the human laughter which the Enchantress, at peace as she was, so much envied in *The Island of Statues*, and the song which the happy shepherd sings. With that laughing and singing we have come almost full circle, and this is the mature vision of the "human condition" Yeats offers but a decade or so before he died. It is true that Yeats was often bitter; so was Freud: neither might have believed so much in Eros and in self-forgiveness had they not been spared the horrors of the war that was to come. Yet even now, when hatred and guilt rule over Eros, their vision can still teach. Their acceptance of life was not stoical: it was the plea for "Mehr Licht" of the dying Goethe, the benediction of sweetness and light of Arnold, the celebration of Hellenic light which Pater expressed so eloquently. Yeats chooses as his "emblem" of life the day against the night, the shining, razor-keen blade of Sato's sword, "still like a looking glass / Unspotted by the centuries. . . ."

The recently published *Concordance* of Yeats's poetry confirms his reputation as a man of dualistic vision for, give or take a few variants, "light" and "dark," "life" and "death" occur with almost equal frequency in his poetry. Certainly Yeats was aware of Death and of the price of mortality as a very young poet, which is not to say that he had not *been* in Arcadia: he was there, as were Goethe and Pater. But Yeats's Arcadia, as a fallen Eden, makes mortality worth its own rewards, and the "fall" is therefore "fortunate." I do not know what his dying words were, but "Mehr Licht" would have suited him as well as they had Goethe. After all, for all the use Yeats makes of the moon it is the full moon which brightens all into perfection and beauty. Nor would we expect Yeats to forget the

light of day, "solar light, intellectual light; not the lunar light, perception."
Upon that solar light he bestowed the quality of "changeless purity."[19]

Notes

1. Edmund Wilson, *Axel's Castle*, New York, 1931, 1954, p. 30.

2. Arthur Symons, *The Symbolist Movement in Literature*, London, 1899, pp. 171–2.

3. Walter Pater, *The Renaissance*, London and New York, 1893, pp. 212–13.

4. The Celtic Element in Literature," *Essays and Introductions*, London, 1961, p. 182.

5. *Introduction* to *Fighting the Waves, Wheels and Butterflies*, London, 1934, p. 65.

6. *The Renaissance*, pp. 240–2.

7. "Pages from a Diary written in Nineteen Hundred and Thirty," *Explorations*, London, 1962, pp. 302–3. (Hereafter cited as *Diary*.)

8. *The Renaissance*, p. 244

9. *Diary*, p. 299.

10. *The Renaissance*, pp. 244–6.

11. *Ibid.*, pp. 251–3.

12. *Diary*, p. 331; Symons, p. 175.

13. Erwin Panofsky, "*Et in Arcadia Ego*: Poussin and the Elegiac Tradition," *Meaning in the Visual Arts*, New York, 1955, pp. 295–320.

14. Richard Ellmann, "Yeats Without Analogue," *Kenyon Review* (Winter, 1964), pp. 30–47.

15. Allen Tate, "Yeats's Romanticism: Notes and Suggestions," reprinted in *The Permanence of Yeats*, ed. James Hall and Martin Steinmann, New York, 1950, p. 105.

16. David Daiches, "The Practical Visionary," *Encounter*, xix (September, 1962), p. 71.

17. *Civilization and its Discontents*, tr. and ed. James Strachey, New York, 1961, pp. 62, 69.

18. "A Dialogue of Self and Soul."

19. *A Vision* (1937), p. 220.

"Among School Children" and the Education of the Irish Spirit   Donald T. Torchiana*

I

One Monday morning in February 1926, a present member of the Convent of Mercy, Waterford, at that time a thirteen-year-old student, watched from a window as Senator W. B. Yeats, in soft hat and with magisterial presence, took his distinguished way up the driveway of St.

*From *In Excited Reverie: A Centenary Tribute to William Butler Yeats, 1865–1939*, ed. A. Norman Jeffares and K. G. W. Cross (London: Macmillan; New York: St. Martin's 1965), 123–50.

Otteran's School. His famed turkey strut — a gait combining short, jerky steps with body erect, head thrown back and hands clasped behind his back — was unforgettable. He had already visited the school, often known as the Phillip Street National Schools, the previous day with his wife. They had been regaled with the kind of overflowing dinner that Ireland does so well and spent the afternoon visiting the empty classrooms prior to an equally extraordinary tea. The visit had been private and unheralded, but St. Otteran's as a model school was important to Yeats, for he was on a government committee pledged to investigate the conditions of schools in Ireland.

There may also have been another reason for Yeats's enthusiasm and curiosity in accepting the invitation from the Superior, the Rev. Mother de Sales. Trained by a sister of the Abbot Marmion (a noted Belgian educator), she inaugurated in St. Otteran's, on St. Patrick's Eve 1920, the Montessori method for teaching four- to seven-year-olds,[1] in which Yeats was particularly interested. Hence on Sunday, he had seen the characteristic long Montessori classroom with its chosen emblem, Raphael's "Madonna della Seggiola." He had also learned that children from eight on were offered the system named for the Parents National Education Union. Here, in addition to the Montessori emphasis on spontaneity and a training of the senses to prepare for and reinforce a child's first intellectual ventures, each child was encouraged to read his own choice in books, then allowed to narrate his reading, to write about it — or even to make a poem from his impressions. Senator Yeats, without his wife this Monday morning, now visited the school full of children.

After seeing the primary grades, Yeats entered the schoolroom of the thirteen-year-old watcher, now a teacher in the school. She was one of those asked to recite a poem before the great man. Yet even more fortunate was her class neighbour who had chosen *Gulliver's Travels* for her reading book and poem. Yeats commended her verses on the little people, read her poem aloud himself, and remarked enigmatically that her performance reminded him of one of his friends. He could hardly believe, as he told his wife later, that the children's recitations had not been specially got up for him. But they had not. As he proceeded from classroom to classroom — the children standing as he entered each room — the Rev. Mother Philomena, Mistress of Schools, answered his questions, as did the Rev. Mother de Sales before and after his tour. The Montessori children had been particularly occupied with their sums and singing, while the P.N.E.U. children had also been rendering an account of their reading and history lessons. All, from seven years on, had been taught to cut and sew their own school bags and even more difficult articles. Neatness was, of course, a watchword in the school. Moreover, according to the present member of the Mercy community, Yeats asked repeated questions on the children's preparations in art. Later in the day he paid a visit to the Ursuline convent in the same city, where again the primary school was run on Montessori lines. Yeats left Waterford without so much as a brief notice in the *Waterford Star* or in the *Munster Express* to mark his stay. But for the observant thirteen-year-old, all are gone today from that religious community and school who might have remembered him. Yeats's visit, however, is fixed indelibly in the opening stanzas of one of his greatest poems, "Among School Children."[2] Hence, with this visit in mind, along with Yeats's speeches, essays and reading on education at the time, I would like to take one more look at the poem, despite the previous dazzling glances by Cleanth Brooks, John Wain and Frank Kermode.[3]

II

Beyond his consuming desire after the Treaty to help to educate the new Ireland artistically, and aside from his equally powerful Shandean preoccupation with his own growing children, Yeats on this trip — one of many in Ireland — was also marking his official concern with Irish education.

Yeats made three important Senate speeches on the Irish schools during March and late April of 1926. They came close to his Waterford trip and close also to the time when the idea of the poem first struck him. The last two, on the 30th of March and the 28th of April, were desperate pleas for a national loan to ensure that schools would be in good repair, clean and habitable — worthy to be centres of culture, and cheerful ones at that. But Yeats's most important speech on education had come on 24 March. Remarking on the primitive condition of many Irish schools, he contrasted a shabby Dublin school with St. Otteran's in these words: "I have seen a school lately in a South of Ireland town managed by the Sisters of Mercy, and it is a model to all schools."[4] Then, after objecting to the out-of-date system of education that imposed the usual harsh strain on both teacher and child, Yeats bluntly questioned the whole scheme of education. These remarks, especially, compel our attention. The first looks at a child, like the young Maud Gonne of Stanza II, under a harsh system:

> Whether it [schooling] is good for the children or not depends not only on the building but on the nature of the system under which they are taught. I am sure for a child to spend all day in school with a stupid, ill-trained man under an ill-planned system, is less good for that child than that the child should be running through the fields and learning nothing.[5]

A second passage asks Ireland to consider the Italian system, which included the Montessori ideal, so ably established by Gentile, the Italian Minister of Education:

> I should like to draw the attention of the Government to one nation which has reformed its educational system in the most suggestive and profound way; that is Italy . . . now teaching a system of education

adapted to an agricultural nation like this or Italy, a system of education
that will not turn out clerks only, but will turn out efficient men and
women who can manage to do all the work of the nation. This system
has been tried in Ireland. There are some schools carrying it out. There
is one large primary school managed by nuns in the South of Ireland
which has adopted practically the entire Italian system and which is
carrying it out with great effect. . . .[6]

Finally, there is Yeats's closing thought, to my mind extremely important
in understanding his poem:

I would like to suggest another principle, that the child itself must
be the end in education. It is a curious thing how many times the
education of Europe has drifted into error. For two or three centuries
people thought that their various religious systems were more important
than the child. In the modern world the tendency is to think of the
nation; that it is more important than the child. . . . There is a
tendency to subordinate the child to the idea of the nation . . . we
should always see that the child is the object and not any of our special
purposes.[7]

The aim is the development of national excellence by the best modern
education available. Yet with equal insistence Yeats asks that the growing
child be guided towards self-fulfillment without being sacrificed to the
codes of any particular religious or patriotic abstraction.

III

Behind the faint light of these Senate speeches, three essays of these
years also throw distant beams on "Among School Children." "Compulsory
Gaelic," appearing in the *Irish Statesman* on 2 August 1924, remains to
this day a seldom-read symposium of Yeats's own conflicting thoughts on
the Irish language. Cast in the form of a dialogue, it asks that Ireland
avoid the usual school-book apathy associated with compulsory study and
that it not become "a little potato-digging Republic" cut off from Europe.
The most provocative statements on education are put into the mouth of
Timothy, described as "an elderly student," who, in his convictions about
the uncertainty of life, seems the speaker most like the real Yeats. On the
last page of the essay he declares his faith:

I have no practical experience, but perhaps it might be possible to
choose a schoolmaster as we choose a painter or sculptor. "There is so-
and-so," we would say, "who thinks that Ireland should be Gaelic-
speaking, and because he is a very able, cultivated, and learned man,
we will give him a school and let him teach. . . ." I am not sure that I
like the idea of a State with a definite purpose, and there are moments,
unpractical moments, perhaps, when I think that the State should leave
the mind free to create. I think Aristotle defined the soul as that which
moves itself, and how can it move itself if everything is arranged
beforehand?[8]

Such a teacher, like a pleasant guest, would neither bore nor tyrannize.[9]

Yeats's third and last essay on education appeared in the *Dial* for February 1926. At its centre lies an angry protest against the ignorance of a clergy, specifically the Christian Brothers, who had condemned as blasphemous an old carol, to be found in Irish and English, that celebrated the Incarnation. Yeats's condemnation of their condemnation is focused in this passage:

> There is the whole mystery — God, in the indignity of human birth, all that seemed impossible, blasphemous even, to many early heretical sects, and all set forth in an old "sing-song" that has yet a mathematical logic. I have thought it out again and again and can see no reason for the anger of the Christian Brothers, except that they do not believe in the Incarnation.[10]

To these notions of the child as a guest of a creative education, of the "sing-song" logic of a verse that presents the Incarnation through a child, or of education as a matter of gracious cultivation before an uncertain future, I should like to add some considerations from Yeats's second and most important essay on education, "The Child and the State," delivered first as a lecture to the Irish Literary Society in London on 30 November 1925.

Yeats makes several recommendations here that are near a good many of his thoughts in "Among School Children." In the first place, he asks again that educational practice he revised according to methods already used in Italy and, incidentally, long advocated in the teaching of art:

> The tendency of the most modern education, that in Italy, let us say, is to begin geography with your native fields, arithmetic by counting the school chairs and measuring the walls, history with local monuments, religion with the local saints, and then to pass on from that to the nation itself. That is but carrying into education principles a group of artists, my father among them, advocated in art teaching. These artists have said: "Do not put scholars to draw from Greek or Roman casts until they have first drawn from life; only when they have drawn from life can they understand the cast." That which the child sees — the school — the district — and to a lesser degree the nation — is like the living body: distant countries and everything the child can only read of is like the cold Roman or Greek cast. If your education therefore is efficient in the modern sense, it will be more national than the dreams of politicians.[11]

Striking here are the possible analogues between the capture of the living body in art — as music might hold a dancer — and the tactile progression of the child from the immediate to the distant in time and space — after the manner of a tree's growth. Nor is the mention of inert casts, Greek, Roman or otherwise, completely irrelevant.

The conclusion is extremely provocative, if we keep in mind the last two stanzas of the poem:

The proper remedy is to teach religion, civic duty and history as all but inseparable. Indeed, the whole curriculum of a school should be as it were one lesson and not a mass of unrelated topics. I recommend Irish teachers to study the attempt now being made in Italy, under the influence of their Minister of Education, the philosopher Gentile, the most profound disciple of our own Berkeley, to so correlate all subjects of study. I would have each religion, Catholic or Protestant, so taught that it permeate the whole school life . . . that it may not be abstract, and that it may be part of history and of life itself, a part, as it were, of the foliage of Burke's tree. . . .

Every child in growing from infancy to maturity should pass in imagination through the history of its own race and through something of the history of the world, and the most powerful part in that history is played by religion. Let the child go its own way when maturity comes, but it is our business that it has something of that whole inheritance, and not as a mere thought, an abstract thing like those Graeco-Roman casts upon the shelves in the art schools, but as part of its emotional life.[12]

After this insistence on unity in education, and after the equally direct references to Gentile and the Italian system of education, it will be worthwhile to briefly sketch Yeats's reading in these matters. It may also do no harm to conclude this briefest of surveys with but a glance at another spirit, presence or memory that hovers over the poem, that of Maud Gonne.

IV

Although Yeats may not have read any of Dr. Maria Montessori's own work, he had, according to his wife, made himself thoroughly familiar with literature on the Montessori method in education. From his remarks, speeches and essays on education, one would expect Yeats to observe to his wife that Dublin boys might well learn arithmetic by counting Guinness barrels, and he did. Hence, though his exact reading in the literature remains unknown, he doubtless agreed to most of the major points of Dr. Montessori's book, *The Montessori Method*.

The counting of Guinness barrels would be part and parcel of the Montessori emphasis on reality brought to the child through sense training and spontaneous work, those ultimately self-disciplining activities. Freedom and discipline, exactness and spontaneity, reality and spiritual growth go hand in hand in the Montessori system. The appeal, as Eleanor Gibbon, Montessori representative in Ireland during Yeats's time, put it, is to a "sense of symmetry—an Ancient Irish trait."[13] Yeats would have seconded Miss Gibbon's statement in her speech in Waterford in 1919 when she summed up the system by calling it "a training for life as it is actually lived in the workaday world."[14] The children worked as might the poet or artist himself — with easy confidence and a naturally motivated inner force.

Liberty likewise becomes a matter of "form, what we universally consider good breeding."[15] Nor does the educator confuse the good child with the passive, inert child, the bad with the active. Further, the hope is not for an intellect that separates man from the world but for one that through work and liberty will bring the whole being into biological and social acquaintance with the world. The hallmark of the Montessori-trained child should be "a special grace of action which makes his gestures more correct and attractive, and which beautifies his hands and indeed his entire body now so balanced and so sure of itself; a grace which refines the expression of his face and of his serenely brilliant eyes, and which shows us that the flame of spiritual life has been lighted in another human being."[16] If this description recalls Yeats's dancer and "brightening glance" at the end of the poem, how truly relevant is this one:

> I have seen here [at the "Children's House"], men of affairs, great politicians preoccupied with problems of trade and of state, cast off like an uncomfortable garment the burden of the world, and fall into a simple forgetfulness of self. They are affected by this vision of the human soul growing in its true nature, and I believe that this is what they mean when they call our little ones, wonderful children, happy children — the infancy of humanity in a higher stage of evolution than our own. I understand how the great English poet Wordsworth, enamoured as he was of nature, demanded the secret of all her peace and beauty. It was at last revealed to him — the secret of all nature lies in the soul of a little child. . . .
>
> Truly our social life is too often only the darkening and the death of the natural life that is in us. These methods tend to guard that spiritual fire within man, to keep his real nature unspoiled and to set it free from the oppressive and degrading yoke of society. It is a pedagogical method informed by the high concept of Immanuel Kant: Perfect art returns to nature."[17]

I have reserved for an all too brief discussion Yeats's reading of Gentile. Mrs. Yeats had extracted and translated for her husband a good many bits and pieces from the work of this writer and other Italian writings on education. Thus, for instance, Yeats had also some knowledge of Gentile's work on secondary education. But the book he had sought after most, according to Joseph Hone, during his stay in Italy in 1924, was Gentile's *The Reformation of Education*.[18] This he found and read in Dino Bigongiari's translation, with an "Introduction" by Benedetto Croce. A total reading of the book strikes me as the best preparation for re-reading the poem, for it offers not only much of the matter that Yeats came to use, but, in one chapter, it virtually furnishes his poem's organization.

Although this book is the key to the philosophic background of the poem, its treatment of education is much like that of Dr. Montessori, though more profoundly idealistic. To start with, the chapter on "The Spirituality of Culture" takes us into the real drift of Gentile's subject, for it demonstrates that only our thought can give material reality any true unity. Otherwise matter as multiple is merely an abstraction. Here then Gentile can conclude—and I have already oversimplified his argument— that

> The world then is in us; it is our world, and it lives in the spirit. It lives the very life of that person which we strive to realise, sometimes satisfied with our work, but oftener unsatisfied and restless. And there is the life of culture.[19]

This idea of culture as activity or a constant becoming, the life of the spirit, is described like Yeats's dancer at the end of the poem: "in no manner comparable to a moving body in which the body itself could be distinguished from motion" (p. 126). In the chapter, "The Attributes of Culture," culture is equated with the whole body of education, and yet is not considered a *thing* to be located in schoolrooms or libraries but only existing in so far as it continues to form, develop, become, and thus to live. At one point, having called this dance of the spirit "motion without mass," Gentile goes on to refine his argument by terming "the spirit a gazing motion" (p. 132). Constant becoming would presumably brighten that gaze or glance. This gaze is also one of joy, for the life of the spirit, culture, is a drama of self-awareness, our work is our own blossoming, and like music it is *ours*. Culture, according to Gentile, "is not simply effort and uneasy toil, it is not a tormenting restlessness which we may sometimes shake off, from which we would gladly be rescued. Nor is it a feverish excitement that consumes our life-blood and tosses us restlessly on a sick-bed" (p. 133). It is rather a kind of beatification. In this process of constant realization of self, culture aspires to a truth which is good, answers a call to duty shared by all men. So education, at least by this argument, is both ethical and divine.

In his chapter on "Character and Physical Education," Gentile offers this central example of the soul's preponderance in the body. The picture is very close, again, to another central image in Yeats's poem:

> The mother who tenderly nurses her sick child is indeed anxious for the health of the body over which she worries, and she would like to see it vigorous and strong. But that body is so endeared to her, because by means of it the child is enabled to live happily with her; through it his fond soul can requite maternal love by filial devotion; or in it he may develop a powerful and beautiful personality worthy to be adored as the ideal creature of maternal affection. If in the bloom of physical health he were to reveal himself stupid and insensate, endowed with mere instinctive sensuality and bestial appetites, this son would cease to be the object of his mother's fondness, nay, he would arouse in her a feeling of loathing and revulsion. It is this sense of loathing . . . that we . . . feel for the human corpse from which life has departed; for life is the

basis of every psychological relation, and therefore of every possible sympathy.[20]

To repeat, then, "the spirit is the root and possibility of every unification" (p. 195). This idea is Greek in the best sense: The soul and body are one, with "gymnastics. . . . the essential complement of music, including in music all forms of spiritual cultivation" (p. 195). Moreover, Gentile conceives of physical activity as Christian, especially after the Italian Renaissance; consequently, the emphasis is on the spirit, the body by his argument being itself spirit.

The central chapter is that entitled "The Ideal of Education," subtitled "Art and Religion." It is primarily a defence of education as a becoming of the spirit before the objections of so-called realistic educators and the more old-fashioned pedants of sheer multiplicity. Gentile's ideal education, where "the spirit *is* in that it *becomes*, that it becomes in so far as it acquires self-consciousness, that its being therefore is consciousness in the act of being acquired" (p. 226), identifies the subject with the object, the spirit with its culture, the pupil with his education. Here, too, we come to an important idea, which Yeats seems to have made full use of in the last enigmatic line of his poem:

> The spirit's being is its alteration. The more it *is*, — that is, the more it becomes, the more it lives, — the more difficult it is for it to recognise itself in the object. It might therefore be said that he who increases his knowledge also increases his ignorance, if he is unable to trace this knowledge back to its origin, and if the spirit's rally does not induce him to rediscover himself at the bottom of the object, which has been allowed to alter and alienate itself more and more from the secret source of its own becoming. Thus it happens, as was said of old, that "He that increaseth knowledge increaseth sorrow." All human sorrow proceeds from our incapacity to recognise ourselves in the object, and consequently to feel our own infinite liberty.[21]

Gentile goes on to say, almost immediately, that "the reality of the spirit is not in the subject as opposed to the object, but in the subject that has in itself the object as its actuality" (p. 229). There then follows what I take to be an elaboration of this reality and, even more important, an explanation of what came to be the organizing principle of "Among School Children." This long passage can be said to lie at the heart of the poem:

> This dialectic in which the spiritual becoming unfolds itself (subject, object, and unity of subject and object), this self-objectifying or self-estrangement aiming at self-attainment, — this is the eternal life of the spirit, which creates its immortal forms, and determines the ideal contents of culture and education. The spirit's self-realisation is the realisation of the subject, of the object, and of their relationship. If of these three terms (the third being the synthesis of the first and second) any one should fail, the spiritual reality would cease to be.
> This threefold realisation admits empirically of a separation that

makes it possible to have one without the others. On the strength of this triple division we speak of art, of religion, and of philosophy, as though each of them could subsist by itself.

. . . .

But in reality they are so indissolubly conjoined, that separation would destroy their spiritual character, and put in its place mechanism, which is the property of all that is not spirit.

Art is the self-realisation of the spirit as subject. Man becomes enfolded in his subjectivity, and hears but the voice of love or other inward summons. . . . He simply spreads out over his own abstract interior world, and dreams; and as he dreams, he escapes from the outer bustle into the seclusion of his enchanted realm, which is true in itself until he issues from it and discovers it to be a figment of his phantasy. This man is the artist, who, we might say, neither cognises nor acts, but sings.

. . . .

This lyrical bent, peculiar to the artist who enhances himself by exalting his own abstract individuality, is in direct contrast with the tendency of the Saint, who crushes and annihilates this same individuality in the face of his God, — that God who infinitely occupies his consciousness as the "other" in absolute alterity to him, so that the subject is hurled into the object in a total self-abstraction. . . . So he deifies this other self, places it on the altar, and kneels before it. Thus the saint's personality is nullified; or rather, it is actualised and realised in this self-annulment, which is the theoretical and practical characteristic of mysticism and the specific act of religion.

. . . .

The nature then both of art and of religion implies a flagrant contradiction which comes to this, — that the subject to be subject is object, and the object to be object is subject. Hence the torments of the poet and the spasms of the mystic.

The concrete spirit is neither subject nor object. It is a self-objectifying subject, and an object which becomes the subject in virtue of the subjectivity that alights on it as it realises it. The spirit is therefore a becoming. It is the synthesis, the unity of these two opposites, ever in conflict and yet always intimately joined. And the spirit, as this unity, is the concreteness both of art (reality of the abstract subject) and of religion (reality of the abstract object). It is philosophy.[22]

The gist of Gentile's discourse is clear. The first of the triad, art, allows the spirit to realize itself as subject; but to avoid the mere retreat into dream, with the consequent pain of return to reality, the subject must objectify itself. The religious man, on the other hand, banishes the subject by completely identifying it with the object, God. In both cases, the images of the artist and the saint are literally self-born. The unifier of these two poles, subject and object, is the concrete spirit which can be neither one nor the other but is a synthesis, a becoming, in short both. It goes by names of the third member of the triad—philosophy. Religion and art, unless they inform each other, become abstractions that leave the self

in a despair of egotism or a sacrifice to an ascetic illusion. Nor is the
philosophy which brings them together the arcane profession of the
specialist. Yet something of a paradox remains. For this ideal philosophy
"is never finished, never completed, for it is his [man's] own spirit, his very
self, which to live must grow, and which must constitute itself as it
develops. And therefore this philosophy cannot help being man's ideal,
which is always being realized and which is never fulfilled" (p. 239). But it
is those fragments, those incomplete men — "the aesthete, or the supersti-
tious worshipper, or the star gazer, always unaware of the pit under his
feet" — who are most to be pitied. Gentile labels them nuisances to be
contrasted in "strength, agility, balance" with the rounded spirits (p. 244).
The aim of Gentile's education would seem to be an exalted, superhuman,
cosmic dancer attuned to the infinite vibrations of life at every moment of
its becoming.

V

Maud Gonne herself tells us in *A Servant of the Queen* that by her
mother's wish she had no formal schooling but was taught privately by a
slow-witted English governess in Ireland and later by a more witty lady in
France. Her early memories are those of virtually running wild over the
hills and heather of Howth with the native Irish. Her childhood there had
been like that depicted in those other dancing girls — Iseult Gonne and
Margot Collis — that Yeats celebrated. Her beauty was girlish, combining
the symmetry of Greek statuary, the pride of a Pallas Athene, and what
Yeats called a "classical impersonation of the Spring."[23] Like "A Woman
Homer Sung," Maud is inevitably described in Yeats's verse as "half lion,
half child," or as possessed with "the simplicity of a child," or as an Irish
Helen learning her tinker's dance, "part woman, three parts a child." Not
only did he associate her with light and blossoms, but according to Mrs.
Yeats, he held in memory the beauty of the flowering chestnut trees in the
Paris springtime as a remembrance of her beauty then. Moreover, her love
of birds — including a Donegal hawk — was shared with an equally powerful love of children. She had organized the Daughters of Ireland. Though
she cannot be called the wisest of mothers, she once said to Yeats after a
trip to Italy that she loved the cascades of Italian children, the large
families so much like those in Ireland.[24] During the 1913 Strike her special
concern was the feeding of the workers' children.[25]

There is even something childlike in her relationship with Yeats: she
had once believed that they had been sister and brother; they once
acknowledged themselves spiritually married.[26] Between the two a remarkable harmony remained, despite periodic exasperations on both sides.
Yeats could say, for instance, in an early unpublished draft of his
Autobiographies:

My outer nature was passive but for her I should never perhaps
have left my desk, but I knew my spiritual nature was passionate even
violent. In her all this was reversed, for it was her spirit only that was
gentle and passive, & full of charming fantasy as though it touched the
world only with the point of its fingers. . . .

I who could not influence her actions, could dominate her inner
being. I could then have use [of] her clairvoyance to produce forms that
would arise from both minds. . . . There would be, as it were, a
spiritual birth from the soul of a man & a woman.[27]

And, curiously enough, their relationship sometimes reminds one of the
two elder children of Lir, once described thus: "Fionnuala was the eldest
and she was as beautiful as sunshine in blossomed branches; Aodh was like
a young eagle in the blue of the sky."[28] Not only does their love, their
transformation to swans, their tragedy, and their reunion in the Tir-na-
nOg vaguely relate to the poem, but this description also recalls Yeats's
own memory of Maud in 1889, published in 1921: "Her complexion was
luminous, like that of apple-blossom through which the light falls."[29] His
own self-identification with the eagle is well enough known. I have,
moreover, purposely taken this description of Fionnuala and Aodh from
Ella Young's *Celtic Wonder-Tales* because there among Maud Gonne's
decorations and illustrations is one recurring motif, original with her so far
as I can tell, of a sphere containing two swans intertwined, ultimately
blent as one, an obvious symbol of kindred souls. This, but one more of
Maud's gifts for children, Yeats knew and may have consciously remembered. Perhaps then, a child's "colour upon cheek or hair" and "Plato's
parable" in the poem are even more widely suggestive than we had
thought.

Hence as perennial subject for Yeats's verse, as lover of children,
spiritual counterpart, classic living beauty (even in sibylline old age),
epitome of blossoms, dancing, light and flowering chestnut, perhaps even
as imagist for children, Maud Gonne belongs to the poem. She loved best
Yeats's poem about her, "The Two Trees." Did she see that both trees lived
on in "Among School Children?"

VI

It is best to introduce the poem itself with a caveat Yeats made at the
beginning of his essay on Berkeley. There he admitted the utility of various
abstractions — among them the educational notion that those who could
not read might be called degraded. Such abstractions, he declared, helped
maintain community life. They were useful if not final. But truth itself,
Yeats warns us, "is always mothlike and fluttering and yet can terrify."[30]
Thus in turning to "Among School Children" we must face not only Yeats's
hopes for education in Ireland but also his ultimate feelings about
generation and becoming. Something of this truth appears in a passage in

a white vellum notebook begun 7 April 1921. The passage seems to have been written in March 1926, some time close to the 14th. Here it is:

> Topic for poem—School children &
> the thought that live [sic] will waste them
> perhaps that no possible life can fulfill
> our dreams or even their teacher's
> hope. Bring in the old thought that
> life prepares for what never happens.[31]

The whole poem resolves the praise of a practical ideal of education as shown in Stanza I and the reservations about this revealed in Yeats's journal.

The first stanza of "Among School Children" strikes me initially as not at all ironical in its context. With thinly veiled references to place and time, it presents us with an occasion—an Irish Senator visiting a model school. Both the long room and the children's co-ordinated activities suggest the Montessori and P.N.E.U. systems. The standing children stare for a moment, but the assumption is that they have been preoccupied and presumably happy at work. The "kind old nun" rounds out the religious and divine coif, hinted in her white hood, that seems to crown their labours. Nor do I find any immediate mockery in "the best modern way." We are ushered into an excellence on the corporate and communal level. The questions, the kindly replies, and the public smile among the happy children are a prosy homage to an ideal that at least tries to face life's uncertainties, if not the truth that is "mothlike" or terrible. Perhaps such mixed thoughts, along with mention of Yeats's age, also suggest the beginning of the faint poetic ache which is elaborated time and again in the succeeding stanazas. Yet is must be insisted upon that these children would not be better off running wild in the fields. Most important, however, they with their singing, ciphering, reading, history, home-making and religious instructions have silently provided the poet in this first stanza with all the strands of his three themes—art, religion and philosophy, as they present themselves alone, and then together united by the divine philosophy of the concrete spirit.

The second stanza offers a contrast with the first. The pain that arises from poor or obsolete education is revealed in the poet-Senator's reverie. In contrast to the children of the first stanza, Maud Gonne is recalled as a young woman confiding in a half-lit scene the educational stupidity that had made a day of her childhood tragic. In this dream or reverie, Yeats also remembers how for that moment their natures *appeared* to be one, as though sympathy had brought their complementary natures together as one soul. Such are the dangers of artistic fantasy, as Gentile warned: the subject fixes on itself, on what might have been when—both young and handsome and of the same mind—Yeats had given reality to a dream of Maud that was not to be.

In an effort to objectify — as Gentile might say — his reveries, the poet looks at the children, only to be made even more wildly and painfully aware of Maud's beauty as a child, for both she and they are birds of a sort, though of different kinds. Then, in his wondering — the children's had been momentary — still in his partial dream, she appears as a child. But this appearance gives way in the fourth stanza to something else. This third and present image is obviously that of Maud in her sixties: "with her great height and the unchangeable lineaments of her form, she looks the Sibyl," as Yeats wrote in those years.[32] There is a contrast then in images, even in beauties, that is immediate and powerful. A Quattrocento finger might well have fashioned the girlish Maud as well as it had fashioned a Leda, any number of Madonnas, babes and assorted gods and goddesses. A Botticelli, a da Vinci (in earlier versions and drafts), even a Raphael might have done justice to this Flora, this "classical impersonation of the Spring" and luminous creature.[33] But Maud's present image is a special, difficult kind of beauty, the very essence of what Yeats meant by Quattrocento art. For this image is of "intellectual beauty," or "the victory of the soul" during a time when "the Mother of God sat enthroned" amid the "Soul's unity."[34] This is what Quattrocento art could do, according to Yeats, to celebrate the marriage of earth and heaven. These are also the aesthetic properties of ideal becoming. A Botticelli had seemed to combine the motifs of Porphyry's Cave and the Holy Manger, both great emblems of the soul's entry into the world, in a "Nativity" Yeats had seen in the National Gallery.[35] Such a finger might have fashioned this image from hollows and shadows, precisely as Yeats does. After all, Maud combined, for him, as we have seen, the pagan and Christian virtues of classic beauty and Madonna. The beauty he finds in this sixty-year elegance is truly their spiritual child, though he creates it out of near despair. He has it both ways. There is a contrast in the years and yet she is to him still transcendently beautiful. Otherwise, looking about him, he realizes that before the children both he and she are scarecrows, another rude jar to his reverie nearly objectified in the classroom.

So far then, after the introductory stanza, we have read three more that have dealt with the lonely singer, as Gentile might say, the lyric poet in his reveries filled with the pain of his passion before living change that mocks the permanent image of his dreams. If there is a beauty in the language that can describe Maud's present skeletal image, it derives from a poet-artist in torment before the imagined child and the actual aged woman who was never truly his. His corrective, so to speak, lies in the children who also sing and whom he would not frighten. Their singing, in contrast to his, does not retreat to dreams and subjective memories. It is a balancing part of their daily multifarious labours.

In the fifth stanza, Yeats turns from his first theme of art, as exemplified in the passion of the artist, explicitly the poet himself. He turns here not to his other major themes of religion and philosophy, but to the human becoming that both practise on—in the role of Madonnas or philosopher-teachers—the becoming that commands the greatest earthly affection, a mother's hopes. Such affection is fixed upon the growing babe, who according to Porphyry and Wordsworth, has ventured from a better world of the pure soul to a lesser one. Yet a mother, no matter what the pain of birth and bruise of body, imagines in the healthy shape a coming burgeoning of soul in human activity, perhaps even greatness, which may never be achieved. As children learn cutting, sewing and neatness among their studies, so they prepare for responsible parenthood. Yet a mother's generative endeavour, considered alone, is no less painful to her than is his song to the solitary singer. This stanza implies that time has also provided other betrayals here, perhaps three: that of the babe, the mother and the mother-to-be who would make generation the narrowed beauty of her life. For maternal affection is born in pain, hemmed in by uncertainties, and might well be broken by the sight of the child grown old. Before these realities, the pleasuring of a mother's soul must depend upon more than the hopes of a bruised maternity. The child must be more than neat, the mother more than mother.

The sixth stanza discovers another kind of affection, that of the so-called wise teacher. As an example of mistaken wisdom or philosophy, or a kind of misdirected affection, the stanza has an overlapping relation to Stanza VIII and its philosophy of unity. The philosophic teacher, if he has not begotten a scarecrow-to-be or even become one himself, by his very specialization has created one to frighten birds of any heritage. As Yeats wrote at the time: "Aristotle and Plato end creative system—to die into the truth is still to die—and formula begins. Yet even the truth into which Plato dies is a form of death, for when he separates the Eternal Ideas from Nature and shows them self-sustained he prepares the Christian desert and the Stoic suicide."[36] All three men fail as philosophers and teachers. The ciphering child has turned into the specialist who fails with Alexander, as did Aristotle—a bircher; who separated reality into the one and the many as did Plato (and not Berkeley and Gentile); or who reduces flow to rigid integer, as did Pythagoras. Such misbegotten wisdom destroys unity, never makes the jump between subject and object, between pupil and culture, ideal and nature—or sing-song and logic.

In Stanza VII we turn to religion as the objectification and virtual denial of self. The focus is on saintliness, the perfection sought after in the cloister rather than the worship of the ordinary man. The image of the artist had been of a past life negated by a real present. The mother's image had been a singular projection of the present negated by a likely future. That of the nun is of an eternity—bronze or marble and in repose—which human life negates at each moment. The flesh that kneels before candles or bronze and marble images is not only bruised, it can also have its heart broken by a perfection that man can at best only strive for. Appropriately at this point, Yeats looks back to all those Presences—those projections of the spirit, those avenging angels which we image forth: passion knowing the form of a Ledaean body that Quattrocento art had glorified in Madonna and pagan Goddess; affection creating the vision of the grown child based on the shape that innocently invests a newly arrived soul, or affection expressed in the taming of nature, kings and music in the fond hope that they will body forth design, reason and mensuration; and piety emulating a Mary or Madonna that ensures the eternal presence of God. All such Presences are born of the self that images them forth—in pure subjectivity or objectivity—and yet those Presences, while symbolizing heaven, also mock the fragmentary, incomplete nuisances we have become, no matter what our industry or labour.

The proper beginning of the concluding stanza is then most certainly with the word "Labour." For it signifies both the birth-struggle, that never stops in earthly becoming, and that task to which all of us are consigned. Yet "labour" may truly be said to blossom and dance in an ideal culture, or education, if you will. Here art and religion (if we can accept both nuns and mothers as worshippers) are unified by an ideal philosophy that does not merely divide, coerce or measure the world. In an ideal culture, the tendance of the soul need not sacrifice the body, for religion will be properly tempered with an artistic regard for self. Nor need beauty necessarily be got from a despair of contrasts, since religion may help us see beauty in even a partially obviated or dilapidated self. Nor will the wisdom that brings art and religion together be that of the guest who excludes himself from life's feast. This ideal of roundness—spiritual and physical, in any case ideal—Yeats had caught a glimpse of in the first stanza. Among the children, song, measurement, domestic chores and religion were one. And now he apostrophizes that unity.

From a nation's point of view, as complement to the child's, reading books and studying history and religion together may provide a total view of a district, the nation and even the world. They may also include Greek philosophers, the story of Christ, the Italian Renaissance, and a poet's memories. This unity of study provides a civic view of the nation where past, present and future are one much in the same way that bole (past), leaf (present) and blossom (future) merge in a chestnut tree. This "great-rooted blossomer" is rooted in spirit or the ideal, which gives unity to multiplicity, does not separate them as Plato did, and, as object of a child's contemplation, keeps all his future studies and years living and unified. The chestnut tree, itself like a living body, the symbol of an ideal civic culture under the aegis of religion, also has its artistic complement. I speak of that other symbol taken from those ciphering and singing Montessori children of the first stanza. Song and number realize the complementary artistic ideal of the dancer whose "gaze of motion" is constantly brightening with the increased grace of a child's proper becoming or growth. Here is "aimless joy" and "pure activity," yet also discipline. Like the image of the eighteen-year-old dancer that Yeats requested in 1926 from T. Sturge

Moore as the design for a book-plate for Anne, this dancer would be just as likely to be pictured dancing between the earth and the moon.[37] She brings both together. She too is a symbol from life in motion—"what a child sees"—not a Graeco-Roman cast on a shelf. The music is the formal complement of the soul during its dance of life. Musical number provides the dancer with a measured motion rather than arresting her or abstractly reducing her to counting fixed intervals on a stick or string.

Yet there is one more line and that line maintains the tragic plaint of wasted human endeavour apparent in even the original idea of the poem. Already in the question "Are you the leaf, the blossom or the bole?" Yeats seems not only to have commended the ideal of a unified civic education— to the benefit of child and state—but he also suggests its inherent limitation. For if a child discovers himself at one with the organic, virtually timeless, growth of the nation, how can he know or understand the uniqueness of his own historical moment? Thus, in the last line, Yeats makes an even more insistent reservation on what might be called man's finest concept of education. The line reminds us that even ideally, even in the new friendly long Montessori classroom, the superchild-to-be must still face those limitations of his humanity, as have those burdened specialists, whether artists, mothers, philosophers or nuns. This last line merely repeats much more finely the paradox voiced by Gentile of a philosophy which in fulfilling itself cannot be realized, the paradox of an ideal identification of subject and object—the child and his culture—where the self is liable not to be discerned, where the child cannot know his infinite liberty, here in space. The lovely merge of dancer and dance, like the difficult beauty of a sixty-year-old woman, may yet also break hearts. As Gentile observed, "He that increaseth knowledge increaseth sorrow." After all then, there may be just the slightest touch of irony in the conclusion of that first Senatorial stanza. Then, too, the presence of Maud Gonne, whether as disappointed child, divine mother, soul's companion or beloved witness to Parisian springtime, lends fragile human grandeur to what might have otherwise been the irony of the inconsolable.

VII

In 1937, A. N. Jeffares, then a student at the High School on Harcourt Street, Yeats's old school, rang up Yeats and, as editor, asked for a poem as a possible contribution to the April issue of the *Erasmian*, the school publication. After some thought Yeats selected a poem called "What Then?" that looked to his own youthful designs, labour, later accomplishments and successes that had brought him friends, home, family and even some perfection in his own work—and these in the face of the buffoonish detractors that Dublin can always offer. Yet the refrain ending each stanza of the poem remained the same: *"What then?"* This sentiment had been the impetus of his own growth. As a scholar at the

Godolphin School, Hammersmith, he had been virtually at the bottom of his class.[38] Nor had Yeats distinguished himself academically at the High School. He had, however, done something more. Lacking the patience for a grammatical adventure with the classics, he had readily surrendered himself to cribs and bad marks, yet, as John Eglinton has gone on to remind us:

> Yeats in the High School was kind of super-boy, who enjoyed an enviable immunity from the various ignomies of school discipline. . . .
>
> His privileged standing among the boys was due, no doubt, to some arrangement with his father, who had applied certain educational principles to his children's upbringing, of which spontaneous development was the essential: and Yeats was really an unusually well read young man of about 19, with a conscious literary ambition.[39]

The point is best made in Yeats's own youthful remarks to J. B. Bury, editor of Gibbon: "I know you will defend the ordinary system of education by saying that it strengthens the will, but I am convinced that it only seems to do so because it weakens the impulses."[40]

Finally then, irreverently perhaps, one cannot help musing over Trinity's thoughts of granting Yeats a professorship in literature in 1913, he who could not have passed the entrance examination as a nineteen-year-old, and then, of course, going no further with that appointment. Nor, in the same year, does U.C.D. seem to have given the same matter much more thought. Nor can one forget the ever-buoyant remarks of the two present Irish literary greats, remarks directed at Yeats as a poet during the very gestation period of "Among School Children." The first was by Frank O'Connor, who said, "Now, what do I find wrong with Yeats? I find this: that never, at any time or for any occasion whatsoever, does his art come into touch with life, with the world around us."[41] Sean O'Faoláin merely endorsed O'Connor's fantasy when in the next month he called Yeats's poetry that of "passing moods," to be compared unfavourably with native Gaelic poetry, "that of basic emotions."[42] One wonders what they came to think "Among School Children" was about? Otherwise, in later saying that "Man can embody truth but he cannot know it," Yeats was but ascertaining once again part of his own life's work: the imaginative bodying forth of an ideal Irish culture while never ceasing to try to explain it to himself. Consequently, in even so exciting and exacting a problem as the education of the young, his final position in "Among School Children" realistically remained that of metaphysical mystery.

Notes

1. Eleanor Gibbon, *Ireland, Freedom and the Child*, Waterford, undated, pp. 9, 18.

2. The information in this section was gathered from conversations with Mrs. W. B. Yeats or with members of the Convent of Mercy, Waterford. The member of this community

who witnessed Yeats's visit must remain, by rules of the Order, anonymous. See also Joseph Hone, *W. B. Yeats, 1865–1939*, London, 2nd ed., 1962, pp. 373–4.

3. See *The Well Wrought Urn*, New York, 1947, pp. 163–75; *Interpretations*, London, 1955, pp. 194–210; and *Romantic Image*, London, 1961, pp. 83–91, 163–4.

4. *The Senate Speeches of W. B. Yeats*, ed. Donald R. Pearce, Bloomington, 1960, p. 108.

5. *Ibid.*, p. 110

6. *Ibid.*, pp. 110–11.

7. *Ibid.*, pp. 111–12.

8. "Compulsory Gaelic," *Irish Statesman*, 2 August 1924, p. 652.

9. *Ibid.*

10. "The Need for Audacity of Thought," *Dial* (February, 1926), p. 116.

11. *Senate Speeches*, pp. 170–1. As early as 1906 Yeats had held something of the same beliefs. In a newspaper interview on the proposal to hand over the Hibernian Academy to the Agricultural and Technical Department, he could say: "It does not matter to the Dublin student whether he gets his art teaching in the Academy or from a Professor of Painting at an Art School. What does matter is that he shall not be put under any sort of official system, and that there is a living model for him to draw from daily. No doubt a powerful personality will teach after some system, but it will be a personal one. Anything like the South Kensington routine, which bores a student out of his wits with drawing from the flat, drawing from the round, drawing from the antique for several years before it lets him get to Nature, destroys the student. . . ." Unidentified clipping, December–January, 1906–7; in possession of Mrs. W. B. Yeats.

12. *Senate Speeches*, pp. 173–4.

13. *Ireland, Freedom and the Child*, p. 19.

14. *Ibid.*, p. 20.

15. *The Montessori Method*, translated by Anne E. George with an Introduction by Professor Henry W. Holmes, London, 1912, p. 87.

16. *Ibid.*, p. 353.

17. *The Montessori Method*, translated by Anne E. George with an Introduction by Professor Henry W. Holmes, London, 1912, p. 377.

18. Joseph Hone, *W. B. Yeats*, p. 368. Yeats's enthusiasm for Gentile's theory of unified education is, of course, part of the poet's enduring preoccupation with unity of being, voiced, as recent to this narrative as 1919 in his essay "If I Were Four-and-Twenty." See *If I Were Four-and-Twenty*, Dublin, 1940, pp. 1–21.

19. *The Reformation of Education*, London, 1923, p. 108.

20. *The Reformation of Education*, London, 1923, p. 194.

21. *Ibid.*, pp. 228–9.

22. *Ibid.*, pp. 230–6.

23. *Autobiographies*, p. 123.

24. Information from Mrs. W. B. Yeats.

25. "Meals for School Children," *Irish Times*, 29 October 1913, p. 8. Maud once "drafted a parliamentary bill for meals for school children," Hone, *W. B. Yeats*, p. 151 n.

26. Unpublished draft of Yeats's *Autobiographies*. All unpublished material in this essay is copyright © Michael Butler Yeats and Anne Yeats 1965.

27. *Ibid.*

28. Ella Young, *Celtic Wonder-Tales*, illustrated and decorated by Maud Gonne, Dublin, 1910, p. 145.

29. *Autobiographies*, p. 123.

30. "Bishop Berkeley," *Essays and Introductions*, p. 400.

31. Unpublished journal. See *Letters* (ed. Allan Wade), p. 719; for a thoughtful discussion of this note and early versions of the poem, see also Thomas Parkinson, "Vestiges of Creation," *Sewanee Review*, lxix (Winter, 1961), pp. 92–111. A journal begun in December 1908, from which the passages in *Estrangement* are taken, contains this unpublished entry dated 6 September [1909]: "I thought of this house [Coole] slowly perpetuating itself & the life within it, in ever increasing intensity of labour, & then of its probably sinking away through courteous incompetence or rather sheer weakness of will for ability has not failed in young Gregory, and I said to myself "Why is life a perpetual preparation for something that never happens? Even as Odysseus only seems a preparation to think of ruin or remembrance. Is it not always the tragedy of the great and the strong, that they see before the end the small & the weak, in friendship or in enmity, pushing them from their place, & marring what they have built, & doing one or the other in mere lightness of mind."

32. *Autobiographies*, p. 123.

33. *Ibid.*

34. *A Vision* (1925), pp. 203–4.

35. *Ibid.*, p. 202.

36. *Ibid.*, p. 183.

37. *W. B. Yeats and T. Sturge Moore, their Correspondence, 1901–1937*, ed. Ursula Bridge, New York, 1953, pp. 60, 90, 91, 113.

38. Godolphin School Reports, 1878, in the possession of Mrs. W. B. Yeats.

39. "Yeats at the High School," *Erasmian*, xxx (June, 1939), p. 11.

40. "I Become an Author," *The Listener*, 4 August 1938, p. 218.

41. "What Is Irish Literature," *Irish Statesman*, 12 December 1925, p. 430.

42. "Irish and Anglo-Irish Modes in Literature," *Irish Statesman*, 9 January 1926, pp. 558–9.

Deirdre: **The Rigour of Logic**   David R. Clark*

I

The action of a typical Yeats play is not to demonstrate purpose or to express passion but to reveal perception. The particular form this action takes in *Deirdre* is to discover the tragedy of trust. This play, however, uses both the syllogistic progression of logical relationships and the qualitative progression of feeling.[1] These are present as the necessary conditions of moments of revelation. Reason demonstrates its narrowness and superficiality; passion expresses its undirected force. The insufficiency of either is momently revealed. Their opposition causes repeated deadlocks during which the characters pause in their acting or suffering, startled by sudden insights which correct their previous misapprehensions of life.

In this play each character shares with the others in four fatalities—

*Reprinted from *W. B. Yeats and the Theatre of Desolate Reality* (Chester Springs, Pa.: Dufour Editions; Dublin: Dolmen Press, 1965), 26–42. © 1965 by David R. Clark.

each is fated to trust another, to betray and to be betrayed; to be motivated by a love, and to shape (or distort) that love to fit the requirements of a code.

Because of his love for all men, which appears in the form of optimistic good faith, Fergus must trust Conchubar and be betrayed by him. Moreover, Fergus must unconsciously betray others through lack of insight. Naoise must trust in Fergus, and through him in Conchubar, not only because of his warrior's code of honor but also because of his friendship for Fergus and his love for Deirdre. This love takes the shape of expecting ideally honorable behavior from both her and himself. Thus he cannot stoop to the dishonorable doubt which would save him. Therefore he must be betrayed and must involve Deirdre in the same fate in spite of her warnings. That his honor is based on her love is shown by the change in him when she pretends to care for Conchubar.[2]

Deirdre must trust Naoise because she loves him and thus must be fellow victim with him of Conchubar's betrayal. Even though her love makes her more fearful and perceptive than the others, it also binds her to assume the honorable pose Naoise believes in. In her death, however, her love takes its honor and dignity from its own integrity. And yet Deirdre too must betray. Her love for Naoise has made her deceive Conchubar once. At the end of the play she again escapes to her lover by deceiving the king. She has even pretended to betray Naoise, at points in the play, but she can never actually do so, even to save him, because the love to which she is true assumes an ideal honor between the lovers.

Conchubar's love for Deirdre is distorted by his sovereign pride. This pride forces him to betray the lovers in order to get Deirdre back and to punish Naoise. Yet it forces him to trust them, too. His intrigue depends on the good faith of Fergus and the honorableness of Naoise. His pride forces him to trust Deirdre at the end and brings about his betrayal by her and her suicide. He is surrounded by "traitors" as Fergus brings in the aroused people.

The theme of the play seems to be something like this: The movement of the whole soul in romantic love gives truer knowledge, nobler courage, and more controlled passion, than do abstract public virtues such as humanitarian good faith, kingly pride, and even heroic honor. Each of the four fatalities, while found in all four chief characters, is most fully dramatized in one. To betray is Conchubar's chief action. To trust is Fergus's. To love is Deirdre's. And to adhere to a code of honor is Naoise's. Yet in the deepest sense, Deirdre is the most successful of the four chief characters in remaining true to trust, although seemingly she is the one most moved by other motives: fear and passion. She fears lest she not be allowed to keep faith with Naoise. Her passion is a faithful love for Naoise.

Naoise is a person of great nobility whose public code (he must behave honorably with Conchubar) comes into conflict with his private faith-keeping with Deirdre. In a sense he betrays her by leading her into the unfortunate situation in which we find them. But one cannot seriously blame him. He has the vice of his virtue: nobility.

Fergus stands surety for the lovers and for the King. He tries to keep faith with both. If he admits the validity of Deirdre's fear, he has to admit the baser motives in Conchubar. Then the pattern of decorum will break down, fear and anger will be admittedly stronger than honor, reason and policy. Being a humanitarian, he cannot admit this possibility without cancelling his fundamental assumption — that decorous (but unsacrificial) righteousness and goodwill unfailingly bring out those qualities in others. Therefore, he deceives himself constantly. There is no sufficient recognition of evil in him, no recognition of the risk, or of the complete willingness to renounce and sacrifice which his attitude must involve in order to work. There is perhaps, too, not a sufficient awareness of the sacrifice he is requiring Conchubar to make.

Conchubar has been betrayed, he feels. But his self-centeredness has caused the betrayal. His love is self-centered. An old man choosing a young girl for bride is not thinking of her happiness. His honor, too, is more a dedication *to* self than a dedication *of* self. He breaks faith, yet maintains that it was only honorable for him so to do. He has his kingly office from which to rationalize his self-centeredness. It was treason for Deirdre and Naoise to run away. It was to keep faith with his office that he should choose "her most fitting to be Queen," and conspire to get her back. It was a king's duty also to punish treason, to let "no boy lover take the sway."[3]

Both he and Deirdre are willing to break faith, but in different senses. In being true to himself and his office, he must betray the lovers, or so he feels. Deirdre betrays to be true to another. Deirdre's love is for Naoise, not for herself. She does not hate even Conchubar. Her honor too is a dedication of self. She is willing to sacrifice the appearance of it, in order to have the reality.

Naoise, similarly, feels no responsibility to die in a great display of physical courage. He would rather die quietly, exercising a genuine moral courage. Yet if Conchubar would fight him chivalrously, he would be glad; more glad to share with his enemy an honorable code than to display individual honor, whether publicly on the field or privately by playing chess to the end with Deirdre.

The fact that Fergus rallies fighting men to the defense of Deirdre and Naoise perhaps shows that his values are changed. But he was never pacifist, merely long-suffering and over-trusting. His uprising, it may be noted, accomplishes no end. Conchubar's motives are indeed unchanged. He learns the consequences of his selfish pride, but he does not reject it. The discovery that each character makes (with the exception of Fergus) is that, although he was "right" in his values, he was incompletely aware of the price of living by them. In the case of Deirdre and Naoise, their struggle purifies their motives, leading them to reject all other values. It does not change their values.

Oedipus' proud purpose, in *Oedipus Rex*, is to find the murderer. His resulting *pathos* is to suffer disruption of his confident kingship. His perception is to discover his own guilt. In *Deirdre*, where the action for each of the characters is to discover the tragedy of trust, only the optimism of Fergus and the pride of Conchubar are qualities capable of bringing about a Sophoclean tragic rhythm, and these are not the chief tragic characters. Trust is not a vice, but a virtue. Naoise's honor is not a mistake, nor is Deirdre's love. What does each perceive but what he already knows? The characters do not undergo any fundamental changes in moral being — they are merely perfected and pay the price of their finishing.

The function of the chorus in this play will be different from that in Greek tragedy because of the difference in the sort of action imitated and the difference in the conception of tragedy. It will be different also from the use in Neoclassic French drama. Fergusson says that the Neoclassic tragedians did not know what to do with the chorus because they imitated action as rational.

> The pathos pictured by the Sophoclean chorus is a moment of change in the moral being: it includes the breakdown of one rational-ized, moral *persona*; the suffering of feelings and images suggesting a human essence capable of both good and evil, and always underlying the individual with his desperate reasons and his fragile integrity. The Sophoclean pathos can only be conveyed by the chorus, with its less than individual mode of being; its musical and kinesthetic mimicry, and its sensuous dreamlike imagery, precisely because it has to convey a change in the highly realized and rationalized individual moral being.[4]

The "chorus" of women musicians in *Deirdre* has no great function to perform in representing the breakdown of the rationalized moral beings of the characters. Its functions are to hold before characters and audience the outcome of the drama, the recognitions that they will soon experience. In the very opening lines of the play, the musicians hold before us the action as fiction, as artistically (if not actually) completed story or song.

> I have a story right, my wanderers,
> That has so mixed with fable in our songs
> That all seemed fabulous.[5]

The First Musician has "entered hurriedly" to announce to the others her discovery that they are "come, by chance, into King Conchubar's country" where "Queen Deirdre grew," and she tells the familiar story up to the elopement of Deirdre and Naoise. Then the musicians gather around her to hear a close secret about present developments in that affair. Conchubar's house is being elaborately prepared and in particular one "great room"[6] — but here the entrance of Fergus interrupts them, turning what was to have been a narrative into a dramatic showing forth of the remainder of the tale.

That the imminent revelation of Conchubar's evil purpose by the First Musician is prevented by Fergus' interruption does not merely mark the place where exposition leaves off and drama begins. It establishes a pattern basic to the play in which again and again the revelation of Conchubar's intent is frustrated by characteristic attitudes and actions of Fergus or Naoise. When, a little later, the First Musician attempts to tell Fergus about that "great room" he will not listen. We must wait until Deirdre is left alone with the musicians to discover the untold secret: In that room is a bed into which are sewn "strange, miracle-working, wicked stones" which have power "to stir even those at enmity to love."[7] This is evidence enough of Conchubar's plot. The musicians are consciously aware of the impending danger. Their conscious awareness points up the unconscious fear from which the other characters suffer. They hold in our attention the consequences of trust, the price these characters, including Conchubar, will have to pay. They also hold up, in their lyrics, an ideal of behavior for Deirdre and Naoise. The heroic and all-sufficient marriage of love and honor is praised by them before Naoise and Deirdre dramatize it in their lives. Thus the outcome of the tragedy, both in terms of the catastrophe and of values displayed, is present from the beginning in the persons of the musicians, who never leave the stage.

The musicians, then, are there partly to put the audience into a frame of mind in which they will accept the legendary material: This is a tale which Irish minstrels have handed down. But further, the tale is one of lovers whose lives seemed shaped by characters and events into a structure like that of art. Deirdre's death seems an artistic achievement, and the form implicit in it cries out — as she herself does to the musicians — for representation in song.

Still further, the musicians combine the function of chorus with that of seer. Their knowledge is a surer one than the narrow reasoning of a Fergus, a Naoise or a Conchubar. Only Deirdre, who thinks with her emotions as well as her head, shares it.

Acting mainly as seers, the musicians oppose their arguments to those of Fergus. Thus they demonstrate a reasoned purpose contrary to his. Acting mainly as chorus, they express for Deirdre and Naoise their passion and devotion. But acting as spectators and transmitters, artistic apprehenders and perfecters of the story, they discover the meaning of the whole. They always know first what is going to happen and what it means. They wait from the beginning in expectancy of a fitting end to the story which is already a legend even before it is over. They are the discoverers of the tragedy of trust. The other characters act that the musicians may see, remember and praise. The musicians' revelations are the discoveries of poetry, however, not of philosophy or science; they are not, on the other hand, the revelations of religion. The musicians are not oracles, only artists. The discoveries represented by the play are terminal stages in movements alternating craft and feeling—as if the characters were periodically granted insights as they practised the art of their lives, training their passion to the model of some form of decorum. Further aspects of the working out of this pattern may be seen as we go through the play in more detail.

II

The scene of *Deirdre* is a guest house in a wood near Conchubar's palace. ". . . *Through the doors and some of the windows one can see the great spaces of the wood, the sky dimming, night closing in.*"[8] The perspective through the window is symbolically important. The woods and the approaching darkness remind us of "that first night in the woods" when Deirdre and Naoise

> . . . lay all night on leaves, and looking up,
> When the first grey of the dawn awoke the birds,
> Saw leaves above. . . . .[9]

and of their death together when they are gone "Into the secret wilderness of their love."[10] The perspective draws our mind off towards "the things [which] come after death."[11]

The interior arrangement is also symbolic as well as functional:

> *There is a door to right and left, and through the side windows one can see anybody who approaches either door, a moment before he enters. In the centre, a part of the house is curtained off; the curtains are drawn. There are unlighted torches in brackets on the walls. There is, at one side, a small table with a chessboard and chessmen upon it. At the other side of the room there is a brazier with a fire; two women, with musical instruments beside them, crouch about the brazier.*[12]

The guest house is a trap, a cage. The perspective without of the darkening woods represents a liberty to be achieved only in a love-death. They mysterious glimpses through the windows of whoever approaches either door provide moments of ominous suspense and focus the attention on the threat from the hunter, Conchubar, who will soon come to claim his quarry.

The curtain closing off the central part of the house is also mysterious. What is behind it? Why is it there? In the context the audience cannot avoid a certain alarm about this question. Both the characters and the audience examine the interior of the room for evidence of Conchubar's intention, or for any hint of what is to come. Nothing waits behind the curtain, however, except the fate of Deirdre and Naoise, who will die there and the fate of Conchubar whose purpose will be defeated there. The curtain will deceive Deirdre while Naoise is murdered, and will deceive Conchubar while Deirdre kills herself. The curtain conceals the unexpected and shocking tragedy, which is not recognized until too late, but for which destiny and the dramatist have reserved a place from the beginning.

The betrayal of guests in a guest-house would be one of the most treacherous sorts of fraud, yet there has been an ominous lack of preparation for these guests. The torches are unlighted, though it is getting dark. An old chess board has not been moved for their coming. The only fire has been prepared by wandering musicians whom chance has made the only persons ready to receive the lovers. The unlighted torches convey the sense of dismal loneliness. The lovers suffer from this fear and depression until they finally see Conchubar's purpose. Then they prepare to meet death in an heroic spirit. At the point Naoise cries, "Light torches there and drive the shadows out. / For day's grey end comes up," [13] and the musicians light the torches in the sconces. The falling darkness, then, suggests the "grey end" of their coming death, the torchlight their growing courage. Later when Deirdre's triumphant death is taking place behind the curtains, Fergus enters with the people, Deirdre's friends, armed. Then *"The house is lit with the glare of their torches."*[14] Life burns highest in these last minutes.

The brazier around which the wandering musicians crouch is the source of the torchlight — both literally and figuratively. The fire of the brazier suggests natural instinctive emotion — the desire to live, the fear of death, and above all the passion of love. This is a woman's play and the fire is a visible symbol of a woman's sensibility. The musicians about the brazier make that space the women's side of the stage. The men's side is over by the chess board, which represents sometimes code and decorum, sometimes craft and the struggle of wills.

The women are wanderers like Deirdre. Like her they value only love. "There is nothing in the world" says the First Musician, "That has been friendly to us but the kisses / That were upon our lips."[15] The women are low born and need not consider honor as a motive. Thus their direct apprehension of the situation is not confused by noble scruples. Naoise finds Deirdre unqueenly in listening to them. They are musicians, and, according to Fergus, full of

> wild thought
> Fed on extravagant poetry, and lit
> By such a dazzle of old fabulous tales
> That common things are lost, . . .[16]

Yet the imaginative truth which they grasp proves more trustworthy than the "truth" based on reason and code. They are simultaneously the sympathetically suffering chorus of this tragedy and the Tiresias or Cassandra whose warnings, unheeded, prove to have a deeper truth than that of reason.

In short, they and their brazier externalize Deirdre's passion, fear, and demanding vitality. It is meaningful that Deirdre and Naoise have been "paid servants in love's house / To sweep the ashes out and keep the doors,"[17] that after their death Deirdre and Naoise will be "Imperishable things, a cloud or a fire"[18] And that the musicians, showing Deirdre's token in afterdays will find "the doors of kings / Shall be thrown wider open, the poor man's hearth / Heaped with new turf."[19] The torches of Deirdre and Naoise's spiritual triumph are lit by these women from their symbolic brazier.

On the opposite side of the stage is the chess table suggesting that the action has many qualities of a game played according to rules. Although, as has been said, the men usually stand near the chess table and the women near the brazier, Deirdre moves back and forth as she fluctuates between passion and craft, fear and honor. When Deirdre and Naoise first enter, Deirdre has gone toward the women, who put her jewels on her as she expresses her fear of Conchubar. *Naoise has stood looking at her, but Fergus brings him to the chess-table.*[20] Naoise says: "I have his word and I must take that word, / Or prove myself unworthy of my nurture."[21] Fergus replies "We'll play at chess" and argues that both Deirdre's fear and Conchubar's tardiness have an innocuous explanation. The chessboard thus externalizes Naoise's heroic honor and Fergus' statecraft based on optimistic good faith. Naoise, whose code does not require him to deceive himself as Fergus' does, notes that the chessboard is an ominous sign:

> It is the board
> Where Lugaid Redstripe and that wife of his,
> Who had a seamew's body half the year,
> Played at the chess upon the night they died.[22]

The chessboard thus becomes an objective correlative for their complete tragedy. Like Lugaid Redstripe and his wife they will play a game of honor and good-faith while they are being betrayed.

Deirdre senses Naoise's apprehension of danger, and now the whole stage becomes a chessboard on which passion and honor oppose each other. Deirdre protests her fear; Fergus and Naoise leave rather than listen to her unqueenly distrust. Then she must evoke and sift the hints of the musicians who are afraid to tell her what they suspect. When she has won that knowledge, she calls back Naoise. He again counters her fear with his honorable scruples, but she tricks him into thinking she cares for Conchubar and thus makes him jealous. When Fergus makes her see the vanity of this action, she is ready to blacken her beauty and thus avoid Conchubar's passion. All this were like an intense game, were it not also like the struggle of a bird in a net.

Conchubar's servant enters and announces that Deirdre is invited to Conchubar's table and his bed, but that Naoise is to be held as a traitor. This event is the betrayal foreshadowed by the earlier reference to Lugaid

Redstripe. Conchubar's cold craft is now added to the suggestions emanating from the chessboard symbol. Conchubar has cheated in the game.

An extension of the impersonal and inexorable quality of the chess game is found in the foreign mercenaries hired by Conchubar to carry out his intention. They are foreigners using force, in security, for gain. They are the opposite of the musicians, who are of the Irish people, yet insecure wanderers, and who act for love. Note also that the mercenaries are opposed at the end not by an Irish army, but by the aroused, undisciplined, people. The confusion of the "reaping-hooks"[23] stands partly for the insufficient preparation of a Fergus in the face of evil, but also for the natural and instinctive horror of evil as opposed to Conchubar's calculation.

When "the game is up," so to speak, Naoise desires to die, not "fighting and passionate" but like "Lugaid Redstripe and that wife of his" who

> Sat at this chess-board, waiting for their end.
> They knew that there was nothing that could save them,
> And so played chess as they had any night
> For years, and waited for the stroke of sword.
> I never heard a death so out of reach
> Of common hearts, a high and comely end.[24]

Deirdre agrees to play, saying,

> . . . Though I have not been born
> Of the cold, haughty waves, my veins being hot,
> And though I have loved better than that queen,
> I'll have as quiet fingers on the board.

The torches are lighted, and they play. The musicians sing at the bidding of the lovers:

DEIRDRE: What is it but a king and queen at chess?
> They need a music that can mix itself
> Into imagination, but not break
> The steady thinking that the hard game needs.[25]

This scene is of the highest importance, for it brings together the images of fire, light, music and womanly passion with the images of the hard masculine game. The substance of Deirdre's passion is being given the form of Naoise's honor.

She breaks off the game, not to lapse back into fear, but to prefer a higher game, the game of love. Deirdre's victory over fear is passionate, and therefore superior to that of the stoical sea-mew's victory.

> I cannot go on playing like that woman
> That had but the cold blood of the sea in her veins.

NAOISE: It is your move. Take up your man again.

She does do, but in the game of love, not chess. She says:

> Do you remember that first night in the woods
> We lay all night on leaves, and looking up,
> When the first grey of the dawn awoke the birds,
> Saw leaves above us? You thought that I still slept,
> And bending down to kiss me on the eyes,
> Found they were open. Bend and kiss me now,
> For it may be the last before our death.
> And when that's over, we'll be different;
> Imperishable things, a cloud or a fire.
> And I know nothing but this body, nothing
> But that old vehement, bewildering kiss.[26]

Death is here figured as a dawn rather than a sunset. A transformation has taken place. Deirdre has joined to her passion the language of honor which Naoise uses in referring to the sea-mew and her lover:

> . . . Those two,
> Because no man and woman have loved better,
> Might sit on there contentedly, and weigh
> The joy comes after.[27]

In this game of love Deirdre and Naoise have been opposites, he honorable and she passionate. But now she has penetrated into his area of this psychological chess board and he into hers. From this time on she is heroical and controlled. Love appears in her speeches now in the forms of decorum, honorable courage, and masterful craft. He, on the other hand, becomes passionate in his desire to kill Conchubar, losing his earlier determination not to "die like an old king out of a fable / Fighting and passionate."[28]

The temptation comes in the form of honor. Conchubar appears, seemingly inviting Naoise to the noble game of single combat.

NAOISE «LAUGHING»:   He has taken up my challenge;
> Whether I am a ghost or living man
> When day has broken, I'll forget the rest,
> And say that there is kingly stuff in him.

Conchubar, however, disappears. It is not the game of war he is playing, but the ignoble one (when human beings alone are involved) of hunter and hunted.

NAOISE: A prudent hunter, therefore, but no king.
> He'd find it if what has fallen in the pit
> Were worth the hunting, but has come too near,
> And I turn hunter. You're not man, but beast.
> Go scurry in the bushes, now, beast, beast,
> For now it's topsy-turvy. I upon you.[29]

This angry lack of restraint leads to Naoise's capture.

CONCHUBAR: He cried "Beast, beast!" and in a blind-beast rage
              He ran at me and fell into the nets.[30]

From this moment on there is no conflict, in Naoise's speeches, between honor and love, the law of one being the law of the other, both games following the same rules. Deirdre is ready to sacrifice herself to Conchubar to rescue Naoise. This sacrifice Naoise will not accept:

NAOISE: If you were to do this thing,
           And buy my life of Conchubar with your body,
           Love's law being broken, I would stand alone
           Upon the eternal summits, and call out,
           And you could never come there, being banished.[31]

Deirdre bows to his decision; she obeys always the law of love.

As Deirdre begins her dignified and decorous pleading, she stands on the women's side of the stage and slowly approaches Conchubar who is on the other side. When she kneels before Conchubar, asking for him to pardon her obedience to the law of love, she has come completely across the stage — from the side of fear and passion to the side of honor. Naoise is then killed. Deirdre staggers back to the other side with the musicians.

Now she opposes to Conchubar's seven-year game of plotting her own skillful deception. She beings to move again toward the center of the stage. She pretends to a passion she does not feel — "There's something brutal in us, and we are won / By those who can shed blood," and a conventional honor with which she is not concerned —

              I shall do all you bid me, but not yet,
              Because I have to do what's customary.
              We lay the dead out, folding up the hands,
              Closing the eyes, and stretching out the feet,
              And push a pillow underneath the head,
              Till all's in order; and all this I'll do
              For Naoise, son of Usna.[32]

Earlier she used her sophistry to get Naoise to give in to her fears. Now she uses it to deceive Conchubar and achieve an honorable love-death.

She appeals to the code of love — "It is so small a gift and you will grant it / Because it is the first that I have asked." Conchubar is not moved. She appeals then to selfish pride and wins her end.

CONCHUBAR: He trembled at the thought of a dead face!"
DEIRDRE: . . . . He shall be mocked of all.
              They'll say to one another, "Look at him
              That is so jealous that he lured a man
              From over sea, and murdered him, and yet
              He trembled at the thought of a dead face!"

[She has her hand upon curtain.]

CONCHUBAR: How do I know that you have not some knife,
And go to die upon his body?

DEIRDRE: Have me searched,
If you would make so little of your queen.
It may be that I have a knife hid here
Under my dress. Bid one of these dark slaves
To search me for it.

[Pause]

CONCHUBAR: Go to your farewells, Queen.[33]

Deirdre now goes behind the curtain from the women's side, as Naoise has been dragged from the men's. The curtain is halfway between the symbols of brazier and chessboard. Deirdre stabbing herself upon the body of Naoise, has played her game of honorable love and won. Fergus enters with rescuers, playing out his game of keeping faith. He will not allow Conchubar to touch the body of Deirdre, for which he still stands surety. Conchubar's game, that of deception used to enhance his sovereign pride, is lost. However, even he feels justified by the rules.

CONCHUBAR: I have no need of weapons,
There's not a traitor that dare stop my way.
Howl, if you will; but I, being King, did right
In choosing her most fitting to be Queen,
And letting no boy lover take the sway.[34]

The whole play has been a tragic chess game in which each player followed the rules sacred to him: Conchubar sovereign pride, Fergus statesmanly good-faith, Naoise heroic honor and Deirdre the laws of love. In a sense the finish was determined before the start and all the action was like that of Lugaid Redstripe and his bride: "They moved the men and waited for the end."[35]

Just as legitimately, however, one could say that the whole play has been a rising fire of passion against the night sky of death. In terms of stage properties the fire spreads from the brazier, to the torches in the sconces, to the torches in the hands of Deirdre's belated defenders. All four chief characters show themselves in an intensity both of passion and of control in that last flaring scene.

The stage movement, like the psychological movement of the whole play, follows that of a pendulum. The early scenes show a great distance between Deirdre's passion and Naoise's honor and the action shifts obviously back and forth from one side to the other. These movements, both physical and psychological, become briefer and briefer as passion becomes honor and honor passion and as Deirdre and Naoise converge upon their place of death and triumph behind the central curtain.

III

Deirdre, like the plays of the theater of reason, never allows the rationalized moral persona to be completely dissolved in passion. On the other hand it is destructive of all codes but a completely individualistic ethic. Fergus and Conchubar are wrong. Naoise and especially Deirdre — whose code is a truth to individual emotion — are right. To be most human, according to the play, is to trust to feeling, not to abstract conceptions of social duty. (Naoise's honor is individualistic, not social.)

This play, then, is not for the theater of reason; nor is it for the theater of passion. It borrows elements from both and attempts to fuse them. They become each other. Naoise's loyalty to his honor is motivated by his love. His purpose gives form to an ideal wholeness. Deirdre's passion provides the content, inseparable from the form in that whole.

The play says that honorable purpose and passionate love are both essential to an ideal relationship, but that the two are in practice incompatible in life. The hero and heroine achieve this ideal relationship only in death. The way of knowing which the play underwrites is neither that of reason nor that of passion but that harmonious movement of the whole soul indicated in the perfect love of Deirdre and Naoise and in the symbol of music and poetry.

The play presents not a genuine tragic rhythm of purpose, passion and perception, but the discovery that the first two are complementary parts of the third. . . . Yeats has still to create the heroes whose central reality would be — not to demonstrate reason, or express emotion — but to see, to recognize, to discover the tragedy of vision.

Notes

1. "Mr. Kenneth Burke, in an essay entitled 'Psychology and Form,' distinguishes two kinds of literary composition, 'syllogistic progression,' in which the reader is led from one part of the composition to another by means of logical relationships, and 'qualitative progression' . . . in which the reader is led, according to a 'logic of feeling,' by means of association and contrast." Francis Fergusson, *The Idea of a Theater* (Princeton: Princeton University Press, 1972; first published 1949), pp. 80–81.

2. *The Variorum Edition of the Plays of W. B. Yeats*, ed. Russell K. Alspach, assisted by Catharine C. Alspach (New York: Macmillan, 1966), pp. 365–66.

3. *Ibid.*, p. 388.

4. Fergusson, p. 52.

5. *Variorum Plays*, p. 345.

6. *Ibid.*, p. 347.

7. *Ibid.*, p. 361.

8. *Ibid.*, p. 345.

9. *Ibid.*, p. 375.

10. *Ibid.*, p. 387.

11. *Ibid.*, p. 375.

12. *Ibid.*, p. 345.
13. *Ibid.*, p. 374.
14. *Ibid.*, p. 387.
15. *Ibid.*, p. 360.
16. *Ibid.*, p. 351.
17. *Ibid.*, p. 378.
18. *Ibid.*, p. 376.
19. *Ibid.*, p. 377.
20. *Ibid.*, p. 354.
21. *Ibid.*, p. 355.
22. *Ibid.*, p. 355-56.
23. *Ibid.*, p. 387.
24. *Ibid.*, p 373.
25. *Ibid.*, p. 374.
26. *Ibid.*, p. 375-76.
27. *Ibid.*, p. 373.
28. *Ibid.*.
29. *Ibid.*, p. 376.
30. *Ibid.*, p. 378.
31. *Ibid.*, p. 381.
32. *Ibid.*, p. 384.
33. *Ibid.*, p. 385-86.
34. *Ibid.*, p. 388.
35. *Ibid.*, p. 356.

Ez and Old Billyum   Richard Ellmann[*]

Ezra Pound, after attending the service for T. S. Eliot in Westminister Abbey in January 1965, memorialized an even older association with W. B. Yeats by visiting the poet's widow in Dublin. His friendship with Yeats began in 1908, six years before he met Eliot. In a shrunken literary scene, it is tempting to try to piece together the substance of this once drastic connection, now diminished to history.

At the time of their first meeting in London, Pound was twenty-three to Yeats's forty-three. He did not, like Joyce six years earlier, find Yeats too old to be helped. Instead, he declared, with humility and yet some arrogance of his own, that Yeats was the only poet worthy of serious study,[1] and in later years he recalled without chagrin having spent the years from 1908 to 1914 in "learning how Yeats did it."[2] What he learned was the "inner form of the lyric or short poem containing an image,"[3] as in

[*]From *Eminent Domain: Yeats among Wilde, Joyce, Pound, Eliot, and Auden* (New York: Oxford University Press, 1967), 57–87.

"The Fish" ("Although you hide in the ebb and flow / Of the pale tide when the moon is set"[4]), and "the inner form of the line"[5] (probably its rhythmical merger of "dull, numb words,"[6] with unexpected ones). Yeats offered further an example of "syntactical simplicity"[7]; he had, for example, cut out inversions and written with what Pound as late as 1914 considered "prose directness," in "The Old Men Admiring Themselves in the Water": "I heard the old, old men say, / 'Everything alters.' "[8]

That Pound had already studied Yeats intently before coming to London is disclosed by the volume *A Lume Spento*, which he published in Venice on his roundabout way to England from Wabash College, and republished in 1965 with a new preface describing the poems as "stale cream-puffs." They are so, but show something anyway about the confectioner. The second poem, "La Fraisne" (Old Provençal for ash tree), has a long "note precedent" in Latin and Old Ezraic. Before explaining that the speaker in the poem is Miraut de Gazelas when driven mad by his love for Riels of Calidorn, Pound indicates that he wrote the poem in a mood like that of Yeats's *The Celtic Twilight*, a title which was intended to suggest a vague borderline between the physical and metaphysical worlds. He felt himself "divided between a self corporal and a self aetherial," or, as he defines it further, "trans-sentient as a wood pool." Such states, in which time is contained and transcended, possess Pound again, most notably in the descriptions of paradisal moods in the *Cantos*, but "La Fraisne" itself does not offer this pitch of feeling. In the course of his self-exegesis, Miraut identifies himself with the ash tree; at one time he was a wise councillor, but now he has left "the old ways of men" to lose himself in sylvan metamorphosis. He seems to follow the lead of two characters in Yeats's early poetry: Fergus, who abdicated to drive his brazen cars in the forest,[9] and another royal abdicator, Goll, who belongs to the same dynasty as Arnold's "Mycerinus." Pound's line, "Naught but the wind that flutters in the leaves," echoes "The Madness of King Goll," where the refrain is: "They will not hush, the leaves that round me flutter—the beech leaves old."[10] Miraut's thought that he is merging into the boles of ash wood owes something, like Pound's other early poem, "The Tree," to Yeats's poem, "He Thinks of His Past Greatness When a Part of the Constellations of Heaven": "I have been a hazel-tree and they hung / The Pilot Star and the Crooked Plough / Among my leaves in times out of mind. . . ."

Other lines in "La Fraisne," where Miraut has "put aside this folly and the cold / That old age weareth for a cloak," and where he announces, "For I know that the wailing and bitterness are a folly," echo words like "wail" and "folly" from the diction of Yeats, and derive more particularly from his poem, "In the Seven Woods," where the speaker has "put away the unavailing outcries and the old bitterness / That empty that heart." Blistered in Provence, Miraut has been patched and peeled in Yeats's first, third, and fourth volumes of verse, as well as in *The Celtic Twilight*.[11]

Yet the proximity to Yeats does not prevent "La Fraisne" from being

identifiably Pound's configuration. Yeats portrays the madness of King
Goll as a heroic state of mind superior to sanity, while Councillor Miraut's
mental condition is more equivocal, even pathetic. Pound diverges also,
after three stanzas, from the formal regularity on which Yeats always
insisted, so that he can attempt to capture his hero's incoherence. In a
passage, bold in 1908, he makes use of a series of broken sentences:

> Once when I was among the young men . . .
> And they said I was quite strong, among the young men,
> Once there was a woman . . .
> . . . but I forgot . . . she was. . .
> . . . And I hope she will not come again.
>
> I do not remember. . . .
>
> That was very long ago.

These are perhaps the most important dots in English poetry. They show
Pound already essaying what in *Mauberley* he calls a "consciousness
disjunct." In the later poem the pauses represent hesitations instead of
panicky repressions:

> Drifted . . . drifted precipitate,
> Asking time to be rid of . . .
> Of his bewilderment; to designate
> His new found orchid. . . .

In the *Cantos*, like Eliot in *The Waste Land*, he usually leaves out dots, as
if no one expected any longer the considerate guidance that prevailed in
earlier poetry. But this mode begins in "La Fraisne."

If Pound translated Yeats, then, like one of his troubadours, sometimes literally and sometimes freely, Yeats responded to the change in
atmosphere with which Pound surrounded his borrowings, and he did not
dismiss him as an imitator. When he read *A Lume Spento*, with which
Pound must have introduced himself, he called it "charming," an adjective
Pound knew to be reserved.[12] Still, Yeats could hardly have read the poem
entitled "Plotinus" without being tempted to rewrite it, syntactically and
otherwise:

> As one that would draw thru the node of things
> Back sweeping to the vortex of the cone. . . .
>
> And then for utter loneliness, made I
> New thoughts as crescent images of *me*.

The vortexes are premonitory of Pound's later vorticist movement, but
they also, with cones and crescents, anticipate metaphors of *A Vision*.
Pound cannot be said to have put them into Yeats's head, for Yeats knew
Plotinus well already, but he must have given them a new spin.

Yeats liked better Pound's book *Personae*, which appeared in April of
the following year, 1909. The title proudly drew attention to the very

point that had vexed William Carlos Williams in the first book, the assumption of a series of exotic roles.[13] For Pound, it was an attempt, by encompassing more situations and moods, to follow Walter Pater's advice and extend the self horizontally. Yeats's purpose in the seemingly similar doctrine of the mask, which he was then cultivating in early drafts of *The Player Queen*, and must have discussed with Pound, was a vertical deepening of the self by fusion with its opposite. For Yeats, Pound's theory, like Arthur Symons's version of Pater's impressionism, was too volatile and rootless, and suspiciously international. But, beyond the theory, he detected the young man's extraordinary talent; and Pound wrote elatedly to Williams, just after *Personae* was published, "I have been praised by the greatest living poet."[14] This snub almost silenced Williams.

Yeats was in fact as pleased with his new friendship as Pound was. In December 1909, he wrote Lady Gregory that "this queer creature Ezra Pound . . . has become really a great authority on the troubadurs."[15] So much erudition of course amused him a little, too, and now or later he humorously accused Pound of trying to provide a portable substitute for the British Museum.[16] He liked the way Pound devised to recite verse so that it sounded like music, with strongly marked time, yet remained intelligible, and he credited it with being a better method than that of Florence Farr, which a decade earlier he had so highly praised. But he noted also that Pound's voice was poor, sounding "like something on a bad phonograph."[17] It may have been just the American accent emigrating to an Irish ear. Pound, for his part, thought Yeats's method of "keening and chaunting with a *u*" absurd, and while he could effect no improvement, he obliged Yeats to admit, after half an hour's struggle, that poems such as those of Burns could not be wailed to the tune of *The Wind among the Reeds*.[18] Each poet enjoyed condescending to the other.

Pound, as he began to flabbergast London with his passionate selections and rejections, found that his allegiance to Yeats was not shared by other writers whom he respected. The movement away from nineteenth-century poetry had begun. As John Butler Yeats wrote his son, "The poets loved by Ezra Pound are tired of Beauty, since they have met it so often. . . . I am tired of Beauty my wife, says the poet, but here is that enchanting mistress Ugliness. With her I will live, and what a riot we shall have. Not a day shall pass without a fresh horror. Prometheus leaves his rock to cohabit with the Furies."[19] The vogue of ugliness was sometimes companioned by an insistence on man's limited and finite condition. T. E. Hulme was already in 1908, when he and Pound met, denouncing the romantic bog and leading the way to the classical uplands; by his rule, Yeats was wet and dim when he should have been dry and clear.[20] On still other grounds T. S. Eliot, who battled Yeats for Pound's soul a few years later, declared Yeats an irrelevance in the modern world.[21] By 1912 D. H. Lawrence, originally an admirer of Yeats, could say, "He seems awfully queer stuff to me now — as if he wouldn't bear touching,"[22] and he objected to Yeats's method of dealing with old symbols as "sickly."[23] Another friend of Pound's, Ford Madox Ford, though not unreceptive to other monstrosities, informed Pound that Yeats was a "gargoyle, a great poet but a gargoyle."[24]

Pound's determination to make it new combined with this voluble pressure to stint a little his admiration of Yeats as a model. Writing in *Poetry*, the then new Chicago review, in January 1913, he explained that Ford and Yeats were diametrically opposed because one was objective, the other subjective. While he grandly pronounced Yeats to be "the only poet worthy of serious study," he felt compelled to warn that the method of Yeats "is, to my way of thinking, very dangerous." The magistrate was severe: "His art has not broadened much during the past decade. His gifts to English art are mostly negative; i.e., he has stripped English poetry of many of its faults."[25] Yeats continued to fall short. In 1913 Pound wrote Harriet Monroe that Ford and Yeats were the two men in London, "And Yeats is already a sort of great dim figure with its associations set in the past."[26] In the *Pisan Cantos* (LXXXII), the two men are weighed again,

> and for all that old Ford's conversation was better,
> consisting in *res non verba*,
> > despite William's anecdotes, in that Fordie
> > never dented an idea for a phrase's sake.
>
> and had more humanitas

Such reservations did not prevent Pound from regarding Yeats as a splendid bridge from Mallarmé and the symbolists,[27] which he could afford to cross on his way to founding imagism and then vorticism. These movements, full of don'ts, extolled light, clarity, and in general a Polaroid view of the verse line.[28] Pound knew, however, as Hulme, Lawrence, and Ford did not know, that Yeats was still adaptable, and as eager to leave the '90s behind as they were. The books of verse he published in 1904 and 1910 reacted against his early manner, but he was still dissatisfied, and kept looking about for incitements for further change. Pound was a perpetual incitement, mixing admiration with remonstrance.

Another spur, now improbable, was Rabindranath Tagore, whom Yeats met in June 1912. Tagore's poetry brought together, Yeats felt, the metaphors and emotions of unlearned people with those of the learned, coupling the fastidious with the popular[29] in the way that he had commended to Joyce ten years before. Yeats remarked to Pound, unhinged by the same enthusiasm, that Tagore was "someone greater than any of us — I read these things and wonder why one should go on trying to write."[30] Pointing to a description in Tagore's poem, "The Banyan Tree," "Two ducks swam by the weedy margin above their shadows, and the child . . . longed . . . to float like those ducks among the weeds and shadows," Yeats proclaimed, "Those ducks are the ducks of real life and not out of literature."[31] His friend Sturge Moore was helping Tagore with the translation, and Yeats joined in the task, arguing with Moore about words."[32] (He allowed Tagore to use the word "maiden," though in a later stage of dictional disinfection, when he was translating the *Upanishads* with another Indian, he insisted upon the word "girl."[33]) Soon he recognized that Tagore was "unequal" and sometimes dull, but he saw mainly "great beauty,"[34] and wrote a fulsome introduction to *Gitanjali*.

Pound's own role in the modernization of Yeats began at first, like that of most mentors, uninvited. In October 1912 he persuaded Yeats to give *Poetry* a start with some new poems. Yeats sent them to Pound for transmittal, appending a note to ask that the punctuation be checked. The note was bound, as Pound said ruefully later, to "create a certain atmosphere of drama."[35] He could not resist exceeding mere compliance by making three changes in Yeats's wording. In "Fallen Majesty," he impudently if reasonably deleted "as it were" from the final line: "Once walked a thing that seemed as it were a burning cloud." In "The Mountain Tomb," he worried over the lines, "Let there be no foot silent in the room, / Nor mouth with kissing or the wine unwet," and altered "or the" to "nor with." Then, with "To a Child Dancing upon the Shore,"

> Being young you have not known
> The fool's triumph, nor yet
> Love lost as soon as won,
> Nor he, the best labourer, dead,
> And all the sheaves to bind,

Pound thought long and deep and then changed "he" to "him."

At peace, he sent the poems to Harriet Monroe with the comment: "I don't think this is precisely W. B. Y. at his best . . . but it shows a little of the new Yeats — as in the 'Child Dancing.' 'Fallen Majesty' is just where he was two years ago. 'The Realists' is also tending toward the new phase."[36] Pound, though he had liked the hardness of "No Second Troy,"[37] was weary of prolonging the celebrations of Maud Gonne as she had been twenty years before. On the other hand, he welcomed the increasing directness that Yeats now usually aimed at. He conveyed something of these opinions to Yeats, and at the same time duly informed him of the small changes he had made. To his surprise, Yeats was indignant at this American brashness, and Pound had to carry out mollification proceedings as recorded in his letters to Miss Monroe. For rhythm's sake Yeats insisted upon restoring the spiritless "as it were" to "Fallen Majesty," though a year later he rewrote the line to get rid of it. But Pound's other two revisions shook him. At first he modified the second passage to read, "Nor mouth with kissing nor *the* wine unwet," but by the proof stage he recognized that unwet wine would not do, and Pound's version, "nor with wine unwet," appears in *Poetry*. In the third instance the battle of the pronouns, he insisted upon "he" rather than "him," but, made aware of the grammatical sin, put a period after the third line to replace the comma. On November 2, Pound transmitted these partial restorations to Miss Monroe with the remark, "Oh *la la*, ce que le roi désire!"[38] Later the same day, he reported a last change, eliminating "Nor" before "he":

> Final clinic in the groves of philosophy.
>
> Love lost as soon as won. (full stop)
> And he, the best labourer, dead
>
> peace reigns on parnassus.[39]

Still enthralled by Tagore's verse, and still stung by Pound's criticism, Yeats felt the challenge to his powers. It was probably now that he confided to Pound, "I have spent the whole of my life trying to get rid of rhetoric. I have got rid of one kind of rhetoric and have merely set up another."[40] For the first time in years he asked for help, as his letters to Lady Gregory of 1 and 3 January 1913 make clear. In the former he writes: "I have had a fortnight of gloom over my work — I felt something wrong with it. However on Monday night I got Sturge Moore in and last night Ezra Pound and we went at it line by line and now I know what is wrong and am in good spirits again. I am starting the poem about the King of Tara and his wife ['The Two Kings'] again, to get rid of Miltonic generalizations,"[41] (Pound had made "Miltonic" a derogatory epithet.) He was later to redefine what he and Pound had crossed out as "conventional metaphors,"[42] presumably those turned abstract by overuse. In his second letter to Lady Gregory he indicates that the whole experience has given him diarrhea:

> My digestion has got rather queer again — a result I think of sitting up late with Ezra and Sturge Moore and some light wine while the talk ran. However the criticism I have got from them has given me new life and I have made that Tara poem a new thing and am writing with a new confidence having got Milton off my back. Ezra is the best critic of the two. He is full of the middle ages and helps me to get back to the definite and the concrete away from modern abstractions. To talk over a poem with him is like getting you to put a sentence into dialect. All becomes clear and natural. Yet in his own work he is very uncertain, often very bad though very interesting sometimes. He spoils himself by too many experiments and has more sound principles than taste.[43]

A letter which Pound sent Harriet Monroe summarizes the sound principles if not the questionable taste he must have communicated to Yeats. In terms ostentatiously graceless he called for "Objectivity and again objectivity, and expression; no hind-side-beforeness, no straddled adjectives (as 'addled mosses dank'), no Tennysonianness of speech: *nothing* that you couldn't in some circumstance, in the stress of some emotion, *actually say*. Every *literaryism*, every book word, fritters away a scrap of the reader's patience, a scrap of his sense of your sincerity."[44] Though Yeats had been able to reconstruct much of his diction, he needed a jolt to complete the process. This Pound, by virtue of his downrightness, his good will, his unintimidatable character, his sense of himself as shocker, was peculiarly fitted to administer. For him, as for Auden later,[45] poems were contraptions, and most of them were inefficient and needed overhaul. He had trained himself, like no one else, for the very task Yeats demanded of him. That Pound was able to give advice, and Yeats, notwithstanding age and fame, to take it and to admit having taken it, made their friendship, unlike many relations of literary men, felicitious.

The experience was, like most medicine, more than a little painful for Yeats; having requested Pound's help once, he had to submit to occasional further reproofs. He showed Pound "The Two Kings" when it was finished, and Pound informed him (and said later in a review of *Responsibilities*[46]) that it was like those *Idylls* written by a poet more monstrous even than Milton. Yeats wrote his father of this harsh verdict, and his father reassured him by saying that the poem had supremely what Tennyson never achieved — namely, concentration. Yeats took heart and believed that Pound this time was wrong. But he was nonetheless gratified when Pound, on reading the untitled last poem in *Responsibilities*, and especially the last lines — "till all my priceless things / Are but a post the passing dogs defile" — remarked that Yeats had at last become a modern poet.[47] An image of urination had finally brought Pound to his knees.

Yeats, while acknowledging Pound's critical penetration and quite liking him as a person, was perplexed about his poetry. He quarreled with the rhythms of its free verse as "devil's metres."[48] Many of the poems did not seem to Yeats fully achieved. When in 1913 Harriet Monroe offered him a prize for "The Grey Rock," Yeats urged her to give it to Pound instead; he said candidly, "I suggest him to you because, although I do not really like with my whole soul the metrical experiments he has made for you, I think those experiments show a vigorous creative mind. He is certainly a creative personality of some sort, though it is too soon yet to say of what sort. His experiments are perhaps errors, I am not certain; but I would always sooner give the laurel to vigorous errors than to any orthodoxy not inspired."[49] Although Pound's work was not to Yeats's taste any more than Joyce's, he could not fail to sense that here, too, was a kind of alien talent. The following year he spoke at a *Poetry* dinner in Chicago, and said again of Pound, "Much of his work is experimental; his work will come slowly; he will make many an experiment before he comes into his own." But he read two poems which he judged of "permanent value," "The Ballad of the Goodly Fere" and "The Return." The latter he complimented, in that slightly histrionic rhythm for which Joyce mocked him in *Ulysses*, as "the most beautiful poem that has been written in the free form, one of the few in which I find real organic rhythm."[50] He quoted it again later in *A Vision*,[51] where it jibed with his theory of cyclical repetition. He was consciously, doggedly allowing virtue in Pound's work, though he had no wish to enroll in the new school which his former pupil had opened. On many matters they continued to dispute, and Pound summarized almost with satisfaction the quarrelsomeness of a meeting the next year: "The antipodes of our two characters and beliefs being in more vigorous saliency."[52]

During the winter of 1913–14, and the two following winters, Yeats wished to be away from London with a secretary who could do some typing and also read to him Doughty's poems and (anticipating Auden) Icelandic sagas. He had formed the plan with Pound as companion in mind,[53] and Pound with misgivings agreed to put himself out for the sake of English letters. He expected that Yeats would sometimes amuse him but often, because the occult was so irresistible a subject, bore him.[54] To his partial surprise, life with Yeats in a four-room Sussex cottage proved contented and placid. He wrote Williams that Yeats was "much finer *intime* than seen spasmodically in the midst of the whirl."[55] With more polish he described life at Stone Cottage nostalgically in Canto LXXXIII:

There is fatigue deep as the grave.
The Kakemono grows in flat land out of mist
        sun rises lop-sided over the mountain
            so that I recalled the noise in the chimney
as it were the wind in the chimney
            but was in reality Uncle William
downstairs composing
that had made a great Peeeeacock
        in the proide ov his oiye
            had made a great pcccceeeecock in the . . .
made a great peacock
        in the proide of his oyyee

proide ov his oy-ee
as indeed he had, and perdurable

a great peacock aere perennius
        or as in the advice to the young man to
breed and get married (or not)
            as you choose to regard it

at Stone Cottage in Sussex by the waste moor
(or whatever) and the holly bush
        who would not eat ham for dinner
because peasants eat ham for dinner
        despite the excellent quality
and the pleasure of having it hot

well those days are gone forever
        and the travelling rug with the coon-skin tabs
and his hearing nearly all Wordsworth
        for the sake of his conscience but
preferring Ennemosor on Witches

> did we ever get to the end of Doughty:
> The Dawn in Britain?
> perhaps not

While Yeats's aristocratic pride and his reaching over Wordsworth for witches amused Pound still, he recognized that these two foibles received a kind of immortal warranty by their reflection in "The Peacock" and "The Witch."

At Stone Cottage, Pound taught Yeats after a fashion to fence, while Yeats offered reciprocal lessons, as dreaded, in spiritualism and related subjects. These proved, however, more apposite to his own interests than Pound had anticipated. For when Yeats was writing essays for Lady Gregory's *Visions and Beliefs in the West of Ireland*, setting them in the context of the tradition *à rebours*, Pound was devoting himself to editing Ernest Fenollosa's translations of the Noh plays of Japan. These were just as crowded with ghosts and other extraterrestrial creatures. East and West met in the astral envelope as well as in Connemara. In the edition he now made of the Noh plays, Pound refers frequently to parallels furnished him by Yeats,[56] and speaks with unwonted respect of such matters as "the 'new' doctrine of the suggestibility or hypnotizeability of ghosts,"[57] though he preserves his dignity by an alibi: only the merit of the Japanese poetry has brought him to this pass.[58] Pound's versions of Noh convene a kind of grand international festival with entries from India, Japan, England, the United States, and Ireland. The Samurai are particularly at home in Kiltartan or Aran:[59]

> I've a sad heart to see you looking up to Buddha, you who left me alone, I diving in the black rivers of hell. Will soft prayers be a comfort to you in your quiet heaven, you who knew that I'm alone in that wild, desolate place?[60]
>
> Times out of mind am I here setting up this bright branch, this silky wood with the charms painted on it as fine as the web you'd get in the grass-cloth of Shinobu, that they'd be still selling you in this mountain.[61]
>
> I had my own rain of tears; that was the dark night, surely.[62]

The Noh plays were more to Yeats's taste than to Pound's: by 1918 Pound was prematurely dismissing them as a failure.[63] He linked them in this disgrace with Yeats's long essay, *Per Amica Silentia Lunae*,[64] which with its hypothesis of antiselves and daimons must still have seemed too occult for the mint assayer's son. Whether he also dismissed the prefatory poem to this work, "Ego Dominus Tuus," is not clear, though his allusion to it as a dialogue of "Hic" and "Willie" (for "Ille")[65] perhaps implies some dissatisfaction, beyond his unwillingness to resist polylingual jokes. He was prepared to believe again, as he said in 1920, that Yeats was "faded."[66]

Yeats had entered a period of much greater assurance. The Noh plays, so fortuitously put in his hands, had won without his being aware of it the battle with naturalistic drama which he had himself been fighting in beleaguered fashion. Here was the authorization he needed for leaving probability in the lurch, by abolishing scenery so the imagination would be untrammeled, by covering faces with masks, by portraying character in broad strokes—emptied of Ibsen's convincing details—through isolating the moment in which some irrevocable deed separates a man from his fellows as well as from his own idiosyncracies. He was also prompted to new and more reckless devices, the symbolic dance as a climax to suggest the impingement of the timeless upon the actual, the preternatural shudder from the sudden lighting-up of a ruined place, the assumption of someone else's human form by a spirit or god. Yeats saw how he might focus an entire play, as he had entire poems, on a single metaphor.[67] That the Noh plays were often blurred in effect did not ruffle him; the form, he saw, could be improved. He kept the strangeness and increased the dramatic tension, splicing natural with preternatural in order, unpredictably, to heighten the human dilemma. The Yeatsian paradox was to explode verisimilitude by miracle for the purposes of a more ultimate realism.

The result was the first of his plays for dancers, At the Hawk's Well, and to some degree almost all his subsequent plays. Happily, Ezra Pound proved to have an aptitude for the criticism of drama as well. He offered many suggestions about scenery and timing;[68] he found the indispensable Japanese dancer Michio Itō; and he helped Yeats to clarify the play. For a time, it seemed that his dramatic ability might receive professional sanction. He wrote a skit which Yeats encouraged him to enlarge, thinking it might be suitable for presentation at the Abbey Theatre, but it was adjudged, by the then manager, too full of indecencies.[69] Then Yeats recommended to Lady Gregory that Pound fill in as manager of the Abbey for a four-month period, but this plan also was vetoed.[70] Surviving these rebuffs, Pound remained indispensable; he observed Yeats locked in struggle with a long-unfinished tragedy, and irreverently proposed it be made a comedy instead. The firecracker went off, Yeats was exhilarated, and The Player Queen reached completion. Both Pound's moral impudence about experience and Yeats's theme in the play—the necessity of lying—would have pleased Wilde.

In the midst of vorticism and daimonism both poets were distracted toward marriage. Yeats had trouble unmaking the fealty to Maud Gonne as symbol, if not as woman, which he had so often declared. He wrote a poem, "His Phoenix" (which Pound dismissed as "a little bad Yeats"[71]) to contrast her more gaily than usual with the current lot of women, "There's Margaret and Marjorie and Dorothy and Nan, / A Daphne and a Mary who live in privacy," with the defiant conclusion, "I knew a Phoenix in my youth, so let them have their day." He was indulging here a private joke by making a list of Pound's girl friends. Among them Dorothy was preeminent. This was Dorothy Shakespear, with whose mother, Olivia, Yeats had been in love during the 'nineties. Pound married Dorothy in April 1914. Then Yeats, after the Easter Rebellion had widowed Maud Gonne, felt duty bound to offer her marriage, though he hesitated to bed an obsessive conviction. (Pound saw her in the same way: when he wished to characterize Yeats's occult interests, just as when Yeats wished to characterize Pound's political ideas, each compared the other to Maud Gonne.[72]) Her refusal was a relief. The next year Yeats married Georgie Hyde-Lees, a cousin and close friend of Pound's wife, and Pound served as best man. The two poets met often after their marriages. After Pound went to the Continent in 1920, they met in Paris in 1922, in Sicily in 1925, in Rapallo in 1928, 1929-30, 1934, and in London in 1938. Yet, as so often, separate households made for a subtle disconnection of friendship.

Pound's work had become more ambitious. After *Lustra*, he wrote *Propertius, Mauberley*, and the first *Cantos*. Yeats disconcerted him in 1916 by saying that Pound's new work gave him "no asylum for his affections." Pound wrote the criticism to Kate Buss, but cautioned her about repeating it.[73] Perhaps in part because he recognized some justice in it, Pound moved away from purely satirical poems like many in *Lustra*, and in the *Cantos* (LXXXI) he subscribes fully to Yeats's principle:

> What thou lovest well remains,
> the rest is dross
> What thou lov'st well shall not be reft from thee
> What thou lov'st well is thy true heritage

It is hard to discover Yeats's views of Pound's new works. He told Pound in 1920 that he liked *Mauberley*,[74] and he tried to suspend judgment about the *Cantos*.[75]

His attitude toward Pound between 1915 and 1925 can however be elicited from *A Vision*, the book he began in October 1917 just after his marriage. In the characterology which formed a large part of this book, Yeats classified contemporaries and men of the past in terms of phases of the moon. Pound was slowly becoming an abstraction, something analyzed at a distance. The early drafts, written between 1918 and 1922, placed Pound with Nietzsche as denizen of the twelfth lunar phase, called the phase of the Forerunner. He is Forerunner to men of fuller consciousness including, with chronological indifference, Yeats himself. But when the book was published in 1926, Pound's name was omitted; Yeats probably feared to give pain. Though Phase 12 was not a bad perch, Pound occupied it in a disharmonious way. The Phase-12 man who is "in phase" follows Zarathustra's exhortation by heroically overcoming himself. (Yeats speaks elsewhere of Pound's effort at total self-possession, but does not seem to have regarded it as successful.[76]) He is thereby enabled to assume his true mask which is lonely, cold, and proud, and to formulate a subjective philosophy that exalts the self in the presence of its object of desire.[77] While Yeats may have thought of imagism as offering an esthetic philosophy of this kind, he had primarily in mind Nietzsche's projection of a superior world. In phase, the Phase-12 mind is a jetting fountain of personal life, of noble extravagance. It loathes abstraction as much as Pound did, and everything it considers comes clothed in sound and metaphor.[78]

But if the man of this phase is "out of phase," the result is much less satisfactory. Unable to discover his true mask, he assumes almost in frenzy a series of self-conscious poses.[79] Here Yeats must have thought of Pound's *Personae*, and perhaps of Pound's own Bergsonian statement in *Gaudier-Brzeska*: "One says 'I am' this, that, or the other, and with the words scarcely uttered one ceases to be that thing. I began this search for the real in a book called *Personae*, casting off, as it were, complete masks of the self in each poem. I continued in long series of translations, which were but more elaborate masks."[80] Always in reaction, yet according to Yeats always hesitant, the out-of-phase man becomes a prey to facts, which drug or intoxicate him. More by chance than choice, he turns to a false mask, which offers instead of splendid loneliness the isolation of some small protesting sect; and he defends this role by "some kind of superficial intellectual action, the pamphlet, the violent speech, the sword of the swashbuckler."[81] He oscillates between asserting some pose or, if preoccupied with outward things, asserting a dogmatism about events which depends too much upon the circumstances that produced it to have lasting value.[82] Yeats is thinking here of Pound's adherence to Major Douglas's theories of social credit.

Even if Yeats penciled Pound into Phase 12, he could not fail to think of him also for Phase 23, which is the phase of our age and of its dominant art. Ultimately, he decided to transfer Pound completely to this later and less desirable phase; he saw him as neither arch-individualist nor forerunner but as a dissolving mind, subject to losses of self-control. What immediately impelled this unhappy demotion was the sight of Pound feeding all the stray cats in Rapallo in 1928. This undifferentiated pity, pity "like that of a drunken man," was quickly connected by Yeats to the hysterical pity for general humanity left over from the romantic movement.[83] He had observed and blamed it in other writers, notably Sean O'Casey and Wilfred Owen.[84] All three now seemed to belong to Phase 23, the theme of which is Creation through Pity.

The man of Phase 23 studies the external world for its own sake, and denies every thought that would make order of it. Instead of allowing the fountain of the mind to overflow, as in Phase 12, he lets the cauldron of the world boil over.[85] Not only is causation denied, as Pound once remarked to Yeats, only sequence being knowable,[86] but even sequence is destroyed. Yeats returned to this idea of *A Vision* in other essays, where he complained of the *Cantos* specifically: "There is no transmission through time, we pass without comment from ancient Greece to modern England, from modern England to medieval China; the symphony, the pattern, is timeless, flux eternal and without movement."[87] In subsequent art, violations like Pound's have ceased to appear violative, but Yeats was not yet accustomed to them. He found an Eastern parallel for such work not in Pound's favorite Easterner, Confucius (who to Yeats seemed an eighteenth-century moralist, pulpited and bewigged[88]), but in Sankara, the ninth-century founder of a school of Vedantism which conceives of mental and physical objects as "alike material, a deluge of experience breaking over us and within us, melting limits whether of line or tint; man no hard bright mirror dawdling by the dry sticks of a hedge, but a swimmer, or rather the waves themselves."[89] The new literature of the *Cantos*, of Virginia Woolf's novels, melted limits of plot, of logic, of character, of nationality, of authorship.[90] In a letter, Yeats complained that Pound and his school prided themselves on what their poems did *not* contain,[91] all that might stop the flood, the conscious mind's capacity for intelligibleness and form.

Remembering his old view that Pound was too preoccupied with experiment, Yeats in *A Vision* asserts that in Phase 23 everything is seen from the point of view of technique and is investigated technically rather than imaginatively. Technical mastery offers the man of his phase his only refuge from masterless anarchy. Denying its subjective life, the mind delights only in the varied scene outside the window, and asks to construct a whole which is all event, all picture. Because of this submission to outwardness, the man of Phase 23 wishes to live in his exact moment of time as a matter of conscience, and, says Yeats, defends that moment like a theologian.[92] He has in mind here Pound's imagist predilection, as well as his forever and dogmatically "making it new."

Yeats noticed also that men of this phase, not only Pound but Joyce and Eliot, were apt to contrast some present scene with a mythical one. By holding apart what should be joined, the Phase-23 mind heralds further loss and eventual extinction of personality, and a world in which rights are swallowed up in duties and force is adored so that society turns into a mechanism.[93] At variance with some of his later prose, Yeats explicitly deplores here an inevitable alliance of this phase and its succeeding phases with a regimented state.

After the first edition of *A Vision* was published early in 1926, Yeats grew dissatisfied with some of it, included the pretense that it was translated from an Arabic manuscript. In 1928 he came to Rapallo intending to work on it some more. He showed Pound a poem he had translated "From the *Antigone*," and was again convinced of his neighbor's critical acumen. After looking over what "the Yeats" (as Pound jocularly called him) had written,

> Overcome, O bitter sweetness
> The rich man and his affairs,
> The fat flocks and the fields' fatness,

Mariners, wild harvesters;
Overcome God upon Parnassus;
Overcome the Empyrean; hurl
Heaven and Earth out of their places—
Inhabitant of the soft cheek of a girl—
And into the same calamity,
That brother and brother, friend and friend,
Family and family,
City and city may contend
By that great glory driven wild—
Pray I will and sing I must
And yet I weep—Oedipus' child
Descends into the loveless dust.[94]

Pound saw that the eighth line must become the second; he changed "And into" to "That in," and dropped "That" before "brother." Yeats accepted the corrections. They may have given him an idea, which was half a jest, of complimenting Pound by prefacing *A Vision* with a series of papers under the common title, "A Packet for Ezra Pound." The irony of this tribute was that of all Yeats's books *A Vision*, with its detailed scheme of life and the afterlife, was most antipathetic to Pound's conception of art as liberated from deliberate rule or abstract theory. So "A Packet" would pit Yeats against his surest castigator.

Acting on this impulse, Yeats began the "Packet" with a description of Rapallo and then a discussion of the poet "whose art is the opposite of mine."[95] He summarized a conversation he had had with Pound about the *Cantos*, and explained the poem enough (as he wrote a friend) to keep Pound neighborly.[96] He did his best, in fact, to present sympathetically Pound's mode of marshaling in spurts certain increasingly enforced themes, though he admitted being unable to overcome his feeling that the *Cantos* were fragmentary, that in them conventions of the intellect were abolished to satisfy an illusion that what is primal is formless, and that discontinuity had become a shibboleth.[97]

Yeats also included in "A Packet" a letter to Pound warning the expatriate against accepting public office: "Do not be elected to the Senate of your country. I think myself, after six years, well out of mine. Neither you nor I, nor any other of our excitable profession, can match those old lawyers, old bankers, old business men, who, because all habit and memory, have begun to govern the world. They lean over the chair in front and talk as if to half a dozen of their kind at some board-meeting, and, whether they carry their point or not, retain moral ascendancy."[98] Pound, deep in correspondence with several senators, was not at all convinced. In Canto LXXX he responded, "If a man don't occasionally sit in a senate / how can he pierce the darrk mind of a / senator?" As for the bankers, Pound's special detestation, he devoted his pasquinade, "Alf's Eighth Bit," in the *New English Weekly* (1934) to reforming Yeats's view of them:

> Vex not thou the banker's mind
>   (His *what?*) with a show of sense
> Vex it not, Willie, his mind,
>   Or pierce its pretence
> On the supposition that it ever
> Was other, or that this cheerful giver
> Will give, save to the blind.[99]

The only other part of *A Vision* on which Pound commented directly was not from "A Packet" but from the ending. Yeats wrote there: "Day after day I have sat in my chair turning a symbol over in my mind, exploring all its details, defining and again defining its elements, testing my convictions and those of others by its unity, attempting to substitute particulars for an abstraction like that of algebra . . . Then I draw myself up into the symbol and it seems as if I should know all if I could but banish such memories and find everything in the symbol."[100] From Pound's point of view, symbols interfered with experience instead of letting experience coalesce into its natural pattern. In Canto LXXXIII he alluded to Yeats's perorative remarks, and connected them with "Sailing to Byzantium" (a poem Pound had published in *The Exile* in 1928), where Yeats had asked to be gathered into "the artifice of eternity." Contrary to Yeats, Pound insisted,

> Le Paradis n'est pas artificiel
> And Uncle William dawdling around Notre Dame
> in search of whatever
>   paused to admire the symbol
> with Notre Dame standing inside it
> Whereas in St Etienne
>   or why not Dei Miracoli:
> mermaids, that carving,[101]

Pound differs with Yeats on architecture as on paradise; he ironically suggests that Mary's presence is diminished rather than enhanced by the symbolic portentousness of her cathedral. He subtly compares her to Yeats ingested into his own cathedral-like *Vision*. As churches, Pound prefers less solipsistic structures like St. Etienne in Périgueux or Pietro Lombardo's Santa Maria dei Miracoli in Venice, and he repeats his earlier praise of Tullio Lombardo's carvings of sirens or mermaids on the latter church.[102] As literature, Pound prefers to *A Vision* those poems of Yeats where there is less sense of the writer's being cocooned. His mild example is "Down by the Salley Gardens," from which he slightly misquotes a few lines later:

>   the sage
>   delighteth in water
>   the humane man has amity with the hills
>
>   as the grass grows by the weirs
>   thought Uncle William . . . .

Yeats did not live to read the mixed blame and praise meted out to him in the *Pisan Cantos*, but he had another occasion to sample Pound's opinion of him. At the age of sixty-nine he wondered if he might not be too old for poetry. Fearing to outwrite his talent, he went to Rapallo in June 1934 primarily to show Pound a new play, *The King of the Great Clock Tower*. Pound was hard to divert from politics; he took the play, however, and next day rendered his verdict, "Putrid!" In recounting this experience, Yeats allowed it to be thought that this was all Pound said, and that it was a sign, like his violent political *parti pris*, of a mind too exacerbated to be reliable.[103] But in an unpublished journal he does Pound more justice. What Pound told him was that the lyrics of the play were written in "Nobody language" and would not do for drama. Far from defying this judgment, Yeats was humbled by Pound's criticism of his diction, willing as always to undergo any indignity for the work's sake. In his notebook he wrote, "At first I took his condemnation as the confirmation of my fear that I am now too old. I have written little verse for three years. But 'nobody language' is something I can remedy. I must write in verse, but first in prose to get structure."[104] He liked the new songs well enough to publish the play with a preface which, without mentioning Pound by name, wryly repeated his verdict. At the same time, as if to guard against any possibility that Pound's criticism might still apply even after revision, Yeats wrote another play on the same theme, *A Full Moon in March*, where the songs of the head (which is lopped off in both plays) are more concrete. He also let Pound know, through Olivia Shakespear, that *The King of the Great Clock Tower* had been his most successful play at the Abbey.[105]

Pound was not abashed; he had reverted to the pejorative view of Yeats's work as "dim" or "faded" that he had taken from time to time in the past, and he wrote Basil Bunting in 1936 that Yeats was "dead," "clinging to the habit of being a writer," that the recent poetry was "slop." In another letter to Bunting he found "increasing difficulty" in "reading the buzzard."[106] For Pound, Yeats, in spite of devoted ministrations, had come alive only for brief intervals. But at the last meeting of the two poets, which took place late in 1938 in London, Pound said he liked very much some of Yeats's recent poems,[107] and Yeats, accustomed to Pound's impertinent rebuff, was proportionately disarmed by his praise. Pound's most recent testimonial of quizzical admiration for Yeats is a parodic version of "Under Ben Bulben" written in a Wabash version of Irish dialect, which he first published in 1958:

> Neath Ben Bulben's buttocks lies
> Bill Yeats, a poet twoice the soize
> Of William Shakespear, as they say
>
> Down Ballykillywuchlin way.

> Let saxon roiders break their bones
> Huntin' the fox
> > thru dese gravestones.

Yeats in his last years made a fresh effort to formulate his view of Pound without recourse, this time, to the symbology of *A Vision*. He was compiling his *Oxford Book of Modern Verse*, and the preface provided a good occasion to fence with his old fencing-master. As he thought about Pound and selected three of his poems ("The River-Merchant's Wife: A Letter," a passage from *Propertius*, and Canto XVII), Yeats remarked to Dorothy Wellesley that Pound's work conveyed "a single strained attitude," that Pound was "the sexless American professor for all his violence."[108] In the preface he said more discreetly: "When I consider his work as a whole I find more style than form; at moments more style, more deliberate nobility and the means to convey it than in any contemporary poet known to me, but it is constantly interrupted, broken, twisted into nothing by its direct opposite, nervous obsession, nightmare, stammering confusion."[109] The trait of nobility mentioned by Yeats was one that Pound had lauded in reviewing *Responsibilities* in 1916;[110] returning the compliment, Yeats prefixed the word "deliberate" to indicate how a consciously assumed role might flag at moments into total disorder. Not having achieved personal unity, Pound, in Yeats's view, had failed in his effort to get all the wine into the bowl.[111] Pound did not respond directly, though in the *Cantos* he remarks briefly, but twice, that Yeats, like Possum (Eliot) and Lewis, and unlike Orage, "had no ground to stand on."[112] Orage stood on the firm ground of Major Douglas's economics.

While not retreating from his innovations, Pound has often owned the tentativeness of the method he adopted for the *Cantos*. When in 1917 he published in *Poetry* the first versions of Cantos, I, II, and III, he was almost apologetic in contrasting their broken form with Browning's: "You had one whole man? / And I have many fragments." At the same time, "the modern world / Needs such a rag-bag to stuff all its thoughts in."[113] After having read and helped revise *The Waste Land*, he wrote Eliot sadly in 1921, "I am wracked by the seven jealousies, and cogitating an excuse for always exuding my deformative secretions in my own stuff, and never getting an outline."[114] This same humility prompted him until 1937 to treat the published *Cantos* as only "drafts," and they became final just by passage of time, not change of heart. In his most recent writing, he returns, as in Canto 116, to his old sense of brave yet possibly unrealized effort:

> but the beauty is not in the madness
> Tho my errors and wrecks lie about me.
> > and I cannot make it cohere.[115]

Pound has, in fact, always recognized some force in Yeats's objections.

For his part, Yeats did not summarily dismiss what Pound was attempting. The Japanese professor Shotaro Oshima went to visit him in the summer of 1938, and expressed dissatisfaction with the poems collected in Pound's *Active Anthology*. Yeats replied, "Even those pieces composed by ellipsis have a triumphant combination of the visual and the imaginative."[116] He had come to identify Pound with ellipsis. In some of his later poems he endeavors to make room for a comparable if not identical agitation, by incorporating in them a direct challenge to the symmetry of the universe. He produces disruption by a refrain that embodies most of the hesitations, denials, and unspoken thoughts which Pound conveyed by ellipsis or discontinuity. So in "What Then?" the ghost of Plato is summoned to question in the refrain everything that has been affirmed in the body of the stanza:

> "The work is done," grown old he thought
> "According to my boyish plan;
> Let the fools rage, I swerved in naught,
> Something to perfection brought";
> But *louder sang that ghost, "What then?"*

With such devices Yeats, who had generally conceived of reality under the figure of a sphere, acknowledges another force, which might be called the *anti-sphere* — a contemptuous, unassimilable force which mocks our enterprise. Plato's ghost is a more reputable symbol for anarchy than Pound would have used, but in its lofty way it counters any hope of accommodation, any content with established forms. Perhaps Pound's liking for Yeats's last poems came from understanding that they were not unconcessive, that they too acknowledged the domain of incoherence.

The relationship of the two men had long ceased to be that of master and disciple. Though Pound referred to Yeats as "Uncle William," or "Old Billyum," it was he who after 1912 often assumed the avuncular role. As a matter of fact, they be uncled each other. The sense that Yeats could profit from his corrections must have reinforced Pound's sense of his own independent talent. To have kept Yeats up to the mark was a heady accomplishment. But Pound went his own way and, notwithstanding his penchant for quoting, and lecturing, Yeats in the *Cantos*, their later work is quite dissimilar. The principal and determining divergence between them remains their conceptions of form, which for Yeats is usually an hourglass, mined until it turns over, while for the later Pound, insofar as it can be characterized at all (and both he and his critics have had difficulty), it is an impromptu breakthrough, not to be prepared in advance or enshrined in retrospect. Yeats was eager to offset Pound's world, one of seeming flow but actually, as he insisted to Stephen Spender, static and tapestrylike,[117] with his own, which brought solids to the melting-point.

The two poets were equally engrossed in what Pound calls "top flights of the mind,"[118] moments often signaled in him by a pool of water, in Yeats by a sense of being blesséd or birdlike or of shaking all over. Their metaphysics are not the same, however, for Pound at least on some occasions insists upon the power of the objective, external image to compel or lure the mind to recognize it, as if he found Yeats too arbitrary in his constructions, while at other times he declares, "UBI AMOR IBI OCULUS EST,"[119] or as he says elsewhere,

> nothing matters but the quality
> of the affection—
> in the end—that has carved the trace in the mind
> dove sta memoria. . . .[120]

The two positions were dovetailed by Pound's insistence that the writer needs above all "continuous curiosity," to insure that enough life will be "vouchsafed" for him to work with;[121] but curiosity and observation are, as he reiterates in the Cantos, only a start, the vital ingredient being love. While Yeats also asserted the importance of love, he meant by it something more ardent, sexual, and individualized, less humanitarian, less cultural than Pound meant. He thought, moreover, that curiosity was too unimpassioned a quality, and that affections which were too eclectic and international could only diminish imaginative intensity.

Both writers agreed that they lived in an age of decline, "beastly and cantankerous" for Pound,"[122] "half dead at the top,"[123] for Yeats. ("My dear William B.Y. your 1/2 was too moderate," the Pisan Cantos admonished.[124]) For Yeats the cure was to condense and arrange experience.[125] Pound thought this procedure could only lead to premature synthesis, born from an insufficient "phalanx of particulars."[126] For Pound, the cure was to probe, experiment, accumulate until things—some things at any rate—shone with their intrinsic light: Yeats thought such experimentation might reach no end. Pound's view of experience is as "improvisatory,"[127] as informalist, as Yeats's is formalist. The city of the imagination for Yeats is Byzantium, taken by assault; for Pound it is Fasa, the African city described by Frobenius, built and patiently built three times again until it becomes "in the mind indestructible," an image of perfection so remote as to carry that special arcane inflection which is Pound's. But while Fasa is, like Ithaca, essential as journey's end, the incidents on the way to it beset Pound's mind with cryptic relevance or with unresolved irrelevance. Helter-skelter may or may not lead to epiphany; it sometimes exists only because Fasa must confront an opposite, and many varieties of helter-skelter will serve. The lack of inevitability is a guarantee of authenticity, of an honesty not to be gulled by esthetics. Pound's art in the Cantos is coagulative, Yeats's in his poems is exploitative; the poets face each other in an unended debate.

Notes

1. Ezra Pound, "Status Rerum," *Poetry* I.4 (January 1913) 123.

2. Letter to Michael Roberts, July 1937, in *The Letters of Ezra Pound*, ed. D. D. Paige (New York, 1950), p. 296.

3. Pound, "Harold Monro," in *Polite Essays* (London, 1937), p. 9.

4. Pound, "The Later Yeats," *Poetry* IX.3 (December 1917) 65–66.

5. Pound, "On Music," *New Age* X.15 (8 February 1912) 343–44.

6. Yeats, *Dramatis Personae* (London, 1936), p. 53.

7. Pound, "This Hulme Business," *Townsman* II.5 (January 1939) 15.

8. Pound, "The Later Yeats," *Poetry* IX.3 (December 1917) 66.

9. Yeats, "Who Goes with Fergus?"

10. The wording of this line was changed somewhat later.

11. "The Madness of King Goll" is from *The Wanderings of Oisin and Other Poems* (1889); "He Thinks of His Past Greatness . . ." from *The Wind Among the Reeds* (1899); and "In the Seven Woods" from the volume of the same name (1903).

12. Pound, letter to William Carlos Williams, in *Letters*, p. 4.

13. Ibid., pp. 3–4.

14. Pound, letter to Williams, 21 May 1909, in *Letters*, pp. 7–8.

15. Yeats, letter to Lady Gregory, 10 December 1909, in Yeats, *Letters*, p. 543.

16. Pound, letter to Sarah Perkins Cope, in *Letters*, p. 257.

17. Yeats, letter to Lady Gregory, 10 December 1909, in Yeats, *Letters*, p. 543.

18. Pound, letter to Felix E. Schelling, 8 July 1922, in *Letters*, p. 180.

19. Letter from J. B. Yeats to W. B. Yeats, 12 March 1918, in J. B. Yeats, *Letters to His Son W. B. Yeats and Others*, ed. Joseph Hone (New York, 1946), pp. 244–45.

20. A. R. Jones, *The Life and Opinions of Thomas Ernest Hulme* (London, 1960), pp. 29–31.

21. T. S. Eliot, "A Foreign Mind," [review of Yeats's *The Cutting of an Agate*], *Athenaeum* 4653 (4 July 1919) 552–53.

22. Lawrence, letter to A. W. McLeod, 17 December 1912, in *The Collected Letters of D. H. Lawrence*, ed. Harry T. Moore (New York, 1962), Vol. I, p. 168.

23. Lawrence, letter to Gordon Campbell, 19 December 1914, ibid., p. 302.

24. Pound, "This Hulme Business," *Townsman* II.5 (January 1939) 15.

25. Ezra Pound, "Status Rerum," *Poetry* I.4 (January 1913) 123–27.

26. Pound, letter to Harriet Monroe, 14 August 1912, in *Letters*, p. 11.

27. Pound, letter to René Taupin, May 1928, in *Letters*, p. 218.

28. "And now one has got with the camera an *enormous* correlation of particulars. That capacity of making contact is a tremendous challenge to literature." Pound quoted in *Writers at Work* (Second Series) (New York, 1963), p. 41.

29. Yeats, "Introduction" to Rabindranath Tagore, *Gitanjali* (New York, 1916), pp. xiii–xv.

30. Pound letter to Harriet Monroe, October 1912, in Harriet Monroe, *A Poet's Life* (New York, 1938), p. 262. Cf. Pound, "Rabindranath Tagore," *Fortnightly Review* XCIII (N.S.).555 (1 March 1913) 571–79.

31. Pound, "French Poets," in *Make It New* (New Haven, 1935), p. 245.

32. W. B. Yeats and T. Sturge Moore, *Their Correspondence*, pp. 22, 190.

33. Yeats, letter to Dorothy Wellesley, 21 December 1935, in Yeats, *Letters*, p. 846.

34. Yeats, letter to Edmund Gosse, 25 November 1912, in ibid., pp. 572–73.

35. Pound, unpublished letter to Harriet Monroe, 4 November 1912, in the University of Chicago Library.

36. Pound, letter to Harriet Monroe, 26 October 1912, in the University of Chicago Library. It is slightly misquoted in Monroe, *A Poet's Life*, p. 264.

37. Pound, "The Later Yeats," *Poetry* IX.3 (December 1917) 66.

38. Pound, unpublished letter to Harriet Monroe, 2 November 1912, in the University of Chicago Library.

39. Pound, letter to Harriet Monroe, also 2 November 1912, but sent separately from above letter, in University of Chicago Library.

40. Pound, "French Poets," *Make It New*, p. 245.

41. Yeats, letter to Lady Gregory, 1 January 1913, in "Some New Letters from W. B. Yeats to Lady Gregory," ed. Donald T. Torchiana and Glenn O'Malley, *Review of English Studies* IV.3 (July 1963) 14.

42. Yeats, "A General Introduction for My Work," in *Essays and Introductions* (London, 1961), p. 525.

43. Yeats, letter to Lady Gregory, 3 January 1913, quoted in A. N. Jeffares, *W. B. Yeats: Man and Poet* (New Haven, 1949), p. 167.

44. Pound, letter to Harriet Monroe, in *Letters*, p. 49.

45. W. H. Auden, *The Dyer's Hand* (New York, 1962), p. 50.

46. Pound, "The Later Yeats," p. 67.

47. Interview with Mrs. W. B. Yeats, 1946.

48. Pound, "The Later Yeats," p. 65.

49. Yeats, letter to Harriet Monroe, ? December 1913, in *A Poet's Life*, pp. 330–31.

50. Yeats, speech given in March 1914, ibid., p. 338.

51. Yeats, *A Vision* (New York, 1938), pp. 29–30.

52. Pound, unpublished letter to Harriet Monroe, 24 December 1915, from Stone Cottage, in the University of Chicago Library.

53. Yeats, letter to J. B. Yeats, 5 August 1913, in Yeats, *Letters*, p. 584.

54. Pound, letter to Isabel Pound, November 1913, in *Letters*, p. 25.

55. Pound, letter to Williams, 19 December 1913, in *Letters*, p. 27.

56. Ernest Fenollosa and Ezra Pound, *"Noh' or Accomplishment* (London, 1916), pp. 27, 44, 91, 106.

57. Ibid., p. 31. Pound was himself prompted to read in occult literature, notably in John Heydon, first mentioned in the discarded Canto III and later in *Guide to Kulchur*, p. 225. While in St. Elizabeth's Hospital, Pound borrowed the book again from Mrs. Yeats, and he quotes from it in Canto XCI.

58. Fenollosa and Pound, *"Noh' or Accomplishment*, p. 44.

59. A point noted by T. S. Eliot in his review, "The Noh and the Image," *Egoist* IV.7 (August 1917) 102–103.

60. Fenollosa and Pound, *"Noh' or Accomplishment*, p. 30.

61. Ibid, p. 132.

62. Ibid, p. 33.

63. Pound, letter to John Quinn, 4 June 1918, in *Letters*, p. 137.

64. Ibid.

65. Interview with Mrs. W. B. Yeats, 1946.

66. Pound, letter to Williams, 11 September 1920, in *Letters*, p. 158.

67. Yeats, "Certain Noble Plays of Japan," in *Essays and Introductions*, p. 234.

68. Two letters from Pound to Yeats, in Mrs. Yeats's possession, deal with the problems of staging the play. One has several sketches included.

69. Pound, letter to Iris Barry, September 1916, in *Letters*, p. 96.

70. Yeats, unpublished letter to Lady Gregory, 21 June 1916, in Mrs. Yeats's possession. Pound had made clear he would not come as a permanent manager.

71. Pound, letter to Harriet Monroe, 17 May 1915, in *Letters*, p. 60.

72. Pound, letter to John Quinn, 15 November 1918, in *Letters*, p. 140; Yeats, letter to Lady Gregory, 1 April 1928, in Yeats, *Letters*, p. 738.

73. Pound, letter to Kate Buss, 9 March 1916, in *Letters*, p. 72. Yeats was quoting a sentence of Tulka which he used as an epigraph to "The Wanderings of Oisin": "Give me the world if thou wilt, but grant me an asylum for my affections."

74. Pound, unpublished letter to Homer Pound, 1 September 1920, quoted by Thomas Parkinson, "Yeats and Pound: The Illusion of Influence," *Comparative Literature* VI (Summer 1954) 256–64.

75. Yeats, "Introduction" to *Oxford Book of Modern Verse*, p. xxv

76. Yeats, Journal kept in January 1929, quoted by Ellmann, *The Identity of Yeats* (New York, 1964), p. 329.

77. Yeats, *A Vision* (New York, 1938), p. 128.

78. Ibid., p. 127.

79. Ibid.

80. Pound, *Gaudier-Brzeska* (London, 1916), p. 98.

81. *A Vision* (1938), p. 128.

82. Ibid.

83. Ibid., p. 6.

84. Yeats quarreled with O'Casey over *The Silver Tassie* on this account; his comments on Owen are in Yeats, *Letters*, pp. 874–75.

85. *A Vision* (1938), pp. 128, 166.

86. Ellmann, *Identity of Yeats*, p. 239.

87. Yeats, "Introduction" to *Oxford Book of Modern Verse*, p. xxiv.

88. Yeats, letter to Lady Gregory, 7 April 1930, in Yeats, *Letters*, p. 774.

89. Yeats, "Preface" to *Fighting the Waves*, in *Explorations* (London, 1962), p. 373. He was alluding to Stendhal's image of the novel as a "mirror moving along a highway."

90. Yeats, *A Vision* (1938), pp. 299–300, 165; "Pages from a Diary Written in 1930," in *Explorations*, p. 294.

91. Yeats, unpublished letter to Harriet Monroe, 8 February 1931, in the University of Chicago Library.

92. Yeats, *A Vision* (1925), pp. 210–11.

93. Ibid., p. 213.

94. In Mrs. W. B. Yeats's possession. Ellmann, *Identity of Yeats*, pp. 131–32.

95. Yeats, *A Vision* (1938), p.3.

96. Yeats, letter to Lady Gregory, 1 April 1928, in Yeats, *Letters*, p. 739.

97. Yeats, *A Vision* (1938), pp. 4–5; "Introduction" to *Oxford Book of Modern Verse*, p. xxiv.

98. Yeats, *A Vision* (1938), p. 26; cf. "Preface" to *The Senate Speeches of W. B. Yeats*, ed. Donald R. Pearce, p. 25.

99. Reprinted in *Personae* (New York, new edition, no date), p. 263.

100. Yeats, *A Vision* (1938), p. 301.

101. Cf. Hugh Kenner, *The Poetry of Ezra Pound* (London: 1951), p. 210, and Donald Davie, *Ezra Pound: Poet as Sculptor* (New York: 1964), pp. 180–81. As Davie notes, *Les Paradis artificiels* is Baudelaire's book about drugs. But the primary allusion would seem to be to Yeats's poem.

102. Canto LXXIV, p. 8; Canto LXXVI, p. 38.

103. Yeats, "Preface" to *The King of the Great Clock Tower* (New York, 1934).

104. Unpublished notebook of Yeats, begun at Rapallo in June 1924.

105. Yeats, letter to Mrs. Olivia Shakespear, 7 August 1934, in Yeats, *Letters*, pp. 826–27.

106. Quoted by Thomas Parkinson, "Yeats and Pound: The Illusion of Influence," p. 263.

107. Parkinson, *W. B. Yeats: The Later Poetry* (Berkeley and Los Angeles, 1964), p. 177.

108. Yeats, letter to Dorothy Wellesley, 8 September 1935, in *Letters on Poetry from W. B. Yeats to Dorothy Wellesley* (New York, 1940), p. 25.

109. Yeats, "Introduction" to *Oxford Book of Modern Verse*, p. xxv.

110. Pound, in "The Later Yeats," p. 67, speaks of "a curious nobility, a nobility which is, to me at least, the very core of Mr. Yeats' production, the constant element of his writing."

111. Yeats, "Introduction" to *Oxford Book of Modern Verse*, p. xxvi.

112. Canto 98, p. 37; Canto 102, p. 80.

113. Pound, Canto I, *Poetry* X.3 (June 1917) 113, 115.

114. Pound, letter to Eliot, 24 December 1921, in *Letters*, p. 169.

115. Quoted by Donald Davie, *Times Literary Supplement* (25 May 1967) 472.

116. Shotaro Oshima, *W. B. Yeats and Japan* (Tokyo, 1965), p. 104.

117. Spender, *World within World* (London, 1951), p. 164.

118. Pound quoted in *Writers at Work*, p. 56.

119. Canto 90, p. 69.

120. Canto LXXVI, p. 35; cf. Canto LXXVII, p. 44.

121. Pound quoted in *Writers at Work*, pp. 41–42.

122. Pound, Canto I (later completely revised), *Poetry* X.3 (June 1917) 115.

123. Yeats, "Blood and the Moon."

124. Canto LXXIX, p. 65.

125. Yeats, *A Vision* (1938), p. 25.

126. Canto LXXIV, p. 19.

127. Yeats, "Introduction" to *Oxford Book of Modern Verse*, p. xxvi.

The Dynastic Theme   Jon Stallworthy*

1

When Beowulf first set foot, with his fourteen companions, on Danish soil and was challenged by the Scylding coastguard, he

> Replied, opening the treasury of words:
> "Men of the people of the Geats are we
> And household followers of Hygelac.
> My father was renowned among the nations,
> A noble chieftain, Ecgtheow by name;
> He lived for many winters, ere he passed,
> An old man, from his dwelling; every sage
> Throughout the world remembers him full well.
> With friendly purpose do we come to seek
> Thy master, the protector of his people,
> Healfdene's son."[1]

The son of Ecgtheow comes in search of Healfdene's son: for man was defined by his lineage in the heroic age where the chief bonds of society were loyalty to one's lord and duty to one's kin. This loyalty and this duty, of course, traditionally extended not only through all the affairs of life, but after life as well. The graves of ancestors were revered, and in early medieval England when a man was killed

> it was the duty of his kindred to take vengeance on the slayer or his kindred, or to exact compensation. The fear of the action of the kindred was originally the main force for the maintenance of order, and to the end Anglo-Saxon law regarded homicide as the affair of the kindred, who were entitled to receive the "wergild," i.e. "man-price," for any of their members slain. Vengeance was no mere satisfaction of personal feeling, but a duty that had to be carried out even when it ran counter to personal inclination . . .[2]

A concern with the ties of blood—what I shall call the dynastic theme—is to be found in one form or another in most "heroic" literatures, and in few more than in old Irish, or Scots, literature. The Irish early in their history, overflowing out of Ireland, occupied the western counties of Scotland and it was there that originated the songs and stories later attributed to the poet Ossian. These came to prominence in the mid-eighteenth century when James Macpherson, who at college between the ages of seventeen and twenty-two is said to have composed over four thousand verses, published his alleged translations, of which the best

*From *Vision and Revision in Yeats's "Last Poems"* (Oxford: Oxford University Press, 1969), 1–19. © 1969 by Oxford University Press. Reprinted by permission of Oxford University Press.

known are *Fingal* (in six books, 1761) and *Temora* (in eight books, 1763). One quotation (from "The Death of Cuthullin") will be sufficient to give an idea of the character of his "translation."

> "And is the son of Semo fallen?" said Carril with a sigh. "Mournful are Tura's walls. Sorrow dwells at Dunscaï. Thy spouse is left alone in her youth. The son of thy love is alone! He shall come to Brogéla, and ask her why she weeps? He shall lift his eyes to the wall, and see his father's sword."

The controversy over the authenticity of Macpherson's Ossian poems contributed to the rising interest in early Irish history and literature. Many ancient manuscripts were edited and translated by such scholars as Eugene O'Curry (1796–1862) and John O'Donovan (1809–61), whose "father . . . on his death-bed repeated several times to his sons who were present his descent, and desired his eldest son, Michael, always to remember it" (*D.N.B.*). The Ossianic Society was "founded on St. Patrick's Day, 1853, for the Preservation and Publication of MSS. in the Irish Language, illustrative of the Fenian period of Irish History, etc., with Literal Translations and Notes." Sir Samuel Ferguson (1810–86) gave fresh impetus to what had been, until the middle of the nineteenth century, a largely academic movement with his popular *Lays of the Western Gael and Other Poems* (1865). The first poem in this book, "The Tain-Quest," opens:

> "Bear the cup to Sanchan Torpest; yield the bard his poet's meed;
> What we've heard was but a foretaste; lays more lofty now succeed.
> Though my stores be emptied well-nigh, twin bright cups there yet remain, —
> Win them with the Raid of Cuailgne; chaunt us, Bard, the famous Tain!"
> Thus, in hall of Gort, spake Guary; for the king, let truth be told,
> Bounteous though he was, was weary giving goblets, giving gold, . . .

Yeats, whose play *The King's Threshold* was to have the same chief characters and the same setting, would not have been blind to the appropriateness of his buying the Norman tower in Gort. This, however, was many years after he had written

> *Know, that I would accounted be*
> *True brother of a company*
> *That sang, to sweeten Ireland's wrong,*
> *Ballad and story, rann and song; . . .*
>
> *Nor may I less be counted one*
> *With Davis, Mangan, Ferguson, . . .*

It is not surprising that a young poet with this ambition should himself attempt a heroic tale: and, true to form, "The Wanderings of Oisin" opens — after the preliminary dialogue between the pagan poet and St. Patrick — with a roll-call of the heroes.

> Caoilte, and Conan, and Finn were there,
> When we followed a deer with our baying hounds,

With Bran, Sceolan, and Lomair,
And passing the Firbolgs' burial-mounds,
Came to the cairn-heaped grassy hill
Where passionate Maeve is stony-still;[3]

The living heroes are forever mindful of the mighty dead. So, when they meet the beautiful Niamh and she asks them why they are downcast, Finn replies

"We think on Oscar's pencilled urn,
And on the heroes lying slain
On Gabhra's raven-covered plain;
But where are your noble kith and kin,
And from what country do you ride?"

She introduces herself in the approved epic style, "My father and my mother are Aengus and Edain," and Oisin is soon bewitched: whereupon

Caoilte, Conan, and Finn came near,
And wept, and raised their lamenting hands, . . .

The names of the heroes and their hounds, recurring through the poem like a refrain,[4] serve to remind Oisin (and the reader) of the world he has left behind him. The warrior-poet's last words echo his first:

when life in my body has ceased,
I will go to Caoilte, and Conan, and Bran, Sceolan, Lomair,
And dwell in the house of the Fenians, be they in flames or at feast.

In his close examination of the sources of this poem, Russell K. Alspach shows Yeats's chief addition to "The Lay of Oisin on the Land of Youth" to be the conception of a third island—the Island of Forgetfulness—where Oisin encounters the ancient heroes, the kings of the Red Branch, and his own Fenian ancestors and companions.

Two heroic legends that were to exert an even more lasting fascination on Yeats's imagination than that of Oisin, Finn, and Oscar were those of Cuchulain and Deirdre. The dynastic theme runs through both tales, especially the former: and "Cuchulain's Fight with the Sea" tells, like Arnold's "Sohrab and Rustum," of a warrior father's killing of the warrior son he did not know he had until the death-blow was delivered. The poem that followed this in *The Rose*, "The Rose of the World," introduces another epic cycle:

For those red lips, with all their mournful pride,
Mournful that no new wonder may betide,
Troy passed away in one high funeral gleam,
And Usna's children died.

His search for a satisfactory metaphor, or basis for comparison, for Maud Gonne, led Yeats to Troy and a tribal vendetta on an even more heroic scale than that in which "Usna's children died." Again and again he returns to the Helen symbol that alone is complex enough to convey his conflicting awe, apprehension, and devotion.

> A girl arose that had red mournful lips
> And seemed the greatness of the world in tears,
> Doomed like Odysseus and the labouring ships
> And proud as Priam murdered with his peers . . .

Of all Yeats's adaptations and explorations of the Trojan story probably the most powerful is "Leda and the Swan," where an entire dynastic theme is telescoped into one of the most brilliant sentences he ever wrote:

> A shudder in the loins engenders there
> The broken wall, the burning roof and tower
> And Agamemnon dead.

2

The poems collected in *In the Seven Woods* (1904) and *The Green Helmet and Other Poems* (1910) mark the main transitional period of Yeats's stylistic development, a transition that he himself summed up in "A Coat." The very title of his next collection, *Responsibilities* (1914), is indicative of the distance he has come since the days when he made his song a coat "Covered with embroideries Out of old mythologies." In the "Introductory Rhymes" with which *Responsibilities* opens, Yeats addresses his *"old fathers"*: *"Old Dublin merchant"* . . . *"Old country scholar"* . . . *"Soldiers"* . . . *"Old merchant skipper"* . . . and *"You most of all, silent and fierce old man."* He asks pardon of Jervis Yeats, the first of the Yeats line to live in Ireland; of his Butler and Armstrong ancestors; of his two great-grandfathers, Yeats and Middleton; and of his maternal grandfather, William Pollexfen:

> *Pardon that for a barren passion's sake,*
> *Although I have come close on forty-nine,*
> *I have no child, I have nothing but a book,*
> *Nothing but that to prove your blood and mine.*

The last line of the poem echoes lines 7 and 8:

> *Merchant and scholar who have left me blood*
> *That has not passed through any huxter's loin,*

and in that repetition of the key-word "blood" is to be found, I suggest, a clue to the ancestry of Yeats's own dynastic theme here making its first appearance.[6] Blood is the chief currency of heroic literature: "blood will have blood"; it is the supreme sacrifice a hero can make; the most prized possession he inherits from his father and in turn hands on to his son. The word runs like a dark thread through Yeats's poetry, the *Concordance* listing ninety-eight appearances (including twenty compound usages) in *The Variorum Edition of the Poems.*

Few works of art introduce a new subject, and few enough introduce a radical rehandling of an old subject: but the latter at least, I think can fairly be claimed for Yeats's "Introductory Rhymes." Whether the subjective application of a theme hitherto reserved for objective narrative can even qualify as a new theme is open to question. Prior to 1914 almost the only appearances of the dynastic theme in English poetry had been in narratives, chiefly epic, told in the third person. In addition, however, to the early heroic poems already discussed and such later members of the same family as "Sohrab and Rustum," Tennyson's "Ulysses," and Morris's versions of Scandinavian sagas,[7] there were a few more domestic tales like Wordsworth's "Michael" or the "Vaudracour and Juliette" episode from *The Prelude.* It is interesting to note that Wordsworth's great autobiographical poem contains only one brief reference to his mother, one to his father (though both, it is true, died when he was young), and none to his forefathers. His "Ode on the Intimations of Immortality" starts from the premiss that "The Child is father of the man," but otherwise has only the most remote relation to the dynastic theme. Looking back, from a point in time when new books of verse containing poems about parents and children probably outnumber those that do not, to the work of the Victorian poets, the Romantics, the Augustans, the Metaphysicals, and the Elizabethans, one notices an almost total absence of such poems. The occasional exceptions — Patmore's "Toys," Arnold's "Rugby Chapel," Coleridge's "Frost at Midnight," Cowper's "On Receiving my Mother's Picture out of Norfolk," and Savage's "The Bastard" — no more than prove the rule that the subjects of blood-ties either did not interest poets or was not considered a poetic theme.

The events of the years 1916 and 1917 accelerated the flow of Yeats's creative energies. His imagination did not change course so much as cut deeper into its former channels. First of all there was the 1916 Easter Rising that seems to have taken him completely by surprise. His great elegy on the executed leaders, "Easter 1916," is also a revealing self-commentary. The "polite meaningless words" uttered against a background of "grey Eighteenth-century houses" or "Around the fire at the Club," the "ignorant good-will," argument, and drunkenness of the leaders show how completely he was deceived by their "casual comedy," how utterly they were transformed. Honour had returned to Ireland: she had found new heroes worthy of Cuchulain and the kings of the Red Branch. In "Easter 1916," "Sixteen Dead Men," and "The Rose Tree" he repeats their names as in "The Wanderings of Oisin" he had repeated the names of the Fenian heroes:

> I write it out in a verse —
> MacDonagh and MacBride
> And Connolly and Pearse . . .

An event of yet greater importance to the poet and his poetry was his marriage in 1917 to Georgie Hyde-Lees. Yeats was over fifty, "the unmentionable odour of death" had for three years blown westward from Europe where a generation was being destroyed, and at home in Ireland a traditional, aristocratic way of life was on the wane. The last two of these factors he translated into characteristically personal terms in "An Irish Airman Foresees his Death," "In Memory of Major Robert Gregory," and "Reprisals":

> Men that revere your father yet
> Are shot at on the open plain.
> Where may new-married women sit
> And suckle children now?

It is worth remembering that Mrs. Yeats was herself "new-married" and expecting her first child on Gregory land when this poem was written. His own passionate attachment to Coole domain was almost equal to Lady Gregory's.

> A spot whereon the founders lived and died
> Seemed once more dear than life; ancestral trees,
> Or gardens rich in memory glorified
> Marriages, alliances and families
> And every bride's ambition satisfied.

The decline and fall of a royal or noble house is a theme as old as tragedy, and there is little doubt that Yeats's poems about the Gregory household owe something of their resonance to his reworking of the Deirdre and Cuchulain stories and his *Sophocles' King Oedipus* "A Version for the Modern Stage." In 1918, with his own marriage only a few months old and the death of his "dear friend's dear son" so recent, it is small wonder that he was increasingly preoccupied with the dynastic theme.

> God grant a blessing on this tower and cottage
> And on my heirs, if all remain unspoiled,

he wrote on taking possession of Thoor Ballylee, and in November of that year[8] addressed his wife in "Under Saturn":

> how should I forget the wisdom that you brought,
> The comfort that you made? Although my wits have gone
> On a fantastic ride, my horse's flanks are spurred
> By childish memories of an old cross Pollexfen,
> And of a Middleton, whose name you never heard,
> And of a red-haired Yeats whose looks, although he died
> Before my time, seem like a vivid memory.
> You heard that labouring man who had served my people.
>   He said
> Upon the open road, near to the Sligo quay—
> No, no, not said, but cried it out—"You have come again,

> And surely after twenty years it was time to come."
> I am thinking of a child's vow sworn in vain
> Never to leave that valley his fathers called their home.

This and the two previous quotations illustrate an essentially primitive concern with place, the "paternal acres," that is frequently related to poetic handlings of the dynastic theme.

In February 1919 Yeats's daughter Anne was born and before she was a month old he was at work on "A Prayer for my Daughter," which was not only to become one of his best and most popular poems, but also—as I attempt to show elsewhere[9]—one of his most influential. Its movement begins with the natural progression of a father's thoughts: will his daughter be beautiful? Better that she should not be *too* beautiful: Helen's beauty, after all, brought her no happiness. At this point Yeats's meditation changes almost imperceptibly into reverse gear, as if the allusion to Helen of Troy in stanza IV had diverted him from the prayer for his daughter's future to a contemplation of Maud Gonne's past, that is at the same time his own. The two strands, precept and example, are beautifully woven together; the poet's voice rising through stanza VII to the bitter vehemence of stanza VIII, his harshness fading through stanza IX as his meditation again changes into forward gear. Maud Gonne, who might so easily have been his daughter's mother, is forgotten as the dynastically minded father concludes his prayer for the child's future:

> And may her bridegroom bring her to a house
> Where all's accustomed, ceremonious . . .

The "Prayer for my Daughter" was followed in December 1921 by the less successful "Prayer for my Son." That year also saw the beginning of Yeats's "Meditations in Time of Civil War" which, though they range far beyond the dynastic theme, start from his contemplation of "My House," "My Table," "My Descendents." In each section his imagination, with its unique ability to interrelate personal and public history, moves effortlessly between past, present, and future. The moorhen is seen to guide "those feathered balls of soot" upon the stream, the honey-bees are bidden to "Come build in the empty house of the stare." In the animal kingdom as in man's domain succession is fundamental to the natural order.

Yeats's concern with dynastic continuity, which reaches its extreme in his advocacy of eugenic reform,[10] is inextricably related to his concern with the continuity of cultural tradition, especially in its more heroic manifestations. He sees the artist, maker of images, as custodian of this tradition and loses no opportunity to celebrate the artist as hero:

> My father upon the Abbey stage, before him a raging crowd:
> "This land of Saints," and then as the applause died out,
> "Of plaster Saints"; his beautiful mischievous head thrown back.

It is his fellow artists that he celebrates in "The Municipal Gallery

Revisited," a poem commemorating the continuity of a cultural tradition, that is followed by "Are You Content?," a poem commemorating dynastic continuity. This, significantly, is given the place of honour at the end of *New Poems* (1938). As in the "Introductory Rhymes" to *Responsibilities*, Yeats again directly addresses his ancestors. One by one he calls them up like the ghosts in "All Souls' Night."

> I call on those that call me son,
> Grandson, or great-grandson,
> On uncles, aunts, great-uncles or great-aunts,
> To judge what I have done.
> Have I, that put it into words,
> Spoilt what old loins have sent?
> Eyes spiritualised by death can judge,
> I cannot, but I am not content.

Action is weighed against "words" as in the earlier poem it was against "a book" and — in the manner of a prosecuting counsel — he asks this jury to "judge" (the word is used twice) whether he has properly discharged his stewardship of the heritage transmitted through their loins. Here, as elsewhere, the succession of family names — Corbet, Pollexfen, Middleton, Butler — has an incantatory effect similar to that of the roll-call of heroes in "The Wanderings of Oisin," "Easter 1916," and "The Rose Tree". It is clear that Yeats intended "Are You Content?," with its recollection of

> He that in Sligo at Drumcliff
> Set up the old stone Cross,

to be followed by "Under Ben Bulben", the opening poem of *Last Poems and Two Plays*. Nothing could be more in character than that he should choose to be buried where he did, and to end his valedictory poem with a celebration of the family connection with that place:

> Under bare Ben Bulben's head
> In Drumcliff churchyard Yeats is laid.
> An ancestor was rector there
> Long years ago . . .

3

Although, as I shall suggest later, the First World War was to have a profound long-term effect on the dynastic awareness of the participating nations, the English-speaking poets who were themselves caught up in it had at the time more urgent themes thrust upon them. The present was too much with them for there to be much thought of their forebears, and their personal future too remote — sometimes too improbable — for them to write many poems about sons or daughters. If, however, the dynastic theme did not find much subjective treatment in their poems of the war period, thoughts of the next generation were none the less lurking at the back of their minds. There is evidence of this in the work of the two best known of the English "War Poets." Rupert Brooke, one of whose last letters asked Dudley Ward to "call a boy after me," wrote—with the bardic voice of 1914—in his sonnet "The Dead":

> These laid the world away; poured out the red
> Sweet wine of youth; gave up the years to be
>   Of work and joy, and that unhoped serene,
>   That men call age; and those who would have been,
> Their sons, they gave, their immortality.

Wilfred Owen—with the very different voice of 1918—ends his bitter adaptation of the Old Testament story of Abraham and Isaac ("The Parable of the Old Man and The Young") with the angel

> Saying, Lay not thy hand upon the lad,
> Neither do anything to him. Behold,
> A ram, caught in a thicket by its horns;
> Offer the Ram of Pride instead of him.
> But the old man would not so, but slew his son,
> And half the seed of Europe, one by one.

Also relevant is the no less bitter conclusion of "Dulce et Decorum Est":

> If you could hear, at every jolt, the blood
> Come gargling from the froth-corrupted lungs, . . .
> My friend, you would not tell with such high zest
> To children ardent for some desperate glory,
> The old Lie: Dulce et decorum est
> Pro patria mori.

Two years after the death of Brooke and one year before Owen's, there was born a poet who in 1968 is already more influential (at least among poets) than either. Robert Lowell, descended from a long line of New England brahmins including—on his mother's side—Edward Winslow, one of the Pilgrim Fathers, spent his childhood on Boston's exclusive Beacon Hill. Endowed with an ancestry, a tradition, and an environment that, one feels, would have had Yeats's whole-hearted approval (not to say envy), Lowell, who clearly learnt a good deal from Yeats, soon showed himself an unwilling inheritor. Hugh Staples, in his informative and perceptive study, *Robert Lowell / The First Twenty Years*, succinctly sums up Lowell's early attitudes:

> Dissatisfied with the Protestantism of his ancestors, he was not content to take up a merely agnostic position—instead he sought for spiritual values in the dogma of the Catholic Church. Finding Harvard, to which his family heritage had consigned him, something less than a nest of singing birds, he removed to Kenyon, where a new creative tradition was being developed by John Crowe Ransom. Unable to

become, like his father, a naval officer, Lowell chose the role of conscientious objector, which he seems to have embraced with the zeal of a Christian martyr. In all these actions, he reveals a deep absorption in the historical sense without which, as T. S. Eliot pointed out in his famous essay, the individual talent cannot grow.

Lowell shows his "deep absorption in the historical sense," as did Yeats before him, both in poems on historical subjects and in poems dealing with family history. At times the two historical frames of reference come together explicitly, and fuse, as in Yeats's roll-call of his ancestors:

> A Butler or an Armstrong that withstood
> Beside the brackish waters of the Boyne
> James and his Irish when the Dutchman crossed;

or Lowell's

> I envy the conspicuous
> waste of our grandparents on their grand tours—
> long-haired Victorian sages accepted the universe,
> while breezing on their trust funds through the world.

More often, however, there is an implied relationship between the two frames of reference; the one underlying the other. So Lowell, writing explicitly of his father's failure and death in "Commander Lowell" and "Terminal Days at Beverly Farms," writes implicitly of the failure and death of a social class.

The central figure in Lowell's poems on the dynastic theme is, however, not his father but his grandfather; just as the presence of Yeats's maternal grandfather, William Pollexfen, overshadows that of John Butler Yeats in the Irishman's poetry and prose. "In Memory of Arthur Winslow" is the central, and many would say the finest, poem in Lowell's first volume, *Land of Unlikeness* (1944). The first of its four parts is entitled "Death from Cancer" and begins:

> This Easter, Arthur Winslow, less than dead,
> Your people set you up in Phillips' House
> To settle off your wrestling with the crab—
> The claws drop flesh upon your yachting blouse
> Until longshoreman Charon come and stab
> Through your adjusted bed
> And crush the crab.

This emphasis on his grandfather's cancer makes one feel that the disease has a symbolic function in the poem: it is as if the terrible physical rotting from within were in some way sign of a spiritual cancer resulting from the family's centuries of brutal materialism ("clippers" and "slavers") censured in parts three and four of the elegy. Like so many of Lowell's poems, this opens with a specific locale: Phillips' House, we learn from Staples, is the private, expensive-division of the Massachusetts General Hospital. The poet's continual reference to recognizable topographical features of "this planned Babel of Boston where our money talks and multiplies the darkness of a land," "these hell-fire streets Of Boston," illustrates that concern with the "paternal acres" that is often associated with the dynastic theme. Lowell shifts the scene in part two of the poem from his grandfather's death-bed to Dunbarton, the family cemetery: "The stones are yellow and the grass is gray Past Concord by the rotten lake." Yellow and gray, the colours of corruption, and "the rotten lake" suggest an extension of the cancer that has brought Arthur Winslow to this

> hill
> Where crutch and trumpet meet the limousine
> And half-forgotten Starks and Winslows fill
> The granite plot . . .

The introduction of the family names reminds one of Yeats's Corbets and Pollexfens, just as the symbolic potency of Dunbarton in a sense parallels that of Drumcliff churchyard: although the very different views that the two poets hold of their ancestors conditions their view of their respective burial grounds.

From the burial service where "The preacher's mouthings still Deafen my poor relations on the hill," Lowell turns in part three, "Five Years Later", to a highly critical meditation on

> the craft
> That netted you a million dollars, late
> Hosing out gold in Colorado's waste,
> Then lost it all in Boston real estate.

Material prosperity is followed by poverty both material and spiritual: and in part four, "A Prayer for my Grandfather to Our Lady," Lowell adapts and joins the story of the raising of Lazarus (John II) and the parable of Dives and Lazarus (Luke 16).

> Beached
> On these dry flats of fishy real estate,
> O Mother, I implore
> Your scorched, blue thunderbreasts of love to pour
> Buckets of blessings on my burning head
> Until I rise like Lazarus from the dead:
> *Lavabis nos et super nivem delabor*

In his alteration of the *Miserere* Latin *me* to *nos* the poet makes it clear that his prayer is for himself as well as for his grandfather.

> "Mother, run to the chalice, and bring back
> Blood on your finger-tips for Lazarus who was poor."

Already in his first book we see the sequence of ideas that he was to explore further in his next three collections: the meditation on his forebears in which he struggles to understand them and, by understanding them, to understand himself.

"In Memory of Arthur Winslow" reappeared in Lowell's second book, *Lord Weary's Castle*, where it was supported by several other explorations of the dynastic theme. "Mary Winslow" also opens with a death-bed scene: the Charles river now is frozen, but again it is identified with the Acheron and "Charon, the Lubber" comes for the poet's grandmother as he came for his grandfather. The poem "Rebellion" Staples describes as an

> enigmatic nightmare-vision of patricide [that] is more than an expression of psychological hostility towards the father-figure as a symbol of authority; the identification of the father with the heirlooms makes it clear that the murder is a rejection of traditions as well:

> > There was rebellion, father, when the mock
> > French windows slammed and you hove backward, rammed
> > Into your heirlooms, screens, a glass-cased clock,
> > The highboy quaking to its toes.

The rebellion is not only against his father, but against his father's fathers:

> > I dreamed the dead
> > Caught at my knees and fell:
> > And it was well
> > With me, my father. Then
> > Behemoth and Leviathan
> > Devoured our mighty merchants.

In the long title-poem of Lowell's third collection to be published in America, *The Mills of the Kavanaughs*, Anne Kavanaugh meditates on the decay of the Kavanaugh fortune. Her husband, a suicide, had like Lowell's father been in the navy, and his signet ring bore the Winslow's motto: "Cut down, we flourish." It is, therefore, perhaps not too fanciful to suppose that Lowell is here carrying one stage further the patricide theme of "Rebellion." The naval father is not only dead, but childless: that his wife is the last of the Kavanaughs gives a grim irony to their motto. In what may be regarded at one level of interpretation as a wish-fulfilment fantasy, Lowell cuts down his family so that it shall no longer flourish. He stands in judgement on his ancestors and finds them guilty: quite the converse of Yeats, who humbly submits himself to judgement *by* his ancestors.

What would appear to be Lowell's final verdict, however, is not the death sentence. In Part Three of *Life Studies*, where he again and even more searchingly reviews his grandparents, parents and himself when young, he begins to find positive values in the lives of his forebears and in the tradition they established, shaped, and he inherited. The affection and nostalgia for the presences of his childhood that were not entirely suppressed in even the most guilt-tormented of his earlier poems now find their true level. Understanding more he forgives more. The eleven titled poems of Part Three are so arranged as to make up one sequence, almost one poem. Each section, though complete in itself, derives strength and meaning from the others, especially the flanking sections. The first is entitled "My Last Afternoon with Uncle Devereux Winslow," but is dominated by Arthur Winslow, as also are the two subsequent sections, "Dunbarton" and "Grandparents." Devereux Winslow "was dying at twenty-nine" "of the incurable Hodgkin's disease;" mention of which, like Arthur Winslow's cancer in Lowell's earlier elegy, seems to hint at some malignant spiritual disorder devouring the family from within. The first section ends with the five-and-a-half-year-old Lowell idly playing with

> piles
> of earth and lime,
> a black and a white pile . . .
> Come winter,
> Uncle Devereux would blend to the one colour.

And the second section coolly opens:

> When Uncle Devereux died,
> Daddy was still on sea-duty in the Pacific,
> it seemed spontaneous and proper
> for Mr. MacDonald, the farmer,
> Karl, the chauffeur, and even my Grandmother
> to say, "your Father." They meant my Grandfather.

Tender recollections of days in his grandparents' house are succeeded by a section whose first line shows them to be dead. Then, in strict time sequence, follow the failure and death of his father, the selling of his "cottage at Beverly Farms," and the death of his mother. "Sailing Home from Rapallo" ends with a view of her coffin, and it is a most dramatic and moving transition to the child's crib that opens the next section, "During Fever."

So Yeats, having for years looked over his shoulder at the somewhat oppressive shades of his ancestors, in "A Prayer for my Daughter" looks forward into the future of his family. Although the greater part of "During Fever" is a monologue addressed to his mother, and "Waking in the Blue" is a reverie from "the house for the 'mentally ill,' " the last poem in this series returns to the subject of his daughter. She is addressed with charming and good-humoured tenderness: "Dearest, I cannot loiter here / in lather like a polar bear." My impression that these poems about his daughter mark Lowell's escape from the valley of the shadow of obsessive guilt, a return to health and hope, is reinforced by the poems in *For the Union Dead* (1964). These are calmer, more confident in tone, and the poet himself — as never before — is the protagonist. His ancestors have played their part and are banished to the wings. Although in "Middle Age" he says:

> At every corner,
> I meet my Father,
> my age, still alive.

he writes now more as husband and father than son and grandson.

It is one thing to plot the development of the dynastic theme through the work of such other contemporary poets as Anne Sexton, Tony Connor, and Anthony Thwaite, but quite another matter to account for it. Though Yeats has been one of the most powerful poetic influences of this century, "a siren whose rock is littered with the bones of lesser poets," one cannot attribute all post-1914 "dynastic" poems to imitation. There has, of course, been an element of this — sometimes a considerable element — but the main cause must lie deeper. One does not, after all, find poems about gyres and the phases of the moon in every second new volume of poetry that one picks up. Yeats himself, I believe, hinted at the main cause when he wrote of "a child's vow sworn in vain Never to leave that valley his fathers called their home." The structure of English society, and Irish society for that matter, changed less in the six centuries prior to the Industrial Revolution than in the century and a half that followed it. Until the end of the eighteenth century people in the main "knew their place," literally and figuratively. Most of them lived where their families had lived for generations before them, as like as not at the same social level. With the progress of the Industrial Revolution this "frozen" society began to thaw. The sons and grandsons of countrymen set off for the towns, on foot, on horseback, and then on the railways, and the distribution of wealth began to change. Through Victorian and Edwardian England the social thaw continued and the First World War further accelerated the processes of change. The battlefields of France took a proportionally heavier toll of the ruling class than the ruled, thus creating a vacuum that did not long remain unfilled.

Yeats then, with his concern for roots, was the first English-speaking poet to give expression to the rootlessness of modern man. Like a sailor establishing his position by the bisection of longitude and latitude, he looked to his ancestors and to his descendants to discover where he stood. If the First World War, as I suggested earlier, intensified the dynastic awareness of the English-speaking world, the Second World War — with its twin spectres of genocide and the atomic bomb — intensified it yet further. These, coupled with the decline of religious belief and the neuroses arising from the discoveries of Freud and Jung, would seem to account for man's present uncertainty as to his nature and his place. The confessional monologue from the psychiatrist's couch (of which an increasing number of writers have first-hand experience) has been adopted as a literary form: though some of its practitioners who subscribe to the view of "poetry as therapy" would object to the phrase "literary form" on the grounds that they have been trying to liberate literature from its forms, bringing it down to earth and back to life. The confessional monologue is, of course, no more an exclusively poetic phenomenon than the dynastic theme itself. Interesting parallels are to be seen in the development of the novel and the increasing popularity of biography and autobiography, but they lie beyond the scope of the present essay. Poetry and prose alike show today the influence of psychiatric method (*A la recherche du temps perdu*) for a psychiatric purpose (the attainment of self-knowledge). Frankness is all: many writers feel that the truth must be found and faced no matter what the cost.

So, paradoxically, at a time when the old morality is under assault from every side, when more is heard than ever before of the isolation of the individual, divorce and the breaking of families, we find the poets concerned — as never since the heroic age — with family relationships. Their message, it would seem, is Auden's: "We must love one another or die." It is perhaps not too fanciful to see a parallel between the society of *Beowulf* and our own: the one with its tribes banded against each other and the terrors of the dark unknown; the other rediscovering its dynastic sense under the threat of atomic war and the extinction of mankind. Consciously or subconsciously giving expression to man's innermost unrecognized hopes and fears, Yeats and the poets that have followed him prove themselves, in Ezra Pound's fine phrase, "the antennae of the race."

Notes

1. Mary E. Waterhouse (transl), *Beowulf / in Modern English*, 1949, lines 259–69.

2. Dorothy Whitelock, *The Beginnings of English Society*, 1952, p 39.

3. These lines did not appear in the poem as first published in 1889: only the three hounds were then named.

4. Book I, line 125; Book III, lines 5, 84, 104, 114, 116, 195, and 224.

5. 'Some Sources of Yeats's *The Wanderings of Oisin*', *P.M.L.A.*, lviii, pp. 849–66.

6. For a discussion of Yeats's genealogical investigations, undertaken with his sister Lily, see Joseph Ronsley, *Yeats's Autobiography*, 1968, pp. 12–13.

7. For the influence of these on Yeats see Peter Faulkner, *William Morris and W. B. Yeats*, 1962.

8. See Ellmann, *The Identity of Yeats*, second edition, 1964, p. 290. Yeats, however, dates it November 1919 in *Michael Robartes and the Dancer*, 1920.

9. An extended version of this essay appeared in *The Critical Quarterly*, vii. 3 (1965), pp. 247–65.

10. See 'To-morrow's Revolution', *On the Boiler*, 1939, pp. 14–21.

"Intellectual Hatred" and "Intellectual Nationalism": The Paradox of Passionate Politics   George Mills Harper*

Although Yeats apparently decided early in his career that "there is no fine literature without nationality,"[1] he was not always certain what nationality meant or what methods patriotic Irishmen should employ to achieve national freedom. He was, of course, consistently concerned with the mythopoeic function of nationality in literature rather than the usefulness of literature as propaganda for nationlistic doctrines. It was that issue which led to his controversy with the Dublin press in the early days of the Irish National Theatre. Arthur Griffith, in *The United Irishman*, was the most vociferous spokesman for the popular patriotic stance: "Did I tell you," Yeats wrote to Lady Gregory, "my idea of challenging Griffith to debate with me in public our two policies — his that literature should be subordinate to nationalism, and mine that it must have its own ideal? I think that a challenge to him would be quite amusing, for his own party sent out so many that he would be a little embarrassed to refuse. I would offer to debate it with him or any other person appointed by his societies."[2] It is not my purpose here to consider the issue of this proposed debate, but rather to point out the gradual emergence of two opposed nationalistic viewpoints and to suggest that Yeats's choice of one over the other was, as Blake would have said, 'uneasy' because he had inclinations towards both. I will suggest also that the great art which developed from his intellectual nationalism would not have been possible without the abrasive stimulant of its opposite, the intellectual hatred of the revolutionaries and the secret societies. Yeats himself vacillated, especially during the nineties. He joined the IRB, and "went hither and thither speaking at meetings in England and Scotland and occasionally at tumultuous Dublin conventions, and endured some of the worst months of my life."[3] But he came to fear the "movement of abstraction and hatred" (A360) which possessed the other party. "I dreaded some wild Fenian movement," he recalled, "and with literature perhaps more in my mind than politics, dreamed of that Unity of Culture which might begin with some few men controlling some form of administration" (A362).

We ought to be grateful, I suppose, that Yeats was a divided man — most great artists are. He was a man of paradoxes and tensions and uncertainties, not the least of which is the ambivalent stance he took on Irish politics. He had learned from William Blake, if he needed a teacher, that "Without Contraries is no progression."

Although Yeats insisted throughout much of his life that he was an intellectual nationalist with little interest in practical politics, he was in

*From *Theatre and Nationalism in Twentieth-Century Ireland*, ed. Robert O'Driscoll (Toronto: University of Toronto Press, 1971), 40–65.

fact obsessed with the subject and sought to create art out of the paradox suggested in these polar opposites, both of which appealed to him. To the public, however, he consistently projected himself as the representative of one pole in diametric opposition to an important but misguided segment of Irish writers and politicians, and the two groups were finally engaged in an increasingly great struggle for the minds and loyalties of the unthinking body politic. In a very real sense almost all his work after the death of Parnell is an attempt to mould the seemingly intractable material of propaganda into living form.

But it might never have become art if the opposition had not been epitomised in Maud Gonne. She was most likely right in her shrewd judgment that Yeats would have been a lesser poet without her opposition, without which, by his own testament, "I might have thrown poor words away / And been content to live."[4] As poet and artist he preferred contemplation; as ardent suitor and student of politics he yearned for action.

To students of literature, it is exciting to imagine what Yeats might have become if Maud had yielded to his entreaties. Would "my movement," as he called his quest for "Unity of Culture," have failed utterly without the leadership he provided? Or was it inevitable that the public stance he assumed should find a champion? Or would he have become an even greater artist through union with his ideological opposite? Such speculations are obviously futile, if not utterly fruitless; and I have no intention of trying to imagine the prayer he might have made for his daughter if Maud had become the mother instead of "an old bellows full of angry wind." Rather, I propose to trace Yeats's own ambivalence towards Maud and Irish nationalism, and to chart briefly his vacillating course in what he was to call the "labour of politics." I want to suggest also the point of view and perhaps counterambivalence of Maud, who stood at times for "intellectual hatred" at its worse, but who was not the only one around with an "opinionated mind." Although most students and critics are readily convinced that Yeats overcame accursed opinions, we must remember that he was constantly besieged by them and would not in all likelihood have been the great poet he became if he had not been forced to struggle. At any rate, it is revealing to watch the battle as he recorded it in action and words.

We may begin with Yeats's vacillation and uncertainty about the Young Irelanders. He was, as he tells us, led to read them through John O'Leary, whose favourite apparently was the national favourite, Thomas Davis; and the source of Yeats's factual information was Gavan Duffy's *Young Ireland* (1880). Duffy was biased, having quarrelled with John Mitchel, the finest writer and most impassioned of the leaders. Whether or not Yeats would have chosen Davis over Mitchel if he had not learned through Duffy, the fact is that Yeats's choice was deliberate. Speaking in 1914 at the Davis centenary meeting in Dublin, Yeats concluded that "the

political influence of Mitchel . . . has been almost wholly mischievous,"
and Yeats's reason is important: "Mitchel played upon international
suspicion and exalted the hate of England above the love of Ireland that
Davis would have taught us, and his gaping harpies are on our roof-tree
now."[5] In his bitter moments, Yeats must have listed Maud among the
harpies and traced her intellectual hatred to the school of Mitchel.

Although the Young Irelanders as a group found a *raison d'être* in
their opposition to O'Connell's policies, including his insistence on non-
violence, Davis belonged to the coterie of Gavan Duffy, who ultimately
split with John Mitchel over the issue of armed revolt. In the words of
Duffy, Davis had "no faith in the Gallic bravado . . . of baptising the
cause in blood." Like Yeats, he feared mob violence and murder: "The
people of Munster are starving," he wrote; "Will murder feed them?" And
like Yeats also, he had faith in the "Aristocracy of Ireland."[6] To Padraic
Pearse, the intellectual nationalist of the Easter Revolution, Davis was
"the first of modern Irishmen to make explicit the truth that nationality is
a spirituality."[7] As a proponent of cultural unity, Davis wanted "not a
Nationality which would prelude civil war, but which would establish
internal independence — a Nationality which would be recognised by the
world and sanctioned by wisdom, virtue and prudence."[8] Even Arthur
Griffith, who sided with Maud and opposed Yeats, praised this strain in
Davis: "When the Irish read and reflect with Davis," he wrote, "their day
of redemption will be at hand."[9]

Of course, such remarks reflect the generalities and abstractions
which irritated Yeats and his followers. But there was a side to Davis
which clearly set him off from most of the Young Irelanders and suggested
him as the model for O'Leary first, then Yeats and his circle; more than
any of the others Davis hoped for Ireland's salvation through unity of
culture. When Douglas Hyde and Father Michael O'Hickey organised the
Gaelic League, they found the perfect expression of their plan "to cultivate
everything that is most racial, most Gaelic, most Irish" in words of
Thomas Davis: "Nationality . . . is the summary name for many things. It
seeks a literature made by Irishmen, and coloured by our scenery, manners
and character. It desires to see art applied to express Irish thoughts and
belief. It would make our music sound in every parish at twilight, our
pictures sprinkle the walls of every house, and our poetry and history sit at
every hearth. It would thus create a race of men full of more intensely
Irish character and knowledge, and to that race it would give Ireland."[10]
Even more like Yeats's thought was the toast Davis proposed at the first
banquet of the '82 Club for "The Advancement of the Fine Arts in
Ireland." "There is a close connection between National Art and National
Independence. Art is the born foe of slavery and of the friends of slavery —
of ignorance, of sensuality and of cowardice. . . . How can he who never
heard the shout of freemen . . . reach the form of a great artist?"[11]
Although Yeats was an artist first and a nationalist second, whereas Davis

was a nationalist who cultivated the arts for his purpose, it is clear that Yeats learned much from Davis.

But he was torn between Davis's intellectual nationalism and John Mitchel's "pure hatred to England," which, as Mitchel suggested to himself in a wellknown passage in the *Jail Journal*, was "a diseased longing for blood and carnage." "And for the *chance* of getting Ireland severed from England in the dreadful *mêlée*," his Doppelganger asks, "do you desire to see all Europe and America plunged in desperate war?"[12] Almost any student of Yeats will respond to that question with his famous line from Mitchel's prayer: "Send war in our time, O Lord!" (V638). At times, certainly, perhaps all his life, Yeats was quite sympathetic to Mitchel's strain of nationalistic fervour, the slogan for which, according to a British historian, "was 'barricades and incendiarism,' a tradition of street warfare which found belated expression in the Irish Rebellion of 1916."[13]

Although many of the Young Irelanders ultimately sided with Mitchel, he was the leader in the break with Duffy, and in the beginning he stood almost alone. When he stopped writing for *The Nation* in late 1847, Mitchel informed Duffy that "the present policy of *The Nation* does not suit me." A few months later he was making it absolutely clear that he would "belong to no society where I cannot express sentiments in favour of absolute tenant-right, and where I cannot recommend the only known method of establishing that right, namely *armed opinion*."[14] In a "Letter to Farmers," written from Newgate Prison, Mitchel declared that "Moral Force and 'Patience and Perseverance' are scattered to the wild winds of Heaven. The music my countrymen now love best to hear is the rattle of arms and the ring of the rifle," and he looked forward to "the crash of the downfall of the thrice-accursed British Empire."[15] In the words of Countess Markievicz, Mitchel was a "queer mixture": "The oddest thing about him was that he was against the freeing of the black slaves in America. Of course his reason was that the English were on the other side." But she liked "his ideas for Ireland" and called him "one of the Divine Ancestors of Easter Week."[16] To Padraic Pearse, likewise, "Mitchel was of the stuff of which the great prophets and ecstatics have been made. He did really hold converse with God; he did really deliver God's word to man, delivered it fiery tongued."[17] And Thomas Carlyle, after warning Mitchel that "he would most likely be hanged," comforted him with the assurance that "they could not hang the immortal part of him."[18] Like James Fintan Lalor, Mitchel was "a passionate hater of tyranny under any form or sky."[19] He was unalterably opposed to any compromise with England, declaring early in his career "that Irish representation in a London Parliament is worse than useless, and that that Parliament is absolutely *nothing* to Ireland save 'an engine of corruption, a workshop of coercion, and a storehouse of starvation.'"[20] Of course, fiery speeches for separation were common in 1848. At one stage Mitchel and his associates became so incensed that they "signed a pledge to refrain from the use of intoxicating drinks until the legislative independence of Ireland had been established."[21]

The story of Mitchel's trial, conviction, and deportation is well known. It is enough, for my purpose, to point out that he became a martyr and a model, his *Jail Journal* the gospel of Irish revolution which the young Yeats, in London, read aloud for many days to his father.[22] Both the man and the book were no doubt exciting, but Yeats had discovered an even stronger attraction in John O'Leary, who had been taught by Davis rather than Mitchel: "For all that is Irish in me," O'Leary recalled, "and above all, for the inspiration that made me Irish, the fountain and the origin must always be found in Davis."[23] Years later Yeats was to pay a very similar tribute to O'Leary.

By the time Yeats met Maud Gonne, he had been exposed to both viewpoints, and had made a choice of the road to travel in carrying out "my mission in Ireland," but the choice had not been easy, and he was never quite sure that he had made the right choice, though he would not have been so uncertain if Maud's road had not crossed his. The stage was set for the ideological struggle at their first meeting. When she called upon Yeats at Bedford Park in London, she brought an introduction from O'Leary, under whose banner she too had enlisted, but without his cultural convictions. Maud was, in her own words, a "one-idea'd" woman, and she constantly reminded all who cared to listen that "there is a perpetual state of war between Ireland and England."[24] At this meeting, Yeats recalled years later, "She vexed my father by praise of war, war for its own sake, not as the creator of certain virtues but as if there were some virtue in excitement itself." The love-struck Yeats supported Maud, excusing himself, in retrospect, with the observation that "a man young as I could not have differed from a woman so beautiful and so young" (A123). Since he was temperamentally opposed to Maud's brand of politics, she brought to his life an ideological and personal tension never wholly resolved in his mind. Although Yeats also must have appeared "one-idea'd" to the political world of Dublin, he acknowledged to himself the abiding paradox of passionate politics which he debated and projected in letters and art.

For several years after that momentous first meeting he sought to enlist Maud in the service of cultural nationalism. Feeling that "I needed a hostess more than a society," he wrote, "I tried to persuade Maud Gonne to be that hostess"; but he found, alas, that "she had already formed a new ambition, the turning of French public opinion against England" (A230). He recorded his disappointment in a harsh condemnation: "Without intellectual freedom there can be no agreement, and in Nationalist Dublin there was not — indeed there still is not — any society where a man is heard by the right ears . . . in its stead opinion crushes and rends, and all is hatred and bitterness: wheel biting upon wheel, a roar of steel or iron tackle, a mill of argument grinding all things down to mediocrity"

(A230–1). Though he referred to Maud in those lines, Yeats managed as usual to include all those who disagreed with his form of nationalism. Another passage in "Ireland after Parnell" illustrates the process of depersonalisation even better: "When we loathe ourselves or our world, if that loathing but turn to intellect, we see self or world and its anti-self as in one vision; when loathing remains but loathing, world or self consumes itself away, and we turn to its mechanical opposite" (A234). Standing alone, of course, such oracular pronouncements seem to have little or only slight relevance to particular people, but the lines following make clear that Yeats not only is thinking of Maud as the mechanical opposite but also is suggesting that the struggle of loathing or hatred versus intellect goes on in his own mind. "The Nationalist abstractions," he continued, "were like the fixed ideas of some hysterical woman, a part of the mind turned into stone, the rest a seething and burning; and Unionist Ireland had reacted from that seething and burning to a cynical indifference, and from those fixed ideas to whatever might bring the most easy and obvious success" (A234).

Yeats is, of course, recollecting events, and may be forgiven if he has over-refined the emotion rationalised in some if never complete tranquillity. But if he had written this section of his autobiography during the nineties, the tone if not the story would have been different, for he made every effort to convert Maud. He induced her to join the Theosophical Society and took her to visit Madame Blavatsky, he urged her to help him create his pseudo-political Castle of Heroes, and he sought her help in organising branches of the Young Ireland Society. But he fought a losing battle: intellectual nationalism lacked excitement for Maud, who thought the whole cultural movement somewhat ridiculous: "Everyone must work according to his own temperament," she recalled in after years. "It was my philosophy of life applied to art and politics. I never willingly discouraged either a Dynamiter or a constitutionalist, a realist or a lyrical writer. My chief preoccupation was how their work could help forward the Irish Separatist movement" (178). In spite of this denial, however, she did discourage "a lyrical writer" by her stubborn insistence that "there must always be war till Ireland is free" (186). Maud was, in her words, "a horse that has to wear blinkers to prevent being side-tracked — I must not look to the right or the left" (176).

She was, in fact, Yeats's opposite in many ways, and they were conscious of being antithetical complements. "I never indulged in self-analysis," Maud recalled, "and often used to get impatient with Willie Yeats, who, like all writers, was terribly introspective and tried to make me so. 'I have no time to think of myself,' I told him which was literally true, for, unconsciously perhaps, I had redoubled work to avoid thought" (308). All the slow process of cultural change Maud was to scorn. In her opinion, the branch of the Young Ireland Society she and Yeats founded "never did much effective work, except sending votes of congratulation (or the reverse) to political groups in Ireland" (170). Her experiment with the occult was motivated by "the hope of gaining power to use for the great objective of my life" (256). When some of the members raised objections to her "political activities," she resigned. She had discovered that "most of the members were Unionists." They were "strictly philosophical and non-political—which," Maud observed, "means non-national" in Ireland (256–7). In the meantime, "persuaded" by Willie again, she had joined the Order of the Golden Dawn, "where more practical magic might be learnt" (257). But the Golden Dawn was also disappointing, and when she discovered its relationship to Masonry she resigned because "Free Masonry as we Irish know it is a British institution and has always been used politically to support the British Empire." As a result she would "have no connection with it." Although "Willie Yeats was very disappointed," Maud was too busy for such child's play. "They could use me," she said; "I could not use them. I have not time to try and learn their secrets" (259–60). It is completely appropriate that Maud should have closed the chapter about her "Occult Experiences" with a withering observation on the Golden Dawn: "The last authentic information I had about the Order was that they were holding ceremonies invoking peace" (260). What more was there to say!

"I have not time" is the refrain running through Maud's account of these experiences, and in fact lack of time is the chief objection to Willie's intellectual nationalism made by all who were "Dancing to a frenzied drum" in those tempestuous and exciting years. Maud's observation about the learning of Gaelic suggests how far apart the two nationalist schools of thought were: "Douglas Hyde . . . believed in the language to free Ireland; to me the method seemed too slow; under his tuition I learned a sentence or two with which to begin my speeches, but . . . I was too constantly travelling from one place to another trying to spread revolutionary thoughts and acts to sit down to the arduous task of learning a language. So Douglas Hyde never succeeded in making me an Irish speaker any more than I succeeded in making him a revolutionist" (98–9). Conscious always that the cultural nationalists "looked down on Constance Markievicz and myself as foolish misguided women" (96), Maud would nevertheless admit that Hyde's *Literary History of Ireland* "supplied the intellectual background of revolt" (99).

But the two groups were still searching for an ideological compromise. Maud, though "suspect to Dublin Castle" and shadowed by two sleuths, was not yet "on the run," and her "rooms over Morrow's Bookshop and Library in Nassau Street" became Dublin's intellectual pub for Yeats, Griffith, Rooney, Hyde, Connolly, MacKenna, and others. "Our talk," Maud recalled, "was the wine on which we used to get satisfactorily drunk. . . . Many now famous poems and plays had their first reading in those rooms in Nassau Street, and many plots were hatched in them"; then she added, in a significant afterthought, "plots for plays and plots for real life" (98). The impassioned debates about politics were clearly leading to two schools of thought with many variations. Indeed, one is tempted to conjecture that Maud's "friends," as she called them all, had perfect agreement on one issue alone: the necessity "to remove from the walls various pictures of British battle-scenes" (98).

Present from the beginning, their philosophic differences led in time to an irreparable breach. Maud was on one side, Yeats on the other; and the tension must have been almost intolerable, to him at least. Maud's "pilgrimage of passion" (84) was not to be his, but he kept hoping that they might be drawn together in the perfect cultural union: after all, he reasoned hopefully, "A beautiful woman is always a little barbarous at heart." When he wrote that sentence, Yeats had been talking with a French woman who was alarmed by "the success of the anti-militarist movement."[25] But he had as usual made the mental transfer to Maud. She was, in fact, so much on his mind that Cathleen ni Houlihan herself took on Maud's archetypal dimensions. Maud had planned to be an actress when she broke away from her family. Prevented by illness, she sought a career working for Ireland's freedom, but she never ceased acting. Although she decided that "going on the stage is infamous" (64), she cast herself in many roles, especially Joan of Arc[26] and Cathleen ni Houlihan. As "a servant of the Queen," she modestly described herself as "one of the little stones on which the feet of the Queen have rested on her way to Freedom," but she pictured Cathleen in her own lineaments: "Then I saw a tall, beautiful woman with dark hair blown on the wind and I knew it was Cathleen ni Houlihan. She was crossing the bog towards the hills, springing from stone to stone over the treacherous surface, and the little white stones shone, marking a path behind her, then faded into the darkness" (vii). She obviously enjoyed the legends which grew up about her: "They are saying," she records, "you are a woman of the Sidhe who rode into Donegal on a white horse surrounded by birds to bring victory. No one can resist this woman" (134).

Since Yeats could not resist her, he tried conversion, but Maud was not vulnerable to his logic. "Willie Yeats accused me of responsibility for encouraging much bad art," she recalled, then added that she knew he would "put up a gallant fight for good art," and her only real concern was getting the message across (282). Yeats apparently thought of the theatre as a means of moving Maud to his viewpoint, and she stubbornly resisted, though she was willing to use the theatre to further the Nationalist movement. Three of Yeats's plays figure prominently in the tug-of-war thus set in motion: *The Countless Cathleen, The Shadowy Waters, and Cathleen ni Houlihan.* Although the story of *The Countess* has often been told, Maud's version has a special interest in this context. On one of those long evenings in her rooms over Morrow's Library, "Willie Yeats had read his play, *The Countess Kathleen*; he wanted to have it produced in Dublin and he wanted me to play in it. . . . I was severely tempted, for the play fascinated me and I loved acting, but just because I loved the stage so much I had made the stern resolve never to act. I was afraid it would absorb me too much to the detriment of my work. I knew my own weakness, and how, when I got interested in anything, I was capable of forgetting everything else — house-building, evicted tenants, political prisoners, even the fight against the British Empire, might all disappear in the glamour of the stage; it was the only form of self-discipline I consciously practised" (176). Maud was willing to use dramatic techniques for Ireland's cause, and even conducted a dramatic class for the Daughters of Ireland, though she refused to act in "any of the plays we used to produce" (177). But several members of her class, including Sally and Mary Allgood, did act in their plays.

On that memorable evening (Maud did not record the date) Yeats must have made his greatest effort to enlist her in the cause of intellectual nationalism, but he failed to touch her "unshakable resolve." "Willie Yeats was sad," she remembered, "and tried hard to persuade me to act the part of Countess Kathleen. 'I wrote it for you and if you don't act it we shall have to get an actress from London to take the part,' which eventually he did with no marked success" (177). According to Maud, both John O'Leary and John F. Taylor, who may have been present that night, approved of her refusal to act because "they probably understood my character and my fear of an absorption which would be detrimental to my work, in which they were interested, especially in its French side, that was beginning to be of real importance to the National struggle." When the last of her friends left as "the dawn was approaching," Yeats was still determined but foiled, though, in her words, "we were all anxious to help. It was part of the movement for capturing the intellectual life of Ireland for the National cause" (177). As usual, Maud was careful to establish the order of priority. On the same grounds also she approved the "new clothes" Willie had put on the fairies and ancient gods, though "the materials for these rainbow garments were not entirely of Irish weave" (178). But she was less certain of "the mists of the Celtic Twilight which shrouded with auras many weak effusions" such as "George Russell's bad paintings" (177).

By this time, surely, Yeats must have agreed with Aleel, in the revised version of *The Countess*, that "Cathleen has chosen other friends than us, / And they are rising through the hollow world." But Maud did yield to temptation just once — to play the lead in *Cathleen ni Houlihan*. Although anyone who reads *A Servant of the Queen* with some attention to Maud's delight in the sensation she was creating in Ireland as well as England and France will feel that vanity had much to do with her yielding, she felt compelled to explain her weakness in other terms: "The only exception I ever made was when I played Cathleen ni Houlihan, and I did it because it was only on that condition that Willie Yeats would give us the right of producing his play, and I felt that play would have great importance for the National movement" (177). After all, how could she resist playing the role of "the tall, beautiful woman with dark hair blown on the wind" (vii). Obviously this description of Queen Cathleen will serve quite as well for the Servant, as she looks in the photo of the frontispiece to Maud's book, at any rate.

Although Yeats gave *Cathleen* to the Fays instead of the Daughters of Ireland, Maud did play the lead and even brought some of her gifted Daughters into the company. If they felt "they had given themselves up to ambition and vanity," there is no evidence that Maud had a troubled conscience. Yeats declared that "she made Cathleen seem like a divine being fallen into our mortal infirmity," and induced her to become a vice-president of the Irish National Theatre.[27]

But life in the theatre was too tame for Maud, and she cared very little for any of Yeats's friends who were not *actively* engaged in the revolutionary struggle. She was glad, she said, that Yeats had found a friend in Lady Gregory, but "feared she would take him away from the fight for Irish freedom." Thinking of herself as Queen Cathleen, Maud contrasted Lady Gregory as "a queer little old lady, rather like Queen Victoria." Maud records that Lady Gregory "had asked me if I would marry Willie Yeats. It did not seem exactly her business, and I had answered rather shortly that we were neither of the marrying sort, having other things which interested us more; and I had thought she seemed rather relieved." Maud was suspicious of Lady Gregory's interest in "John O'Leary's literary group," and even of her entertainment of Willie and his friends in her Galway home: "when these writers came back from Coole," she observed, "they seemed to me less passionately interested in the National struggle and more worried about their own lack of money. . . . Lady Gregory and I were gracious to each other but never friends and in the later struggle in the theatre group, — Art for Art's sake or Art for Propaganda, — we were on different sides." After "Lady Gregory carried off Willie" to Italy, "Willie's national outlook underwent a complete change. There would be no more poems against English kings' visits." Willie was lost to what Maud called the "vehement expression of Irish Independence" (332–3). By this time, apparently, they had given up trying to convert each other, but Yeats urged the cause of union in the hope that he could thereby resolve Maud's bitter battle with the world. According to her dramatic memory, he continued to plead: "Oh Maud, why don't you marry me and give up this tragic struggle and live a peaceful life? I could make such a beautiful life for you among artists and writers who would understand you" (329). Maud knew, of course, that neither Willie nor his friends would appreciate her brand of politics. Since her book was written long after the event, Maud was probably not as perceptive as her celebrated answer proved to be:

"Willie, are you not tired of asking that question? How often have I told you to thank the gods that I will not marry you. You would not be happy with me."

"I am not happy without you."

"Oh yes, you are, because you make beautiful poetry out of what you call your unhappiness and you are happy in that. Marriage would be such a dull affair. Poets should never marry. The world should thank me for not marrying you." (329–30).

And, in fact, the world does thank Maud, for it is more true than she ever imagined that a great poet was almost literally made of his frustrated desire for "A proud woman not kindred of his soul" (V479). Failing to enlist Maud, Yeats conceived her as his symbolic opposite, and much of the poetry after his great disappointment reflects their social and political debate and projects her image—no longer as (V149–50)

> a glimmering girl
> With apple blossom in her hair
> Who called me by my name and ran
> And faded through the brightening air

but "A Helen of social welfare dream [who] climb[ed] on a wagonette to scream" (V626) — which is reminiscent of Miss Horniman's wry comment that "The greatest poet is always helpless beside a beautiful woman screaming from a cart."[28]

Yeats could insist in later times that "we are the true Ireland fighting the false"[29] — meaning thereby the Abbey Theatre versus Maud's cart — but he often seems certain that his choice is the right one only after the alternative is impossible, that is, after Maud's marriage in 1903. Although Yeats and Maud are perhaps idealised as Aengus and Edaine in *The Shadowy Waters*, which he continued to revise, she has a less important place in the plays beginning with *Where There Is Nothing*. Cathleen ni Houlihan married "a drunken vain-glorious lout" in February 1903; the poet reasserted his aesthetic determination, but Maud's shadow was always there. His poetry betrays Yeats's passionate ambivalence over his forced choice: (V495)

> The intellect of man is forced to choose
> Perfection of the life, or of the work,
> And if it take the second must refuse
> A heavenly mansion, raging in the dark.

Even when he seems certain, the lingering doubt remains: (V577)

> "The work is done," grown old he thought,
> "According to my boyish plan;
> Let the fools rage, I swerved in naught,
> Something to perfection brought";
> *But louder sang that ghost, "What then?"*

If Maud was not in fact that ghost, Yeats certainly had her in mind when he suggested the paradox with which he lived from 1903 to the end, and the evidence is clear that he not only understood the political polarities in his life, but also the importance to his work of the aesthetic tensions stimulated by these polar extremes. Seen from this angle, Yeats's verse represents the most significant body of political poetry in our time, possibly in all time.

As Yeats reviewed his own career for American audiences in 1932, he suggested that the whole body of his work should be considered a part of the third "formative movement" of "the modern Irish nation," which began, he said, "almost exactly forty years ago on a stormy autumn morning." Here as always, almost, Yeats's thoughts about nationalism are also thoughts about Maud. On that stormy morning he had gone to meet Maud at the Dun Laoghaire pier, where they witnessed by accident "the arrival of Parnell's body." From the psychic distance of forty years, Yeats looked upon that fabulous day as a symbolic shadowline dividing his earlier work from all that was to follow: "I have tried to explore, for the sake of my own peace of mind, the origin of what seems to me most unique and strange in our Irish excitement."[30] "I collect materials for my thought and work," he reflected, "for some identification of my beliefs with the nation itself."[31] Although Yeats could insist, in 1931, that "the fall of Parnell had freed imagination from practical politics, from agrarian grievance and political enmity, and turned it to imaginative nationalism, to Gaelic, to the ancient stories, and at last to lyrical poetry and to drama,"[32] he was still aware that "Man runs his course" "Between extremities" (V499): "Hitherto we have walked the road, but now we have shut the door and turned up the lamp."[33] "How can they know," he asked, (V398)

> Truth flourishes where the student's lamp has shone,
> And there alone, that have no solitude?

It is ironic, I think, to compare Yeats's confident assertion that the fall of Parnell had furthered the cause of "imaginative nationalism" to Kitty O'Shea's equally confident report that Parnell had "stood appalled at the intensity of the passion of hate that he had loosed, and no one but he — and I with him — knew the awful strength of that force of destruction."[34] Yeats knew the awful strength of intellectual hatred, of course, and was fascinated by it, though he sought (hopefully until 1903) to harness its destructive force. To Maud, in contrast, Parnell "had failed when he had repudiated acts of violence," and she thought that "the funeral of the Parliamentary party should have taken place when [he] was lowered into the grave at Glasnevin" (174).

Many if not all the good poems of *In the Seven Woods* (1903) reflect Yeats's agony over the loss of Maud, associated now with this frustration over cultural integration: (V206–7)

The old brown thorn-trees break in two high over Cummen Strand,
Under a bitter black wind that blows from the left hand;
Our courage breaks like an old tree in a black wind and dies,
But we have hidden in our hearts the flame out of the eyes
Of Cathleen, the daughter of Houlihan.

Having given "all his heart and lost" (V202), Yeats found some comfort in an old man's wisdom that (V208)

> All that's beautiful drifts away
> Like the waters;

and he sought to (V198)

> put away
> The unavailing outcries and the old bitterness
> That empty the heart.

He had in fact "forgot awhile" (V198)

> Tara uprooted, and new commonness
> Upon the throne and crying about the streets.

But not for long because he knew "the folly of being comforted" by rationalisations. Seven years later, in his next volume of poems, many of the lyrics reflect the "reconciliation" Yeats found in the knowledge that "love is the crooked thing" (V268) and that he "may wither into the truth" (V261) through the philosophic conclusion that Maud as opposite sets up the tension necessary to creation: (V256)

> Why should I blame her that she filled my days
> With misery, or that she would of late
> Have taught to ignorant men most violent ways,
> Or hurled the little streets upon the great,
> Had they but courage equal to desire?

He recognises frankly that (V256)

> I have come into my strength,
> And words obey my call,

because "you went from me" (V257).

Several of the lyrics from *The Green Helmet and Other Poems* project a fundamental difference in their approach to social change. To Maud, who was "half lion, half child," the answer to land reform was simple: "Shoot the landlords" (106). This was, to be sure, Maud's solution to all phases of the nationalist problem: "If . . . every Chief Secretary or Lord Lieutenant (or better still, every English king) were shot one after the other," she wrote, "Ireland would soon be free with small sacrifice of life" (347). Yeats, of course, was directly opposed to this resolution by fire: (V264)

> How should the world be luckier if this house,
> Where passion and precision have been one
> Time out of mind, became too ruinous
> To breed the lidless eye that loves the sun?

It was, I suppose, to be expected that one who believed in intellectual nationalism should fear the indiscriminate levelling process advocated by the "other side." Nothng will be acomplished if (V265)

> The weak lay hand on what the strong has done,
> Till that be tumbled that was lifted high
> And discord follow upon unison,
> And all things at one common level lie.

Some twenty-five years later, in a note to "Three Songs to the Same Tune," Yeats was saying the same in even stronger terms: "In politics I have but one passion and one thought, rancour against all who, except under the most dire necessity, disturb public order, a conviction that public order cannot long persist without the rule of educated and able men. That order was everywhere their work, is still as much a part of their tradition as the *Iliad* or the Republic of Plato; their rule once gone, it lies an empty shell for the passing fool to kick to pieces. Some months ago that passion laid hold upon me with the violence which unfits the poet for all politics but his own. While the mood lasted, it seemed that our growing disorder, the fanaticism that inflamed it like some old bullet imbedded in the flesh, was about to turn our noble history into an ignoble farce"[35] (V543). The refrain from the second of the "Three Songs," though referring to an altercation with a neighbour, reflects in its political context Maud's fanatic hatred in contrast to Yeats's passionate conviction that "Great nations blossom above": (V547)

> "Drown all the dogs," said the fierce young woman,
> "They killed my goose and a cat.
> Drown, drown in the water-butt,
> Drown all the dogs," said the fierce young woman.

By this time, ironically, Yeats himself was angry enough to "'Take to the roads and go marching along" because "nations are empty up there at the top" (V548).

He is no longer as certain as he had been in 1913 when he assured his "Companions of the Cheshire Cheese" that they had chosen the right way. "I have kept my faith," he wrote, then added sadly, (V276)

> I am in no good repute
> With the loud host before the sea,
> That think sword-strokes were better meant
> Than lover's music—let that be,
> So that the wandering foot's content.

It is clear, of course, that Yeats was not content. Many of the poems of *Responsibilities* almost shout his discontent that "the blind and ignorant town" (V287) has no "Delight in Art whose end is peace" (V288). He admits, in a note, that "we have but a few educated men and the remnants of an old traditional culture among the poor." Several poems are devoted to a bitter rebuke of "our new middle class . . . showing how base . . . at moments of excitement are minds without culture" (V819).

Insisting that "culture is the sanctity of the intellect," he filled a diary of these years with "my discontents," directly chiefly at "the lower-middle class" in general and Arthur Griffith in particular: ". . . the political class in Ireland," he reflected, "have suffered through the cultivation of hatred as the one energy of their movement, a deprivation which is the intellectual equivalent to a certain surgical operation. Hence the shrillness of their voices. They contemplate all creative power as the eunuchs contemplate Don Juan as he passes through Hell on the white horse."[36] Although the poems on *The Playboy* and Hugh Lane controversies do not seem to include Maud in their condemnation, Yeats was thinking of her. He implies in several poems of *Responsibilities* that she too is disillusioned: he "record[s] what's gone," and comments sadly that (V315)

> A crowd
> Will gather, and not know it walks the very street
> Whereon a thing once walked that seemed a burning cloud.

"She lived in storm and strife" (V317) and will be "broken in the end" (V313), whereas he, though suffering quite as much, can forgive and find peace through "companions / Beyond the fling of the dull ass's hoof," even though (V321)

> . . . all my priceless things
> Are but a post the passing dogs defile.

Between the publication of *Responsibilities* and *The Wild Swans at Coole* (1919) occurred two catastrophes which led Yeats to more profound thoughts on love and war: the Easter Revolution and World War I. Although his initial response to the revolution seems to justify the sacrifice and even suggests it is "enough / To know they dreamed and are dead" (V394), many doubts about the ultimate good of armed revolt remain: "Was it needless death after all?" (V394). The poem to Con Markievicz, who is frequently linked with Maud, suggests sadly that "too long a sacrifice" has made "a stone of the heart," and Yeats recalls (V397)

> the years before her mind
> Became a bitter, an abstract thing,
> Her thought some popular enmity:
> Blind and leader of the blind
> Drinking the foul ditch where they lie?

And one of the poems to Robert Gregory is bitterly ironic over what "we called . . . a good death": "Flit to Kiltartan cross," he advised the dead Robert, (V791)

> and stay
> Till certain second thoughts have come
> Upon the cause you served, that we
> Imagined such a fine affair:
> Half-drunk or whole-mad soldiery
> Are murdering your tenants there.[37]

Admitting to himself by 1916 that "We have no gift to set a statesman right" (V359), Yeats continued to vacillate between nationalistic polarities. One poem, in particular, contrasts his position with Maud's. When he upbraided "The People" and she "answered in reproof," (V352–3)

> All I could reply
> Was: "You, that have not lived in thought but deed,
> Can have the purity of a natural force,
> But I, whose virtues are the definitions
> Of the analytic mind, can neither close
> The eye of the mind nor keep my tongue from speech"

So it was to the very end: "The poet stubborn with his passion" (V356) sang the "victories of the mind" but "dream[ed] of a Ledaean body," frequently managing to suggest in the mind-body dilemma the paradox of Ireland's nationalistic struggle.[38] Although he wanted to believe "there are men who have made their art / Out of no tragic war" (V369), Yeats was not one of these. He felt that he (V384)

> had been undone
> By Homer's Paragon
> Who never gave the burning town a thought;

and he hoped that (V385)

> She would have time to turn her eyes,
> . . . upon the glass
> And on the instant would grow wise.

He never ceased to imagine what might have happened to him and Maud, and to Ireland by extension, if they had been able to avoid the (V506)

> Great hatred, little room, [which]
> Maimed us at the start.

"To be choked with hate," he wrote in "A Prayer for My Daughter," "May well be of all evil chances chief." He expanded this observation with a distinction in kinds of hatred which he increasingly emphasised in his late years: (V405)

> An intellectual hatred is the worst,
> So let her think opinions are accursed.

> Have I not seen the loveliest woman born
> Out of the mouth of Plenty's horn,
> Because of her opinionated mind
> Barter that horn and every good
> By quiet natures understood
> For an old bellows full of angry wind?

In order to justify his own impassioned reaction to social and political affairs, Yeats associated the "arrogance and hatred" of Maud and Con with "the wares / Peddled in the thoroughfares" (V406), in contrast to "the spiritual intellect's great work" (V632). It was the "abstract hatred" of "soldier, assassin, executioner" (V482) in contrast to the concrete wrath of the artist. There were, of course, times during "The Troubles" when Yeats himself, his (V426)

> wits astray
> Because of all that senseless tumult, all but cried
> For vengeance on the murderers of Jacques Molay.

Realising that he was about to fall into the trap he had warned against so diligently, he explained in a note: "A cry for vengeance because of the murder of the Grand Master of the Templars seems to me fit symbol for those who labour for hatred, and so for sterility in various kinds" (V827). It "fed class hatred," the very development he sought to counteract in the Unity of Culture.

Yeats knew from observation, however, that the passion of politics might be unifying, and he had learned from William Blake that "the tygers of wrath are wiser than the horses of instruction." But Blake's "honest indignation" is one thing, "abstract hatred" another. If Yeats was to avoid "the logic of fanaticism" (V837), he needed to assume the mask of (V576)

> Timon and Lear
> Or that William Blake
> Who beat upon the wall
> Till Truth obeyed his call.

Or, of course, Jonathan Swift, to whom he was indebted for (V481)

Saeva indignatio and the labourer's hire,
The strength that gives our blood and state magnanimity of its own desire;
Everything that is not God consumed with intellectual fire.

Tempted perhaps but not fierce enough to mount Maud's wagonette, Yeats nevertheless studied "hatred with great diligence," (V558)

> For that's a passion in my own control,
> A sort of besom that can clear the soul
> Of everything that is not mind or sense.

From this conclusion emerges the teasing paradox that "Hatred of God may bring the soul to God" (V558), which lies at the heart of Yeats's dilemma. As the artist (V637)

> lives and dies
> Between his two eternities
> That of race and that of soul,

he realises that the intellectual tension necessary to the creation of "a rest for the people of God" demands the union of contraries: Davis and Mitchel, Pearse and Connolly, Eva Gore-Booth and Constance, W. B. and Maud. "Under Ben Bulben" is convincing evidence that these nationalistic polarities were urgent to the very end: (V638)

> You that Mitchel's prayer have heard,
> "Send war in our time, O Lord!"
> Know that when all words are said
> And a man is fighting mad,
> Something drops from eyes long blind,
> He completes his partial mind,
> For an instant stands at ease,
> Laughs aloud, his heart at peace.
> Even the wisest man grows tense
> With some sort of violence
> Before he can accomplish fate,
> Know his work or choose his mate.

And it may well be that some degree of intellectual hatred is a necessary complement to any satisfactory scheme of intellectual nationalism. Cathleen ni Houlihan could be "Mother Ireland with the Crown of Stars about her head,"[39] but as Sean O'Casey observed on a riotous night at the Abbey, "one who had the walk of a queen could be a bitch at times."[40]

Notes

1. *Letters to the New Island*, ed. Horace Reynolds (Cambridge, Mass. 1934), p. 6. Compare also pp. 103–4.

2. *The Letters of W. B. Yeats*, ed. Allan Wade (New York 1955), pp. 421–2.

3. W. B. Yeats, *Autobiographies* (London 1956), p. 355. (Hereafter cited in the text as A and followed by the page numbers.) When he looked back upon his experience as a political organiser, Yeats felt "no different for it all, having but burgeoned and withered like a tree," p. 356.

4. *The Variorum Edition of the Poems of W. B. Yeats*, ed. Peter Allt and Russell K. Alspach (New York 1957), p. 256. Hereafter cited in the text as V and followed by the page numbers.

5. *Tribute to Thomas Davis* (Oxford 1947), p. 18. In the light of the ultimate division of Ireland, Yeats's next sentence is suggestive: "How could we learn from the harsh Ulster nature . . . a light that is the discovery of truth, or a sweetness that is obedience to its will?"

6. Quoted by Edward Sheehy, "Davis's Social Doctrines," *Thomas Davis and Young Ireland*, ed. M. J. MacManus (Dublin 1945), p. 30. Hereafter cited as MacManus.

7. *Ibid.*, p. 28.

8. T. F. O'Sullivan, *The Young Irelanders* (Tralee 1944), p. 44. Quoted from the prospectus for *The Nation* (15 October 1942). Hereafter cited as O'Sullivan.

9. Quoted by Frank Gallagher, "Davis and the Modern Revolution," MacManus, p. 9.

10. Quoted by Richard J. Loftus, *Nationalism in Modern Anglo-Irish Poetry* (Madison, Wisc. 1964), p. 6.

11. Quoted by O'Sullivan, pp. 32–3.

12. John Mitchel, *Jail Journal* (Dublin n.d.), p. 80

13. H. B. C. Pollard, *The Secret Societies of Ireland* (London 1922), p. 68. Not confined to Mitchel, this remark is typical of Pollard's bitter denunciation of Ireland's "malignant and terrible secret associations," p. x.

14. Quoted by Kevin B. Nowlan, "Charles Gavin Duffy and the Repeal Movement," (O'Donnell Lecture, University College Dublin, May 1963), p. 19. This excellent article outlines the divisive issues clearly.

15. Quoted by O'Sullivan, p. 143. Compare Yeats's obvious enjoyment of "the words of a medieval Gaelic poet, 'We are a sword people and we go with the sword' " (*Wheels and Butterflies*, London 1934), p. 13.

16. *Prison Letters of Countess Markievicz*, ed. Esther Roper (London 1934), p. 226.

17. Quoted by O'Sullivan, p. 131.

18. *Ibid.*, p. 132.

19. Quoted by Cathal O'Shannon, "James Fintan Lalor," MacManus, p. 70.

20. *Ibid.*, p. 77. From Mitchel's short biography of Thomas Francis Meagher.

21. O'Sullivan, p. 80. At the same meeting Devin Reilly moved and Mitchel seconded a motion "to inquire and report on the best and most effectual means of organising an armed National Guard," p. 80.

22. Yeats, *Letters*, p. 39.

23. Quoted by Sheehy, MacManus, p. 31.

24. *A Servant of the Queen* (London 1938), p. 158. All quotations from Maud are from this book, cited hereafter by page references in the text.

25. "Discoveries: Second Series," *Irish Renaissance*, ed. Robin Skelton and David R. Clark (Dublin 1965), p. 87.

26. Of the many passages in *A Servant of the Queen* which illustrate Maud's delight in casting herself in the role of some mythical heroine, one is especially suggestive. According to Maud, Millevoye, her revolutionary friend whose "whole ambition . . . was to win back Alsace-Lorraine for France," urged her to an action she had no doubt already dreamed: "Why don't you free Ireland as Joan of Arc freed France? You don't understand your own power. To hear a woman like you talk of going on the stage is infamous. Yes, you might become a great *actrice*; but if you became as great an *actrice* as Sarah Bernhardt, what of it? An *actrice* is only imitating other people's emotions; that is not living; that is only being a *cabotine*, nothing else. Have a more worthy ambition, free your own country, free Ireland," pp. 64–5. On still another occasion, at the Bal Irlandais in Paris, a "florid gentleman . . . called for cheers for Ireland's Joan of Arc, which was responded to vociferously," p. 169. George Moore also records that "Maud Gonne believes herself to be Joan of Arc" and suggests that Irish revolutionaries thought she "would prove herself to be an Irish Joan of Arc," *Hail and Farewell*, 1, pp. 78, 91.

27. Joseph Hone, *W. B. Yeats* (New York 1943), pp. 183–4.

28. *Ibid.*, p. 223.

29. Letter to Lady Gregory, in *Our Irish Theatre* (New York 1965), 211.

30. *Irish Renaissance*, pp. 13–14.

31. *Wheels and Butterflies*, p. 7.

32. *Ibid.*, p. 5.

33. *Ibid.*, p. 6.

34. Quoted by Herbert Howarth, *The Irish Writers* 1880–1940 (London 1958), p. 294.

35. The image of the imbedded bullet recalls Maud's pride in a brooch, which she "always wore," made from a bullet found in the grave of a French soldier" who died for Ireland in 1798, p. 229.

36. Quoted by John Unterecker, *A Reader's Guide to William Butler Yeats* (London 1959), pp. 120–1. Griffith was named in the diary but not in *Discoveries*, the published version.

37. Yeats omitted this poem, "Reprisals," from the *Collected Poems* because he feared Lady Gregory might be hurt by the implication that Robert was "Among the other cheated dead."

38. Yeats may have been thinking of himself and Maud in these wellknown lines: (V386)

> Did God in portioning wine and bread
> Give man His thoughts or His mere body?

39. W. B. Yeats, *Essays and Introductions* (London 1961), p. 249. "Miss Maud Gonne could still gather great crowds," Yeats wrote in 1907, ". . . and speak to them of 'Mother Ireland with the crown of stars about her head'; but gradually the political movement she was associated with, finding it hard to build up any fine lasting thing, became content to attack little persons and little things. All movements are held together more by what they hate than by what they love, for love separates and individualises and quiets, but the nobler movements, the only movements on which literature can found itself, hate great and lasting things," pp. 249–50. Here apparently Yeats is not distinguishing between degrees or kinds of hatred, but between the qualities of its objects. The point is that he thought it necessary to distinguish between the hatred engendered by Maud's political movement and that of his movement, and he felt the force of both.

40. *Autobiographies* (London 1963), II, p. 150. O'Casey also is talking indirectly about the two nationalistic groups. Recalling the riots over *The Plough and Stars*, he records: "Sean felt a surge of hatred for Cathleen ni Houlihan sweeping over him. He saw now that the one who had the walk of a queen could be a bitch at times. She galled the hearts of her children who dared to be above the ordinary, and she often slew her best ones. She had hounded Parnell to death: she had yelled and torn at Yeats, at Synge, and now she was doing the same to him. What an old snarly gob she could be at times; an ignorant one too."

Tragic War   Daniel A. Harris*

In "Vacillation" Yeats posed the central question of *The Winding Stair*:

> The body calls it death,
> The heart remorse.

*From *Yeats: Coole Park & Ballylee* (Baltimore and London: Johns Hopkins University Press, 1974), 201–22.

But if these be right
What is joy?

[I]

"A Dialogue of Self and Soul" (1927) and "Blood and the Moon" (1926–27)[1] seek what "Meditations . . ." had failed to wrest from civil war, a tangible joy. Both poems tacitly acknowledge that "The Tower," for all its imaginative scope, is an insular poem whose joy is never tested against present history.

The poems share a background of political violence. On July 10, 1927, the IRA assassinated Kevin O'Higgins, the Minister of Justice, in retaliation for executions of their members. Yeats was shocked; O'Higgins had been a personal friend, "the one strong intellect in Irish public life,"[2] de Valéra's opponent and an intense conservative committed to Anglo-Irish ideals of integrity and service. Yeats, assuming personal responsibility for the tragedy, placed his guilt within so universal a context that it signified the Fall: political experience and Western mythology converged. Feeling "the helplessness of human life,"[3] he recounted to Olivia Shakespear certain premonitions he had disregarded the night before the ambush, and concluded: "Had we seen more he might have been saved, for recent evidence seems to show that those things are fate unless foreseen by clairvoyance and so brought within the range of free-will."[4] Yeats's guilt was not a neurotic self-laceration but a philosophic judgment on the inscrutable byways of the human psyche in relation to the totality of conscious and unconscious thought. Not the post-Treaty political morass but the epistemological failure of humankind to comprehend its own nature was the ultimate cause of O'Higgins's death. "Had we seen more he might have been saved": metaphysical blindness is sin.

That philosophical gloom suffuses the poems. In "A Dialogue of Self and Soul," Self claims that "A living man is blind and drinks his drop" (II.i); intrinsic blindness is less corrigible than the optimistic illusions castigated in "Nineteen Hundred. . . ." Soul terms existence the unredeemable "crime of death and birth" (I.iii); his call to escape the cycles of time reflects Yeats's revulsion. In "Blood and the Moon" the speaker smells "Odour of blood on the ancestral stair!" (III). Derangement and purification are obsessions: "What theme had Homer but original sin?" ("Vacillation," VII). The poem shows how Yeats transformed a public event into private drama. O'Higgins's death, completely assimilated into the tower's ecology, is invisible.[5] The emotions it prompted, the philosophical and religious issues it raised have been molded with intimate passion into generalization: Yeats attributed to the tower the contamination he felt, wrote in "Blood and the Moon" (III) *as if* the event had occurred at Thoor Ballylee, and used that implosive pressure to transmute his own experience into a crisis of the human spirit.

O'Higgins's death catalyzed the increasingly dialectical debate concerning the value of human life which Yeats had explicitly begun in *The*

Tower and its title poem. Soul seeks to transform Self's architectural heritage, the "winding, gyring, spiring treadmill of a stair" ("Blood and the Moon," II.ii), into the spiritual staircase of mystical ascent. The radical repudiation of earthly sanctity, the chief goal of Yeats's speakers, is a logical development in Yeats's exploration of the tower. His architectural iconography shows a clear progression from the tower's earth-bound base to its top, a visionary promontory. "Ego Dominus Tuus" occurs outside; in "A Prayer on Going into My House," the speaker is at the tower's threshold; in "The Phases of the Moon," the poet has reached his second-floor study. The speaker of "In Memory of Major Robert Gregory" is in the ground-floor dining area. "Meditations . . ." contains more dynamic movement than any other of the poems: the speaker begins outside (I, II), goes to his study (III), descends to his doorway to meet the "affable Irregular" and Lieutenant (V), returns to his study (VI), and then — the move is crucial — escapes, for the first time in the poetry, to the tower-top (VII), where he ironically suffers a vision of history so terrifying that he must "shut the door" and "turn" downstairs (VII.v). On the battlements in "The Tower," he *seeks* a visionary understanding and gains, within time, a moment of transcendent joy. The mystical ascent proposed in "A Dialogue of Self and Soul" climaxes Yeats's fascination with the tower's top and what lies beyond it, the contemplative world of the spirit's perfection. Because the poem so emphatically polarizes the tower's base and top, Self's choice not to ascend appears all the more decisive. The poem is Yeats's most blunt, tragic affirmation of existence.

"A Dialogue of Self and Soul" is appropriately the most ethereal of the 'tower' poems. It originates *ex nihilo*, and the unexplained, ghostly beginning shocks. In Marvell's "A Dialogue between the Soul and Body," you accept a motiveless opening because the participants are abstractions. But in Yeats, Soul as well as Self has a body (e.g., "my tongue's a stone," I.v), and you quite properly want to know how he arrived at Thoor Ballylee.[6] The effect of that incongruous reification is spectral. When Soul summons Self (I.i), he explains *what* is happening, but not *why*. Even when he justifies his command (I.iii), he does not satisfactorily indicate why the alternative to earthly meditation should necessarily be a renunciatory devotion to mystical union. That it is usually so in Christianity and sometimes so in Yeats (especially when he pits the swordsman against the saint) are arguments which do not diminish the inscrutability of this poem's drama.

Soul's mysterious visitation occurs because Self is in a trance, a semi-conscious reverie. Like the ghosts who "break upon a sleeper's rest" in "The Tower" (II.ix), he enters because the conscious will, which bars influx of the unknown, is half-asleep. Self, apprehending Soul only instinctively, never addresses him directly; trance produces a curiously diaphanous conversation whose logic of progression is almost always suppressed. Heightening the aura of reverie, Yeats deliberately obscured the spatiotemporal connections expected from earlier poems. The debate, a permanent human struggle, has no particular historical context. All references to weather and landscape at the tower's base, including the familiar storm of earthly complexities, have been omitted; instead, Soul alludes to a shimmering, "breathless starlit air" (I.i). The tower itself has lost its substantiality, and Soul mentions its "broken, crumbling battlement" (I.i) only to convince Self of transience. Compare "Meditations . . ." (VII.i): "I climb to the tower-top and *lean* upon broken stone." That crucial bodily pressure epitomizes the tactility which the dialogue eschews. Soul will not even deign to acknowledge Self's corporeal body; note the ellipsis in "I summon [you] to the winding ancient stair." Yeats, when he presented the tower, saw through Soul's eyes, including nothing to jeopardize an atmosphere conducive to Self's ascent.

Yet before the poem begins, Self has made his "choice of rebirth rather than deliverance from birth."[7] Seated in the tower's lower regions, he stubbornly refuses through his very posture to yield to Soul's temptation. The fact that he triumphs by belief rather than argument raises important questions about Yeats's purpose in writing a "dialogue." Yeats's subject was Adam's curse and the modes of responding to knowledge of sin, and not the *process* of self-affirmation. Dialogue obviously gained him a dual perspective; but the poem's form actually offers *three* opposed visions of temporal reality. Soul's asceticism is plain. Self, however, has two conceptions of his mortal state. The first, in section I, is induced by trance, a partial separation from reality which softens the vision of evil: it is a romantic, somewhat self-deluding fascination with the productions of time. But in his monologue (II), Self is rudely awakened into the purgatory of his own nature. In the passage of *Paradise Lost* to which Yeats alluded in "Under Ben Bulben" (IV), Adam tells Raphael how he dreamed Eden and then

> wak'd, and found
> Before mine Eyes all real, as the dream
> Had lively shadow'd . . .
>   [VIII, 11.309–11]

The discrepancies in vision between Self and Soul, and between Self dreaming and Self waking, result from the Fall, the loss of unitary perception. Through structure, Yeats illustrated within a very brief span the fragmentation which renders all psychic activity conflict and pain (the blindness Self derides in section II is partly his own in section I), and produced an increasingly ferocious account of the price one pays for living.

Unlike the speaker of "Meditations . . . ," Self does not choose between poetic contemplation and action in the world, but between experience (which, as in "The Tower," includes poetry) and a mystical transcendence which denies art. The poet, because he takes his images from the sensuous world, cannot leave it without sacrificing his vocation; he must submit his soul to its chaos. These aesthetic principles are familiar. Yet Self, remarkably, nowhere employs them; nor does he identify himself as a poet. In this respect the poem is unique in the "tower" series.[8] He neither mentions "pen and paper" ("Meditations . . . ," III) nor invokes his literary ancestors ("Ego Dominus Tuus," "Blood and the Moon," II). He makes his choice as a human being. Art is no longer a detached "vision of reality" ("Ego Dominus Tuus") but an organic part of that reality; art and experience, though opposed in many respects, nevertheless join in common, guilty cause to reject the imageless infinite. A decade earlier, Ille had superciliously pitied the fate of the poet who identifies himself with humankind: "The struggle of the fly in marmalade." Self shows no such squeamishness masquerading as hieratic pride. He claims "as by a soldier's right / A charter to commit the crime once more" (I.iv). Soul may usurp the tower, but he cannot erase Self's memory of ghostly "men-at-arms" ("The Tower," II.ix). He cannot, in short, combat the *genius loci* at Thoor Ballylee.

Thus, instead of the shapeless nothing at the "hidden pole" which Soul proffers (I.i), Self contemplates a changeless symbol of "love and war" which unites the world's antinomies in aesthetic form, "consecrated" to Self because it poses an "artifice of eternity" against eternity itself. Sato's sword, though still an emblem of aristocratic perfection, differs fundamentally from the same sword in "Meditations . . ." (III). There is no pretense of identifying the sword's permanence with the "soul's unchanging look." The sword, although "Unspotted" (I.ii), belongs to the fallen realm of blood; it is "razor-keen." Having seen the sword brandished in the apocalypse of "Meditations . . ." (VII.i), Self can no longer blink the tumultuous violence it implies. And compare "A bit of an embroidered dress / Covers its wooden sheath" ("Meditations . . . ," III) with Self's fanciful embellishment, "That flowering, silken, old embroidery, *torn* / From some court-lady's dress. . . ." "Torn," alluding to murder or rape, is rhymed with "adorn"; the juxtaposition accurately defines the sword's mesmeric, "terrible beauty." Self seeks, as from a talisman, a reflection of its power. Lying not on his work-table but across his knees, it has merged with his total bodily figure in a posture of defense. And yet, the symbol continues to express more than Self, entranced, knows — although his evasions are less drastic than in "Meditations . . ." (III). Self recognizes the antinomies it embodies, but not their harshness. "Heart's purple" (I.iv) should be blood of the slain; instead, it is a badge of high passion and a refulgent epithet for the color of the embroidered flowers. Wistful but deliberate vagueness — "Flowers from *I know not what* embroidery" — blurs the truth of the earlier fancy, "torn / From some court-lady's dress." Flowing adumbration of adjectives and lush, incantatory repetition pastoralize the violence. All is seen as a remote chivalric drama.

Were Self less rapt, Soul might wittily have accused him of acting like Falstaff, wenching in his dotages. Instead, he makes an oratorical flourish:

> Why should the imagination of a man
> Long past his prime remember things that are
> Emblematical of love and war?
>
> [I.iii]

The impropriety of Self's egocentric fancy of his own juvenescence is the least of Soul's criticisms. Self has blindly embraced illusion (the sword) instead of reality (the "hidden pole"). Lacking that center of truth, Self's intellect must inevitably wander, as in the reverie itself. Recognizing Self's penchant for antiques, Soul lures him with "ancestral night" (I.iii) — like Phase One of the Great Wheel, a condition of "complete passivity, complete plasticity,"[9] superhuman, amoral. Instead of mere trance, he offers total release from consciousness. Fixing upon Self's occasional longings for annihilation (as in "Nineteen Hundred . . . ," III), Soul insidiously tempts Self with Self's own language of escape, drawn from "Meditations . . ." (VII.iii):

> Such fullness in that quarter overflows
> And falls into the basin of the mind
> That man is stricken deaf and dumb and blind,
> For intellect no longer knows
> *Is* from the *Ought*, or *Knower* from the *Known*.
>
> [I.v]

Soul's central promise is innocence, deliverance from the "crime of death and birth" (I.iii). Self has not fathomed the unreprieved horror of generation and destruction. Will and action have nothing to do with sin: existence is sin. The human power to sanctify — Self has called the blade "consecrated" — is a delusion.

> Only the dead can be forgiven . . .
>
> [I.v]

But Soul's stark pronouncement is ironically more than he had meant to say. He had intended to guide Self to a spiritual purgation which nevertheless left the body intact. Yet as his pessimism overtakes him, the premises of classical mysticism collapse. There is no way out except physical death,

> But when I think of that my tongue's a stone.
>
> [I.v]

Even Soul will not counsel suicide. The stone, hardly the fiery coal which purifies "unclean lips" (Isaiah 6:5; see "Vacillation," VII), symbolizes the spiritual vacuity of Soul's message. Defeated by his own inexorable logic, Soul recoils from despair, his tongue dehumanized; and Self's trance is broken.[10]

In plotting Soul's crisis, Yeats brilliantly hardened the lines of debate within the poem itself, closed off all alternatives to criminal existence except death *or* the affirmation of life despite its criminality. Yet Soul's reversal, while necessary dramatically, is psychologically gratuitous;[11] Self has already reasserted his commitment to the sword:

> and all these I *set*
> For *emblems* of the day against the tower
> *Emblematical* of the *night*,
> And claim as by a soldier's right
> A charter to commit the *crime* once more.
>
> [I.iv]

Self's subconscious assimilation of Soul's vocabulary (italicized) represents his complete acceptance of Soul's judgment on the world. Had he done less, the victorious bluntness of his "choice of rebirth" would have been vitiated. He makes absolutely no attempt to substitute a more palatable euphemism for Soul's piercing word "crime," and indeed uses it in a phrase—"commit the crime"—which evokes the very sexuality Soul abhors.[12] The paradoxical legal language suggests both that Soul's summons violates natural law and that natural law is chaotic: Soul has violated the institutionalized anarchy of existence. Finally, the repetition of "emblems," "Emblematical," scoffs at Soul's Philistinism and asserts the primacy of the imagination; for Soul has proposed questing for a "quarter" where symbol is both unnecessary and impossible.

Self now confronts—without benefit of chivalric fiction—the criminality he has chosen. He is "A blind man battering blind men" (II.iii) in furious flailings. Having willfully imprisoned himself, he executes a typically Yeatsian maneuver: he controls the grotesque absurdity of his experience by embracing it. The definition of humankind is cynically abrupt:

> A living man is blind and drinks his drop.
> What matter if the ditches are impure?
> What matter if I live it all once more?
>
> [II.i]

As he transforms imagery remembered from section I with dazzlingly illogical insight, Self mocks all thought of transcendence. Man, blind in daylight, needs no "ancestral night"; and, dizzy in compensatory stupor, why should he need the trembling ecstasy of the saint? A "drop," moreover, ought to be a drink in a pub; but the snide rejoinder to such implied coziness—"What matter if the ditches are impure?"—twists the landscape into a phantasmagoria where the outcast, animalized, "drinks the green mantle of the standing pool" like Poor Tom (*King Lear*, III.iv.135–36). Soul's asceticism, although rejected, permeates Self's deepest thought. If Self repudiates the Platonic universe and any aesthetic which considers art the twice-removed shadow of an ideal type, he also recognizes that Sato's sword—fostering an illusion of secular purity—has protected him too well. In no other of Yeats's major works is the world's attraction so repugnant.

Unflinching, Self meditates not on a distant aristocracy but on his daily agony, knowing that he must

> Endure that toil of growing up;
> The ignominy of boyhood; the distress
> Of boyhood changing into man;
> The unfinished man and his pain
> Brought face to face with his own clumsiness;
>
> The finished man among his enemies [.]
>   [II.i–ii]

The bitter variation on "Among School Children" (V) is no less than Self's criminal "delivery" into a new cycle. With terrific speed the anticipated future becomes the experienced present. As the crucial demonstrative adjective ("*that* toil") and the minutely sequential discrimination of pains indicate, the stages of what Eliot called "the rending pain of re-enactment"[13] are already vivid to the imagination. Although the passage corresponds to that portion of the afterlife Yeats designated *The Return*, it differs significantly in lacking a teleology.[14] Yeats's theory in *A Vision* sets forth a thoroughly organized process of expiation whereby the Spirit, variously recapitulating its life, finally casts out "remorse" and becomes—temporarily—innocent. The mental suffering entailed is consequently purposive. No such justification of agony graces the passage at hand ("What matter . . . ?"). Not until the last stanza can Self discover a purgative value in the anarchy and guilt he confronts, the inescapable labyrinths of which Soul has warned. The searing relevation, parodying Paul (I Cor. 13:12), ends in a bleak admission of pointless doom. "Finished man," if it recalls Montashigi's completed aristocratic quest, cuts through such remote fictions with a morbid pun—"finished" / "dead"—which evokes a self-mocking parody of heroic combat. For the only time in Yeats's work, completion of the quest is irrelevant, useless.

Silently, Self remembers Soul's promise of deliverance, yet

> How in the name of Heaven can he escape
> That defiling and disfigured shape
> The mirror of malicious eyes
> Casts upon his eyes until at last
> He thinks that shape must be his shape?
> And what's the good of an escape
> If honour find him in the wintry blast?
>   [II.ii]

The exasperation conceals a passion to renege on the choice. But the reiterated rhyme—"shape" / "escape"—defines the prison: even Soul could not surrender his body. Self, moreover, has no particular "shape" to "escape" from. The echoing repetition of "shape" makes nebulous what should be a circumscribed image. Self's shapelessness manifests physically his lack of identity, the lack of unitary self-perception which criminality imposes. Compounded of others' hatreds and his own, he resembles the Hunchback of Phase Twenty-six, nearly the exact opposite of the "perfectly proportioned human body" which signifies internal unity.[15] Only Sato's polished blade, "still like a looking-glass," retains its clear form; but Self has discovered that it reflects neither the world nor his own deformity, but something other and less obtainable. The culminating irony is that Self, spurning mystical ascent because it demands self-dissolution, finds himself already dissolved by irreconcilable perspectives. Yet the indomitable desire for "honour" — the illusion of selfhood — remains: farcical, tragic, hopelessly human. Unlike Yeats's ghost in "Little Gidding" (II), Self never learns that "fools' approval stings, and honour stains."

Superimposing self-pacification in the face of all that is humiliating and absurd, Self reasserts his "right," yet without vaunting any power to "claim": "I am content to live it all again." The contentment is minimal, vile; the galling qualification follows inevitably, quickening into a suicidal embrace of life,

> if it be life to pitch
> Into the frog-spawn of a blind man's ditch,
> A blind man battering blind men;
> Or into that most fecund ditch of all,
> The folly that man does
> Or must suffer, if he woos
> A proud woman not kindred of his soul.
>
> [II.iii]

The compulsive return to the double theme of love and war is the raw climax of the decision made in "The Tower" (II.xiii). Knowing no action can damage a "self" which is but an artificed construct, he plunges into crude generation, lured neither by noble passion nor by deceptive emblems of heroic glory.

Critics have often interpreted all of section II as Self's affirmation both of identity and of experience.[16] But not until the end can Self find valid reasons for his existence or begin what the mystical ascent precludes, the quest for self-understanding:

> I am content to follow to its source
> Every event in action or in thought;
> Measure the lot; forgive myself the lot!
> When such as I cast out remorse
> So great a sweetness flows into the breast
> We must laugh and we must sing,
> We are blest by everything,
> Everything we look upon is blest.
>
> [II.iv]

Contradicting for the first time Soul's judgment on human criminality, Self asserts imagination's power to confer absolution upon experience. Though he shares neither Satan's glibness nor his characteristic evasions of responsibility, Self claims in effect that "The mind is its own place, and in itself / Can make a Heav'n of Hell, a Hell of Heav'n" (*Paradise Lost*, I.254–55). Self-mercy—what Yeats's speakers so conspicuously lack—finally emerges. The desired consequence of such sweet purgation—a remarriage to Soul, suggested by the reiterated "we" and the concluding chiasmic structure—is the earthly re-creation of original Adamic unity. Unlike Coleridge's mariner, who blesses the water snakes before expiating his guilt and thus blesses "unaware" ("The Ancient Mariner," Part IV, 11. 272ff.), Self must cleanse himself first; his consecration will be fully conscious. Yeats's reversals of Coleridge imply his goal: an earned and controlled visionary joy, the capacity to experience in waking perception the awe with which Self initially contemplates Sato's consecrated blade.

What warrant has Self for his warm jubilation? None: the unexplained leap from the self-understanding of an interior hell to self-forgiveness, personal and cosmic blessedness, is essential to the stanza's design. Yeats somewhere cited Tertullian, *Credo quia absurdum*. Knowledge is not enough; Self affirms the consecration of earth because he must, not because it is logically permissible to do so. A strictly trochaic scansion of the counterpointed line, "We must laugh and we must sing," does not adequately render the obligatory force of "must." The time-structure emphasizes the greatness of his need. The future-oriented syntax (e.g. "I am content to *follow*") makes plain that the quest has barely begun.[17] Yet the vision of potential reunification so overwhelms Self that he switches tense:

> We *are* blest by everything,
> Everything we *look* upon *is* blest.

No rhetorically imposed solution, but the mirror of passionate desire, the shift has the suddenness of self-revelation.

Self's radical gesture toward his own secular beatitude is a critical moment in Yeats's career and the tower's history. No claim for the imagination's autonomy is so extensive as this. To create a sacred territory through ritual exclusions, to achieve a timeless moment through the study of history—these characteristic imaginative acts are not of the same order as Self's bestowing of absolution upon himself and "Everything."[18] When Yeats first explored Thoor Ballylee, his imagination—for all its daring—was in part imitative, receptive. He followed Dante, accepted Gregory's counsel, prayed that he might handle nothing "But what the great and passionate have used" ("A Prayer on Going into My House"). The tower's stones were his model; he half expected wisdom, isolate strength, the richness in Irish tradition to emanate from the soil, and sought his own purification by sanctifying his territory. But repeated onslaughts against his space invalidated that imaginative mode. The realization which "A Dialogue of Self and Soul" encompasses is that blessedness cannot be absorbed by osmosis. This poem, consequently, has no territory to speak of, and the tower has nearly vanished. Self's beneficent joy depends upon nothing in the world which Yeats's earlier speakers have meditated into being; it has no objectifications such as the transformed landscape in "In Memory of Major Robert Gregory" (VII) or that in "The Tower" (III); nor is it localized in "a house / Where all's accustomed, ceremonious." The joy is a motion of the spirit which occurs in its own place and time, and no other.

II

"Blood and the Moon" follows the dialogue directly, as if in quarrel. Its speaker faces the difficult responsibility of validating, within historical particulars, Self's ahistorical faith in human sanctity. He understands all too clearly that his "choice of rebirth" compels him to relive more than personal memory. If he cannot exercise his consecrative imagination to redeem the confusions of his national experience, then he must acknowledge, with Soul, the bondage of his supposedly autonomous creativity. The drama thus played out at Thoor Ballylee involves exactly the problem of expiating cultural sin which drives the Old Man in *Purgatory* to kill (murder? sacrifice?) his father and his son.

The speaker begins with a brutally swift ritual of purification immeasurably distant not only from the serene elation in Self's "blest" preception of terrestrial glory but from the modest orthodoxy of "A Prayer on Going into My House":

> Blessed be this place,
> More blessed still this tower;
> A bloody, arrogant power
> Rose out of the race
> Uttering, mastering it,
> Rose like these walls from these
> Storm-beaten cottages . . .
>
> [I]

The consecration, even as it overwhelms all skepticism, anticipates the poem's dark conclusion: the profanation of ground initially made sacred by the speaker's own demand. The growling, dogmatic affirmation wars against a "time / Half dead at the top," strains against the mind's inveterate powerlessness to will sanctity. Flaunting a vengeful pride as he reclaims his usurped tower, the speaker blesses everything Soul had disparaged. He blinks no ugliness, exults in naked physical power (rhymed throughout with "tower"), revels in language designed to affront Soul's sensibilities and thus banish forever the temptations of infinity.

The tower's architectural evolution is Irish history itself, given compact mythological continuity in his own territory. As linear time dissolves in symbol, the Anglo-Norman, Anglo-Irish presence becomes a monolith, rising "like these walls." The tragic paradox, that such a violent mastery ultimately expressed most fully the ethos of the conquered Celtic aristocracy, is reiterated poetically in the speaker's own consecration: as he utters the tower's nature, masters its identity, he reenacts its founding; then, traversing seven centuries, he wheels about to scorn the worthless present:

> In mockery I have set
> A powerful emblem up,
> And sing it rhyme upon rhyme
> In mockery of a time
> Half dead at the top.
>
> [I]

Seemingly, the tower immunizes him against all he despises: violations of aristocratic tradition ("In Memory of Eva Gore-Booth and Con Markiewicz," the opening poem in *The Winding Stair*), emasculation of the heroic ideal ("Statistics"), the decline of literature ("The Nineteenth Century and After"), the "levelling, rancorous, rational sort of mind" typical of modern Irish pettiness ("The Seven Sages"). Consequently deriding foulness, the speaker is hardly "content" to "pitch / Into the frogspawn of a blind man's ditch."

Thus, Thoor Ballylee is both a consecrated place and the epitome of satiric hatred. These irreconcilably opposed definitions haunt the speaker: the mockery may turn corrosively inward, diminish his power to demarcate sacred ground. Is he not, as in "Nineteen Hundred . . ." (V), part of the world he condemns, perhaps its symptomatic figure? The poem dramatizes the appalling paradox of a man so tormented by the smell of mortality that he can seek a saving self-protection only by means wholly subversive of that end: "More substance in our enmities / Than in our love" ("Meditations . . . ," VI.iv). Even at the outset he hides in derision his fear that sanctuary may be impossible. "Half dead at the top," explicitly characterizing the corrupt "time," is also a vertical image of the tower: the image has psychological intensity precisely because it evokes the architectural analogy in ways which the speaker fails to recognize. Not until the terrifying rhetorical question (IV) does his suspicion of the tower's contamination become explicit knowledge:

> Is every modern nation like the tower,
> Half dead at the top?

Yeats marvelously calibrated these sole poetic uses of the tower's topmost Stranger's Room to show the drastic metamorphosis in understanding which finally renders tower and world indistinguishable. As the structure of this simile suggests, the tower has become the source and model of the world's deterioration. Corresponding to "Rose like these walls" (I), it completes the paradigmatic cycle of creation and dissolution which the tower incorporates. The attempt to consecrate ends in renewed consciousness of primal guilt.

As he faces that imminent knowledge, the fear of derangement burgeons. The ghost of Swift in his madness hovers like a fury over this poem even before the speaker names him. Consider Young's anecdote about Swift which spurred Yeats to make his architecture an image of *dementia*: ". . . [I] found him [Swift] fixed as a statue; and earnestly gazing upward at a noble elm, which in its most uppermost branches, was much withered and decayed. Pointing at it, he said, 'I shall be like that tree, I shall die at top.' "[19] This ominous specter, the speaker's *genius loci* and that of Anglo-Irish culture, is sublimally present in the first use of "Half dead at the top." In Yeats's instinctive conflation of tree and tower, Swift's obsessive terror of insanity materializes. The tower, animated with his quietly hysterical prophecy, becomes a person helplessly losing control. The amalgamation of self and architecture is even darker than in "Meditations . . ." (VI.i): "My wall is loosening." To evade it, the speaker turns to consider other towers (II.i), the architectural tradition symbolic of Western thought which Thoor Ballylee now threatens to end. "Alexandria's was a beacon tower" of unimpaired spiritual illumination; Babylon's symbolized not terrestrial convulsions but the rationalized order of the cosmos. Shelley's towers were "thought's crowned powers": the image of the head compensates for the dangerous allusion to Swift by emphasizing the strength of the intact mind; stark "power" is transmuted to "powers," the faculties of the exuberant intellect.

None of these towers resembles the speaker's. Undeterred by the sinister discrepancies, he accepts his dwelling with bitter triumph:

> I declare this tower is my symbol; I declare
> This winding, gyring, spiring treadmill of a stair is my ancestral stair;
> That Goldsmith and the Dean, Berkeley and Burke have travelled there.
>
> [II.ii]

This, Yeats's most radical possession of the tower, is also the most ambiguous. The last clause is self-consciously outrageous, a bizarre consolidation of his Anglo-Irish kin which deliberately contravenes history. Raftery and Mrs. French may well have "passed this door" ("The Tower," II.xi); Swift? Burke?—never. The act of populating Thoor Ballylee, far more compulsive than in "In Memory of Major Robert Gregory" or "The Tower," measures his need to house a quickly disappearing heritage within an impermeable bulwark. But his ancestors inhabit a dangerous environment. The stairwell is neither the defined space of the "narrow winding stairs" ("In Memory of Major Robert Gregory," I) nor the path of mystical ascent ("A Dialogue of Self and Soul," I). It is a maze and prison, the "treadmill" of human life. Its spirit is that of Piranesi or the "cunning passages, Contrived corridors" of history in Eliot's "Gerontion," not that of the diagrams in *A Vision*. Although "winding" refers to the unpredictable path of the Serpent, multiplicity; and "gyring," to the ordered intersection of antinomies in history; and "spiring," to release from the wheel of time — what matters about these adjectives is their cumulative visual effect: rapid, random, confused movement. The circular "treadmill," another conflicting pattern of motion, hoops the others together in an image of nonsensical, dehumanized labor. The stairwell is the physical form of madness.[20] What, then, does it mean that "Goldsmith and the Dean, Berkeley and Burke have travelled there"?

Yeats's prose does not much clarify the rhapsodic catalogue which follows (II.iii–vi). More than the speaker's enumeration of Anglo-Irish ideals and the substantiation of his initial "boast," [21] it switches tone, point of view, and chronology so abruptly, welds together so many contradictory impulses that its ultimate dramatic character is that of an ecstatic mad-song, an extraordinarily distended sentence fragment which ends only when the speaker exhausts himself. With perverse joy he wrenches his ancestors from their rational Augustan couplets, flings aside their masks of courtesy and equipoise. As he celebrates, he imitates — not merely Swift's satiric energy or Burke's proud conservatism or Berkeley's pre-Romantic idealism but their passionate extravagance and wit, their "blood." He delights in Berkeley and Burke's absurd "proofs" which are really metaphors. Created in his image, they all become poets; their derangement is divine *afflatus*. These inspired men herald his own achievement; incorporating them, he stands "massed against the world" ("The Seven Sages").

But this maelstrom has other currents. In *The Words upon the Window-pane*, Mrs. Henderson transmits the following conversation:

> [*In Swift's voice.*] I have something in my blood that no child must inherit. I have constant attacks of dizziness. . . . I had them in London. . . . There was a great doctor there, Dr. Arbuthnot; I told him of those attacks of dizziness, I told him of worse things. It was he who explained. There is a line of Dryden's. . . . [*In Vanessa's voice.*] O, I know — "Great wits are sure to madness near allied."[22]

For Swift, and for the speaker as he envisages Swift, the alliance is too close for comfort:

> Swift beating on his breast in sibylline frenzy blind
> Because the heart in his blood-sodden breast had dragged him down
>   into mankind . . .
>
> [II.iii]

"Blind" is syntactically ambiguous. Does it modify Swift or his frenzy? Is the frenzy truly "sibylline" or is it the "blind" chaotic utterance of madness? As Corbet asks in the play, "Was Swift mad? Or was it the intellect itself that was mad?"[23] Is Swift the satirist so tormented by his own fury that he can no longer conceive the "purity of the unclouded moon" (III)? Or has the moon's very chastity goaded him to rage against

all impurities, himself included? The passion the speaker celebrates is
Swift's enslavement to corruption; yet Swift, had he not despised his
"blood-sodden breast," could not have risen to such imaginative frenzy and
prophesied the coming ruin. Swift, whose need for sanctity counterbal-
ances his satiric hatred, is clearly the speaker's tutelary genius; yet like the
tower in its later stages, he is also a nemesis pointing toward self-
destruction. The speaker is both attracted and repelled; his ironic,
affectionate portrait of Goldsmith, like Ariel "deliberately sipping at the
honey-pot of his mind" (II.iii),[24] seems a suddenly calculated retreat from
Swift's magnetic influence. Repeatedly he alters his distance from his
ancestors, uncertain whether their nonreturnable legacy of passionate
imagination is a blessing or a curse. All four suffer from solipsism, the
recurrent danger of aristocratic isolation and imaginative vigor; "God-
appointed Berkeley" (II.v), despite the comic phrasing, seems like the
speaker himself, threatened by paranoia. With guarded satire the speaker
fends off what his tower presses upon him, the complete identification
with his past that he half desires. Behind the divine *afflatus*, actual
madness remains; and behind the speaker's satire lurks the foreboding that
the real enemy to the consecration of his territory is not external, but
within the rich, blood-sodden Anglo-Irish mind.

Upon these ambivalent, charged responses is imposed another. The
speaker takes his ancestors' masks, despite his misgivings, to gain authority
for his mockery. Yet the mockery shows no real hope of redeeming Ireland
from craven indignity. Like Parnell in "To a Shade," his ancestors return, in
him, to preside in genuine grief and morbid self-satisfaction over the last
enervation of "The strength that gives our blood and state magnanimity of
its own desire" (II.vi). Swift's and Burke's most dire prophecies of political
decrepitude, loss of human liberty, have been fulfilled. The stanza on
Berkeley implies Stephen Daedalus's gruesome, traditional judgment on
Ireland: "the old sow that eats her farrow."[25] As the summoning of
eighteenth-century Anglo-Irish vibrancy closes, the shadow of the assassinated O'Higgins, who also kept faith with his tradition, passes before the
speaker's eyes.

That undertow of pessimism climaxes in section III. The final
definition of Anglo-Irish achievement—"Everything that is not God consumed with intellectual fire" (II.vi)—is also the speaker's own cry for
purification. Such extremities cannot be matched; a sudden emotional
trough follows:

> The purity of the unclouded moon
> Has flung its arrowy shaft upon the floor.
> Seven centuries have passed and it is pure,
> The blood of innocence has left no stain.

And then, as awareness of the assassination intensifies:

> Odour of blood on the ancestral stair!

Nauseated, he recoils from the crushing revelation of his mortal condition. All summonings of Anglo-Irish imaginative strength have failed to create a sacred ground. As the speaker contemplates the inviolable moon, self-loathing mingles with awe. "The purity of the unclouded moon . . . is pure." Not a tautology, this is the grim judgment against earth permitted by the ambiguity of "it" (1. 3). Whatever purity humankind achieves is besmirched, even the exalted Anglo-Irish genius. The tragedy of the "blood-sodden" heart is that, while it seeks purification, it also suffers the equally unassuageable need to pollute what it most loves. Thus, in the tower's history, "Soldier, assassin, executioner" have "shed blood, / But *could not cast* a single jet thereon" (III): the verb conveys nothing less than frustrated desire. "Blood-saturated" man, perpetually trying to recreate the universe in his image, must hate what he cannot obtain. As natural description merges with mythic personification, Diana, murderously innocent, flings her "arrowy shaft" in sexual challenge, tormenting men to madness. Does man murder because he cannot make love to the moon? Do all murderings but displace a greater desire, deliverance from "the crime of death and birth"? Murder becomes a quest for the apocalyptic cessation of time; for "The sun shall be turned into darkness, and the moon into blood, before that great and notable day of the Lord come" (Acts 2:20). Philosophies and psychologies unconsciously seek the same end: Swift's hatred of common humankind, Goldsmith's aversion to raw experience, Burke's metamorphosis of human institutions into permanent organic forms, Berkeley's wish that the world "vanish" (II.v).

Inevitably, the revelation involves the speaker's awareness of his tower. The visceral exclamation, "Odour of blood on the ancestral stair!" is shocking dramatically precisely because the speaker, even as he contemplates earth's impurity, has tried so desperately to believe his territory sanctified. The "bloody, arrogant" spirit of place (I) has ironically turned against its defender; the invasion, more intimately experienced than in any other "tower" poem, systematically erodes the speaker's faith. This is why the word "Odour" is so perfect; it conveys a surreal encroachment, as if the Cloone River's "blood-dimmed tide" were swelling against the tower and its attainted possessor. Yet the speaker must accept the consequences of having made this tower his symbol: all people are Cain's kin, implicated in the fellowship of blood,

> And we that have shed none must gather there
> And clamour in drunken frenzy for the moon.
>
> [III]

Love of the moon again connotes sexual brutality. Caught between antinomies, maddened by knowledge of inexpiable sin, the speaker becomes a parody of Swift his nemesis: "drunken," not "sibylline." Behind the renewed cry for purification lies a political judgment as disturbingly honest as that in "Meditations . . ." (I). Anglo-Ireland, for all its "great-

ness," has finally reaped the proper harvest of "Bitter and violent men":
the "blood of innocence" has been shed in payment for the accumulated
guilt of a "bloody, arrogant" culture. And the speaker, like Swift and the
others, although technically innocent, must share the guilt by virtue of
blood-kinship. The judgment is "Bound neither to Cause nor to State"
("The Tower," III).[26] As the speaker is humbled from "Uttering" the Anglo-
Irish pride of sections I and II, his vision becomes tragic.

An exquisite night-piece deflects the cathartic rage his frenzy inti-
mates:

> Upon the dusty, glittering windows cling,
> And seem to cling upon the moonlit skies,
> Tortoiseshell butterflies, peacock butterflies,
> A couple of night-moths are on the wing.
> [IV]

In this fine mingling of observation and symbol, the butterflies are
traditional emblems of the soul, their ascent aborted by imprisonment
within the tower. But their mediatory stationing ("cling, / And seem to
cling") points, for a vanishing instant, to a universe which harmonizes
lunar and sublunar realms. Like the image of Keats in "Ego Dominus
Tuus" ("face and nose pressed to a sweet-shop window"), the barrier of the
windowpane—demarcating the profane from the sacred—is agonizingly
transparent. Here, however, there is no violent desire; instead, the speaker's resignation to entrapment passes into disinterested love for the
butterflies as creatures. The emotion resembles that felt for the "Magical
unicorns" in "Meditations . . ." (VII.iii) and for the swan and "mother
bird" in "The Tower" (III). Even the aesthetically unattractive moths,
perhaps an ironic self-reference, seem lovely.

In the midst of this sudden calm comes a furious, horrified explosion:
"Is every modern nation like the tower, / Half dead at the top?" This is the
final knowledge: the tower heralds catastrophe—personal, Irish, international. The mood rapidly shifts into bleak gloom:

> No matter what I said,
> For wisdom is the property of the dead,
> A something incompatible with life; and power,
> Like everything that has the stain of blood,
> A property of the living . . .

The judgment transcends neat historical categories to become ethical and
epistemological commentary. Redemptive wisdom is unavailable, an unknown "something." Man's doom is natural blindness: efforts to escape
that condition can only produce a more spectacular failure, a more
elaborate turn on the treadmill. "Blood" and "power," now synonymous
with earth, operate inexorably. The savored pun on "property" (philosophic "attribute"; land, enclosed space) stresses human limitation in
terms of the territorial metaphor. As the Greek in *The Resurrection*

remarks, "Every man's sins are his property. Nobody else has a right to them."[27] That pessimistic irony, reducing identity to guilt, accords wholly with the speaker's vision. Yet the poem's more generous irony, and the one which confers tragedy, is that the speaker, beginning in proud isolation, ends in humbled consciousness of community. Unable to bless his tower, he finally blesses the moon:

> but no stain
> Can come upon the visage of the moon
> When it has looked in glory from a cloud.

As the poem completes its circular form, the violent self-willed consecrations (I) and the drunken clamor (III) ripen into a disinterested emotion of sanctity. How can man bless the infinite? Again, paradox: but what other response is appropriate? Diana, responding to this gesture of awed obeisance, sheathes her "arrowy shaft" to become a mandala of light.

Viewed in relation to the "tower" poetry generally, this small joy which staves off utmost nihilism[28] — the joy of humility, not of self-fulfillment — is all Yeats managed to salvage from the monumental design which first stirred his imagination in "Ego Dominus Tuus" and "A Prayer on Going into My House": the creation of a complete self upon sacred, unfallen ground. Blood has washed away the "Magical shapes" once traced upon the sand; the expectation of prophetic, self-unifying wisdom has given place to knowledge of ignorance; and faith in the power of language to establish boundaries has crumpled.

Notes

1. Richard Ellmann dates the poem July-December 1927 (*The Identity of Yeats* [1954; rpt. London: Faber, 1964], p. 291). Lady Gregory indicates that Yeats began the poem during the summer of 1926, just after he had started "Among School Children" (Unpublished Journals, Book XXXIII, May 28, 1926 [Berg Collection, New York Public Library]).

2. W. B. Yeats, *The Letters of W. B. Yeats*, ed. Allan Wade (London: Hart-Davis, 1954), p. 727.

3. "Sympathy with Mrs. O'Higgins," *Irish Times*, July 14, 1927; quoted by Donald T. Torchiana, *W. B. Yeats and Georgian Ireland* (Evanston: Northwestern University Press, 1966), p. 184.

4. *Letters*, p. 727.

5. Cf. Torchiana, *W. B. Yeats*, pp. 179–80, 320–21. In "Blood and the Moon," the "blood of innocence" (III) is not identified. Had Yeats wanted the poem to assume an explicitly political cast, he would hardly have written so skimpy an introductory note (W. B. Yeats, *The Variorum Edition of the Poems of W. B. Yeats*, eds. Peter Allt and Russell K. Alspach [New York: Macmillan, 1966], p. 831); compare his extensive commentary on "To a Wealthy Man . . ." in the first edition of *Responsibilities*. Nor would he have first published the poem in America (*Letters*, pp. 728–29).

6. Cf. Harold Bloom, *Yeats* (New York: Oxford, 1970), p. 373. Bloom's approach to the poem's origin is biographical: "the poem's genetic impulse belongs to the Soul; Yeats has been

very near the gates of death (having just experienced his first severe illness since childhood) and he turns to consider the Last Things in a very different spirit than that of *A Vision*."

7. *Letters*, p. 729. The poem's structure has been largely misunderstood. Denis Donoghue, "On 'The Winding Stair,' " in *An Honoured Guest*, eds. Denis Donoghue and J. R. Mulryne (London: Edward Arnold, 1965), p. 108, objects that the dialogue is not "an outstanding example of free democratic speech; the casting vote is delivered before the poor Soul has well begun"; he does not ask why Yeats planned it thus. John Unterecker, *A Reader's Guide to William Butler Yeats* (New York: Farrar, Straus, 1959), at the opposite extreme, believes that Soul "eventually loses the debate" (p. 204).

8. "The Black Tower," which might appear to share this distinction with "A Dialogue of Self and Soul," is in a class by itself; it simply does not raise the same kind of questions, nor is the speaker's self-divestiture of his poet's pose an issue. Cf. Ellmann (*The Identity of Yeats*, p. xiii) and Unterecker (*A Reader's Guide*, p. 205), both of whom regard the speaker of the dialogue as an artist.

9. W. B. Yeats, *A Vision* (New York: Macmillan, 1961), p. 183.

10. See Bloom, *Yeats*, p. 375: "The poem's largest irony is that the Soul is an esoteric Yeatsian, and the Self a natural man."

11. Cf. Bloom (*Yeats*, p. 374), who thinks that Soul, as he begins his last speech, has already surrendered.

12. See *King Lear*, III.iv.81–82: "commit not with man's sworn spouse" (Edgar); see also "Consolation," in "A Woman Young and Old."

13. "Little Gidding," *II*, in *Four Quartets*. Richard Ellmann, *Eminent Domain: Yeats among Wilde, Joyce, Pound, Eliot, and Auden* (New York: Oxford, 1967), pp. 93–95, thinks that Eliot was alluding in this passage (beginning "Let me disclose the gifts reserved for age") to Yeats's "The Spur" and "Vacillation." But this stanza in "A Dialogue of Self and Soul" seems a far more likely source.

14. Cf. Holloway, "Style and World in *The Tower*," in *An Honoured Guest* (p. 93): "Yeats is, in fact, conducting a rehearsal, in meditation during this life, of the stages of the Dreaming Back (part II, stanzas 1–3) and the Return. . . ." From a technical point of view, there is no relation between these stanzas and the *Dreaming Back*, which is a nonsequential recapitulation of experience (*A Vision*, p. 226). Stanzas i and ii, in their strict chronology, do resemble the *Return*, but stanzas iii and iv are too generalized to be given precise labels from *A Vision*. The lumping together of stanzas i–iii, moreover, disregards the significant dramatic shift which occurs between stanzas ii and iii.

15. See *A Vision*, pp. 177–78; T. R. Henn (*The Lonely Tower* [1950; rpt. London: Methuen, 1965], pp. 184–85) has suggested additional relationships between the speaker and the Hunchback.

16. See, e.g., James H. O'Brien, "Self vs. Soul in Yeats's *The Winding Stair*," *Eire* 3, 1 (1968): 27–28; Unterecker, *A Reader's Guide*, p. 205.

17. Unterecker (*A Reader's Guide*, p. 205), overlooking the way in which Yeats's verb tenses interact, regards the poem's conclusion as the moment of purification itself; he too remarks on the obligatory force of "must" but conceives it in terms of the poet's irrepressible creative energy.

18. See Bloom's comments on the solipsism of this poem (*Yeats*, pp. 372–73).

19. Edward Young, "Conjectures on Original Composition," in *Works* (London: Dodsley, 1798), III: 196. Young goes on in the next sentence: "As in this he seemed to prophesy like the Sybils. . . ." The comment would seem to be responsible for Yeats's image in section II, "Swift beating on his breast in sibylline frenzy. . . ." Dr. Thomas Sheridan, whose edition of Swift Yeats bought with his Nobel Prize money, cites part of Young's attack on Swift but stops just before Young narrates the incident from which the imagery of "Blood and the Moon" derives (*The Works of Jonathan Swift* [London: Strahan, 1784], I: 512). Mario

Rossi and Joseph Hone also included the anecdote in *Swift, or The Egotist* (New York: Dutton, 1934), p. 364; but Yeats did not see their drafts until several years after writing the poem. A. Norman Jeffares, *The Circus Animals* (Stanford: Stanford University Press, 1970), p. 43, gives the allusion passing mention.

20. Thomas R. Whitaker, *Swan and Shadow: Yeats's Dialogue with History* (Chapel Hill: North Carolina University Press, 1964), p. 212, views the imagery more positively and speaks of the "compelling harmonies of life" in this stanza.

21. Torchiana, *W. B. Yeats*, p. 320; Bloom (*Yeats*, p. 377) has called the passage "rant."

22. W. B. Yeats, *The Collected Plays of W. B. Yeats* (1953; rpt. New York: Macmillan, 1966), pp. 383–84.

23. Ibid., p. 387.

24. See *The Tempest*, V.i.88. The image also refers to Goldsmith's editorship of the short-lived periodical *The Bee*.

25. James Joyce, *A Portrait of the Artist as a Young Man* (1916; rpt. New York: Viking, 1964), p. 203.

26. Torchiana's interpretation of the political judgment (*W. B. Yeats*, pp. 320–21) is more partisan than the one offered here: O'Higgins' assassination represents modern Ireland's "repudiation" of "all those qualities seemingly come down from the world figures of eighteenth-century Ireland to Kevin O'Higgins" (p. 321). He considers the entirety of section III a cry for wisdom and sees in that cry "the possible triumph of the intellectual imagination in the terrestrial realm, a continuous possibility despite the intermittent bloodshed and political roils since the Normans came in" (p. 321). Such an interpretation accords well with Yeatsian history but hardly does justice to the hellish experience the poem creates; surely there is no sense of "possible triumph" in the crazed stupor of the stanza's conclusion.

27. *Collected Plays*, p. 367.

28. Cf. Bloom, *Yeats*, p. 380.

Yeats and the Greater Romantic Lyric

George Bornstein[*]

In the second part of "The Tower" Yeats — as persona — paces on the battlements of his tower, stares at the landscape, and sends imagination forth to encounter it. That series of actions dramatically places him in a central Romantic line of symbol, theme and form; like Thoor Ballylee itself the poem becomes an elaborate stage set for Yeats to sport upon in his true role of modern Romantic. The tower as symbol derives partly from Shelley, as Yeats acknowledged in the related "Blood and the Moon": "And Shelley had his towers, thought's crowned powers he called them once."[1] Yeats adopted both the symbol itself and the notion of varying it from poem to poem which he found in his precursor. Correspondingly, "The Tower" seizes upon the high Romantic theme of mind encountering

*From *Romantic and Modern: Revaluations of Literary Tradition*, ed. George Bornstein (Pittsburgh: University of Pittsburgh Press, 1977), 91–110. Reprinted by permission of the publisher.

the world through imagination. And finally, the second part of "The Tower"—and indeed the whole poem, for the underlying pattern would hold even without the overt triple division—is a Greater Romantic Lyric, in which poetic movement follows a special course of imaginative mental action. Yeats discovered his great mature subject in his relation to what "The Tower" calls "images and memories," and a characteristic means of developing it in the Greater Romantic Lyric. This essay first examines that traditional mode, then pursues the grounds of Yeats's reworking of it in "The Tower, II" and finally surveys his other innovations in that form.[2] In focusing primarily on later poems I do not mean to scant Yeats's early Romanticism but simply assume that topic to be sufficiently established already.[3] My subject here is Yeats's transformation of a Romantic mode—and accompanying Romantic themes—in some of his finest mature work, including "The Tower," "In Memory of Major Robert Gregory," and "The Second Coming."

<h2 style="text-align:center">I</h2>

In the Greater Romantic Lyric, Coleridge, Wordsworth, Keats, and to a lesser extent Shelley evolved a structure suitable to their individual conceptions of mental action: in Meyer Abrams's definition, a speaker in a landscape undergoes "an out-in-out process in which mind confronts nature and their interplay constitutes the poem." The first poem in the new genre, Coleridge's "Eolian Harp," illustrates the pattern: a particular speaker begins by describing the landscape round the cottage with detached affection (out), progresses through an increasingly rapt medita-tion in which he identifies more and more with his own revery (in), and then breaks off imaginative involvement to return to the original scene in a new mentality (out). While Abrams's interest in the doctrine of such poems causes him to describe the "in" phase as a "meditation" through which the speaker "achieves an insight, faces up to a tragic loss, comes to a moral decision, or resolves an emotional problem,"[4] I would substitute "vision" for "meditation" to emphasize the poem's structure as determined by shifting mental modes from observation to increasingly active imagina-tion and then to its subsidence in an interpretive conclusion. In these terms, the poem's structure is description-vision-evaluation. "The Eolian Harp," for example, moves from Coleridge describing his cottage to his imagining first a fairy world, which in turn modulates into a projection of a more general world of "the one Life within us and abroad"; he then imagines himself in a noontime revery on a sunny hillside and finally rises to highest imaginative intensity in envisioning "all of animated nature" as organic harps swept by an Intellectual breeze. He then breaks off the vision and returns to the cottage, where faith, memory, and reason conspire to repudiate his imaginative power for having challenged Chris-tian orthodoxy. Seen doctrinally, the poem "comes to a moral decision";

seen psychologically, it moves through different faculties in a searching presentation of genesis, fulfillment, and exhaustion of imagination.

Like all Greater Romantic Lyrics, "The Eolian Harp" is a poem of the act of the mind. But the genre provides a structure, not a straitjacket, and admits a variety of actions within its basic tripartite pattern. Four representative poems serve as reference points for mapping the grounds on which Yeats built his tower vision—Coleridge's "Frost at Midnight," Wordsworth's "Tintern Abbey," and Keats's "Ode to a Nightingale" and "Ode on a Grecian Urn." Situation, use of memory, and two structural innovations point our attention in "Frost at Midnight," which is in effect a Prayer For My Son. Like Yeats's "A Prayer for My Daughter," a variant on the pattern whose combination of the Atlantic with "Gregory's wood and one bare hill" recalls Coleridge's "sea, hill, and wood," the poem invokes growth in a future environment favorable to imagination for the poet's child, in contrast to the father's own experience. Coleridge's poem opens with a favorite Yeatsian situation—a man meditating at midnight inside his rural home, as in "All Souls' Night" or the more generally nocturnal "In Memory of Major Robert Gregory," two more of Yeats's Greater Romantic Lyrics. Unlike "Eolian Harp," this poem shifts into memory for its first "in" section, where Coleridge creates an image of his past self in remembering dreams prompted by a grate in childhood. Structurally, the vision comes in two parts punctuated by a return to the present, here a brief address to his "Dear Babe," before imagining a future of Hartley's communion with "lovely shapes and sounds intelligible." As Yeats will later sometimes do, Coleridge ends within his vision in impressive rhetoric.

"Tintern Abbey" follows "Frost at Midnight" in offering two visions, making the pattern out-in-out and then back in again, and stresses memory as much as imagination. As in "Coole Park, 1929" (a structurally simpler Greater Romantic Lyric) and in "The Wild Swans at Coole" (which in its original stanzaic order tried to be one as far as its theme of failed imagination would permit), dynamism derives from confrontation with a place important to the speaker in the past. Wordsworth first describes the scene, then imagines a near past when he remembered it and a further past when he first encountered it, comes back to the present, and then imagines a future for Dorothy. His diction rather than his technique of using memory to prepare for imaginative action claims our attention here. He speaks of animated mental images—"the picture of the mind," "beauteous forms," and being "laid asleep in body and become a living soul"—just as Coleridge calls on "flitting phantasies" and "shapings of the unregenerate mind." Although Yeats would have hated the poem's praise of nature, he habitually used similar phrases,[5] most notably "the mind's eye," and interpreted Romantic references to images, phantoms, and other shapes more literally than their creators did. The point is not that he borrowed terms from, say, Wordsworth, but that a drive to render similar mental action causes related phraseology among writers in this genre.

Yeats's two odes return to a normative three-part pattern with obvious links to Yeats's later work but also with those differences of stance which made Yeats cleave more unto Shelley. Unlike Yeats, Keats remains in the present tense, for his poems depict an ongoing struggle to transform current experience rather than to invoke memory. "Ode to a Nightingale" speaks a parable of sympathetic imagination—first bodily quiesence, then imaginative projection into the nightingale ("already with thee"), and final collapse of the vision with a bell-like forlorn "to toll me back from thee to my sole self." This Keatsian out-in-out pattern of interaction with a natural object remained alien to Yeats, who created visions apart from nature. In the Byzantium poems, his desire to reincarnate himself in a golden bird of art both recalls and "corrects" Keats's limitation of merger within natural rather than aesthetic boundaries. But even while divorcing human life from cold pastoral, Keats did allow his imagination to interact with art. In "Ode on a Grecian Urn" he first describes the urn (out), then enters into his vision to imagine a town not actually on the urn (in) at his highest intensity, and then withdraws again to a more distanced perspective (out). That is, he substitutes an art work for an actual landscape to prompt his Greater Romantic Lyric, as Wordsworth did in "Elegiac Stanzas" on Peele Castle. Yeats does not, though poems like "A Bronze Head" or "The Municipal Gallery Revisited" display similar devices. Most strikingly, his imagining of the halfway house in "Lapis Lazuli" parallels Keats's image of the Grecian town—neither exists in the artistic object, but only in the poet's mind. Yeats took from Keats as much as he could without changing from creative to sympathetic imagination.

The Romantics channeled so much creative energy into the new genre because it followed the shape of imaginative experience. More than displaying the results of imaginative creation, it allowed the following through of a mind moving from description or ordinary perception to vision and then back again. Abrams has quoted Coleridge on the return upon itself as a device making for wholeness: "The common end of all *narrative*, nay, of *all*, Poems . . . is to convert a *series* into a *Whole*: to make those events, which in real or imagined History move on in a *strait* Line, assume to our Understandings a *circular* motion—the snake with it's Tail in its Mouth."[6] Experience thus assumes the shape of ouroboros, the tail-eating snake. Equally important, it becomes a cycle and harmonizes with the cyclicity that haunts Romantic thought about both societies and individuals. Often this cyclicity takes a special shape: vision breaks off at its intensest moment and the poet returns to his ordinary state, whether in "The Eolian Harp," "Grecian Urn," or "Nightingale." Inability to sustain imagination in the poems matches our experience in life. Wordsworth minimized the discrepancy and drew new strength from his experience, while Keats stressed the discontinuity. At his most extreme a Keatsian poet is not sure which state is real, the imaginative or the ordinary, and is plagued by doubt and questioning, often ending the poem with an interrogative ("Do I wake or sleep?"). Yet despite the persona's questions, these poems ratify vision de facto, for in all of them vision is more important than natural landscape. The poems exist to present the visions, and interest centers on acts of mind, not narrative description of nature. Significance springs only from mind—the landscapes do not possess meaning in themselves but only that meaning which the poet gives them by his own mental processes. The banks of the Wye interest us only because of Wordsworth's experiences there, and we do not know at all from the poem precisely where Keats encounters his nightingale.

II

Yeats wrote Greater Romantic Lyrics only in his maturity, when he had cast off derivative Romanticism of the nineties and was creating a modern variety. The form suited the intermittent pulsations of his own imagination, and its circular shape harmonized with his antinomies and gyres. By moving into and then out of vision he could hold in a single poem reality and justice, or actual and ideal. Likewise, doubt generated by discontinuity between states matched his own vacillations. Yet he did not simply imitate his predecessors. Instead, he stepped up the importance of vision over nature even further, diminishing description of external scene and preserving only as much of nature as imagination needed. For him vision became a literal summoning of images in nature's spite. In effect, he crossed visionary autonomy from Blake and Shelley with poetic structure from Wordsworth, Coleridge, and Keats, and he infused both stance and form with his own sensibility. The resultant hybrids included many of his best poems between 1918 and 1929.

"The Tower" (VP 409) makes the form an arena for a romantic grappling with the despondency of aging. Unlike Wordsworth, the poet still has both flaming imagination and fervent sense. For Blake, those would have been enough,[7] but Yeats here fears waning of emotion, the third term he introduced into his exposition of Blake. His temptation is abstract argument, for his years demand the philosophic mind, which he conquers through vision. The first five lines of part two present an orthodox beginning for a Greater Romantic Lyric: a speaker looks at a landscape and "send[s] imagination forth" to encounter it. The next line signals a Yeatsian innovation, in calling "images and memories" from the landscape. Were the speaker Keats, he would identify with objects in the scene; were he Wordsworth, he would summon images and memories of his past self. Since he is Yeats, he calls up images and memories mostly of others. With their arrival the "in" part of the lyric begins.

These images divide the great symbols of passion and mood Yeats admired in the Romantics into paired creator and follower—Mrs. French and her serving man, blind poet Raftery and the man drowned in Cloone bog, and Yeats's own characters of old juggler and tricked Hanrahan. Despite his Shelleyan situation on the tower, Yeats here repudiates his youthful Intellectual vision of ascent to the ideal which he had founded upon Shelley. Mrs. French's servant, the drowned man, and Hanrahan all carry over ideal moonlit visions into the actual world ("the prosaic light of day") and so end in disaster. Opposed to that, Yeats now wants moon and sunlight to "seem / One inextricable beam" encompassing antinomies into which all things fall without kindling a mad lust to live only by the moon.

The vision builds to its climax in Yeats's questioning of those images of passion—did they too rage against old age as he does? Just here, in line 101, we suddenly realize what Yeats has done. He has called up the images literally and they stand in front of him:

> But I have found an answer in those eyes
> That are impatient to be gone;
> Go, therefore; but leave Hanrahan.

We understand that Wordsworth imagines his past self near Tintern Abbey, or that Keats imagines himself with the nightingale; but what are we to understand by Yeats addressing images here as though they were present? We can make sense of this in two ways: first, he has slipped into revery and these images "in the Great Memory stored" (line 85) have now entered his individual consciousness. If we do not believe in the Great Memory, then we can say that he has called up images from his own conscious or subconscious memory (Yeats in fact knew a fair amount about the characters in this poem), or else simply created them outright, and in the intensity of his vision addresses them as if they were present, which they are in the mind.

Whatever explanation we choose, the speaker modulates out of vision in questioning Hanrahan, his own creation. His second question signals the change: "Does the imagination dwell the most / Upon a woman won or woman lost?" The "you" in the following line refers more to Yeats himself than to Hanrahan, for this is another of Yeats's continual self-reproaches about his failed relation to Maud Gonne. The lines of the poem,

> If on the lost, admit you turned aside
> From a great labyrinth out of pride,
> Cowardice, some silly over-subtle thought
> Or anything called conscience once . . .

parallel the mixture of pride, timidity, over-subtlety, and conscience in a passage about Maud in the original draft of his autobiography:

And in all that followed I was careful to touch [her] as one might a sister. If she was to come to me, it must be from no temporary passionate impulse, but with the approval of her conscience. Many a time since then, as I lay awake at night, have I accused myself of acting, not as I thought from a high scruple, but from a dread of moral responsibility, and my thoughts have gone round and round, as do miserable thoughts, coming to no solution.[8]

That love, linked by Yeats to his early Romanticism, signifies the same mistake made by the servant, the drowned man, and even Hanrahan, yet its memory is so strong that even the memory reduces him to their condition. With realization in the poem that passion still remembers what was so fugitive, Yeats's obstinate questionings cease. Yet in making this tangent to the Intimations ode he veers off into his own orbit, for he refuses the Wordsworthian comfort of the philosophic mind and, spurred by the renewed sense of loss on which his poetry depends, makes his will in triumph of imagination. Exaltation carries over into the third section, until it subsides again in the closing lines and leaves the poet where he began, though with a difference.

The images summoned in this poem provide one gauge for Yeats's claim to have corrected Romanticism by fastening its visions to a national landscape, and thus reinvigorating them. Unlike Greater Romantic Lyrics of the Romantics themselves, "The Tower" could not be transferred to another setting. Mrs. French, Raftery, and Mary Hynes, the bankrupt ancient master of the house, and others all lived in *this* landscape. Yeats's elevation of major and minor Irish figures into heroic roles has stirred a large controversy in which both its defenders and its attackers overstate their cases. On the one hand, Yeats's allusions to Mary Hynes, or, say, to Maeve, do not make his poems any easier for non-Irish readers (and perhaps not always even for Irish ones); they are, in fact, obstacles to understanding. On the other hand, critics who simply condemn the habit, and Yeats's exaggerated claims for it, miss the point. In "The Tower" he uses them to move away from Romantic subjectivity which made earlier Greater Romantic Lyrics depend only upon the poets' minds and not their environments. Mrs. French and Raftery, or elsewhere MacGregor Mathers or William Horton, are not immediately meaningful for everybody, but they do, at least, link private vision to something beyond the poet himself. In *A Vision* Yeats boasted that he had improved on Blake by turning historical characters into elements of his mythology and so made it more accessible. A romanticist might respond with some truth that the representativeness of Wordsworth's or Keats's mind makes them in fact more accessible than Yeats's quirky Celts, but I think it also true that Yeats's poems do gain both force and a measure of seeming impersonality from his tactic, which the character of his imagination badly needed. Though original Romantics may not have required this attachment, Yeats himself clearly did.

Yeats habitually addresses such images as if they were present and often claims that he sees them "in the mind's eyes." That phrase takes us back to Hamlet, not thin from eating flies but as visionary prince:

HAMLET: My father—methinks I see my father.
HORATIO: O, where, my lord?
HAMLET: In my mind's eye, Horatio.

Yeats used the expression particularly often from about the time of *Responsibilites* through *The Tower*, when it appears in half a dozen poems and frequently in his prose. He connected it especially to seeing images of human forms, for which the allusion to Hamlet provides a cunning context. In Shakespeare's play Hamlet uses his mind's eye to see a mental image of his dead father, but he is shortly to encounter a real ghost. In Yeats's poems speakers summon figures which could be mental images but which also seem, like ghosts, to exist independently. The Shakespearian echo allows us to interpret the images as we choose, with Yeats himself remaining as gnomic as the Delphic oracle.

Because Yeats's chief innovation in the Greater Romantic Lyric was to make vision into a summoning of images, we need to look more closely at these images seen in the mind's eye before turning to more of his work in that genre. They are usually great figures of passion or of mood, like the Romantic questers so dear to Yeats. We meet the first as a completed poet-figure associated with a tower in a sort of Greater Romantic Lyric in prose, related as an incident from a tour of the Appenines:

> I was alone amid a visionary, fantastic, impossible scenery. It was sunset and the stormy clouds hung upon mountain after mountain, and far off on one great summit a cloud darker than the rest glimmered with lightning. Away south upon another mountain a mediaeval tower, with no building near nor any sign of life, rose into the clouds. I saw suddenly in the mind's eye an old man, erect and a little gaunt, standing in the door of the tower, while about him broke a windy light. He was the poet who had at last, because he had done so much for the world's sake, come to share in the dignity of the saint.[9]

Yeats goes on to combine the figure with Jesus in an ecstatic rhapsody in which the old man, a mixture of Athanase and Ahasuerus, becomes a prototype of the poet as successful quester and mage. The passage's embryonic doctrine of poet and mask exfoliates later in "Ego Dominus Tuus" (1917), where Hic argues that Dante "made that hollow face of his / More plain to the mind's eye than any face / But that of Christ" (VP 368). Ille's correction of Hic's oversimple account of how poets create their masks concerns us less than how the masks or images are perceived by observers—in the mind's eye as figures of impassioned questing.

Three other poems in which images appear to be the mind's eye ring changes on the theme of intense desire. In "The Magi" (1914) they are searching again for the divine union of celestial mystery and bestial floor, while in the last section of "Meditations in Time of Civil War" (1923) they are troopers calling for vengeance on the murderers of Jacques Molay. Clearly, the images can represent misdirected as well as admired passion, for Yeats's note to "Meditations" identifies the troopers' cry as "fit symbol for those who labour for hatred, and so for sterility in various kinds" (VP 827). A mixed tone pervades the description of William Horton, first image summoned in the Greater Romantic Lyric "All Souls' Night" (1921). Like early Yeats, Horton had known "that sweet extremity of pride / That's called platonic love" (VP 471). After the death of his lady (Audrey Locke) he fixes "his mind's eye . . . on one sole image," a fusion of her and God.[10] Despite Yeats's ambivalence toward Horton's (and his own) form of quest, concentrated intensity still makes Horton fit auditor of the poem's "mummy truths."

Besides great figures of passion and mood, the mind's eye could summon figures of self-possessed mastery or symbols from esoteric Yeatsism. To the first group belong Major Robert Gregory and his literary forerunner, the fisherman. In "The Fisherman" Yeats calls up an image of a Connemara man who does not exist but is "a dream" as ideal audience for the cold and passionate poetry he wanted to write. Here Yeats gives us a simple account of his genesis — he simply imagined a man. His accounts of the origin of images were not always so direct, whether in poetry or in prose. The Great Memory which he invoked in "The Tower" and the Spiritus Mundi of "The Second Coming" found fuller description in *Per Amica Silentia Lunae*, where Yeats described his own practice of symbolic meditation:

> Before the mind's eye, whether in sleep or waking, came images that one was to discover presently in some book one had never read, and after looking in vain for explanation to the current theory of forgotten personal memory, I came to believe in a Great Memory passing on from generation to generation. But that was not enough, for these images showed intention and choice. . . . The thought was again and again before me that this study had created a contact or mingling with minds who had followed a like study in some other age. . . . Our daily thought was certainly but the line of foam at the shallow edge of a vast luminous sea; Henry More's *Anima Mundi*, Wordsworth's "immortal sea which brought us hither."[11]

The Great Memory gets into the poetry, but the guardedly expressed (not "I believed" but "the thought was before me") remainder does not, except possibly for the Spiritus Mundi of "The Second Coming." The sphinx vision there, like the related one seen by the mind's eye in "The Double Vision of Michael Robartes," will appear in our chronological survey of Yeats's Greater Romantic Lyrics. We have learned enough of the mind's eye and its images to continue.

III

Yeats wrote eight Greater Romantic Lyrics between 1918 and 1929. They divide into four pairs: "In Memory of Major Robert Gregory" (1918) and "All Souls' Night" (1921) summon images of the dead; "The Second Coming" (1920) and "The Double Vision of Michael Robartes" (1919) conjure images from the Great Memory; "The Tower, II" (1927) and "Meditations in Time of Civil War, VII" (1922) stress the tower top; and "Coole Park, 1929" (1931; written 1929) and "The Crazed Moon" (1932; written 1923) offer landscapes uncommonly symbolic even by Yeats's standards. All relate to Romanticism in form and often in theme and symbol as well, as we saw in "The Tower." The earliest of them, "In Memory of Major Robert Gregory," prefigures both the tower symbol and the stanzaic pattern of that poem, for it takes place in the "ancient tower" and uses the same *a a b b c d d c* rhyme scheme which Yeats derived from Cowley's elegiac ode on William Harvey and based two other Romantic poems upon, "A Prayer for My Daughter" and "Byzantium." The Coleridgean situation of Yeats's elegy recalls "Frost at Midnight," while its place in the overall order of Yeats's poems recalls Shelley, for it follows "The Wild Swans at Coole," whose basic image derives from an encounter between poet and swan in *Alastor*.

Mental action in "In Memory of Major Robert Gregory" (VP 323) follows the program of description-vision-evaluation, but a brief return to the present divides the vision itself into two parts, one of Lionel Johnson, John Synge, and George Pollexfen, and the other of Robert Gregory himself. Typically, for Yeats, the vision reverts to the past, counterpointing the spatial out-in-out with a temporal present-past-present sequence. He begins with meditative description of his present situation in the tower, whose subdued symbolic suggestion still alerts us for imminent imagination. In the initial vision, images of "discoverers of forgotten truth" and "companions" come to the speaker's mind. All of them are figures of passion or mood: Johnson brooding on sanctity and dreaming of consummation, Synge finding at last an objective correlative to his heart in passionate and simple Aran islanders, and Pollexfen forsaking physical sport for astrological search. A relapse into the present to mention "all things the delighted eye now sees" prepares for the sustained vision of Robert Gregory. Though described as ideal "soldier, scholar, horseman," Gregory appears mostly as artist, particularly if we remember that the eighth stanza, on horsemanship, was added to the poem later at his widow's request. In accomplishing all "perfectly," Gregory resolves the split between active and contemplative, becoming the kind of possible subject for a poem suggested at the end of Stevens' "Of Modern Poetry." The vision culminates in the eleventh stanza where Yeats subordinates Gregory to symbolic ignition of the combustible world. The question, "What made us dream that he could comb grey hair?" signals the exhaustion of imagination at its intensest moment and prepares us to shift back "out" into evaluation.

The final stanza deserves more attention than it usually receives. Its first two lines, which return us to the original scene, oppose the wind of nature (not inspiration) to mind and suggest that mind creates its images to counterbalance nature, to resist a violence from without by a violence from within. The speaker then reveals his original plan — not just to call up Synge (whom "manhood tried"), Pollexfen (whom "childhood loved"), or Johnson (whom "boyish intellect approved"), but to *comment* on them "Until imagination brought / A fitter welcome." Imagination thus redeems the decay implicit in the chronological sequence love-approve-test. Yeats's always erratic punctuation obscures the syntax here. A comma instead of semicolon after "each" in the first two printings[12] makes it culminate the previous sequence — he thought to comment until imagination would enter in. This Yeats has done most fully for Gregory but also in miniature for Johnson, Synge, and Pollexfen, whom he has turned into images of intensity. But, the last two lines suggest, thought of Gregory's death interrupted a lengthier sequence by discharging Yeats's passion ("heart"). This exhaustion of the heart recurs as problem in "The Tower"; here it marks the end of a remarkable reworking of a Romantic mode.

Similar structure holds together the more abstruse "All Souls' Night," written two years later and eventually made into an epilogue for *A Vision*. Again the speaker summons a trio of dead contemporaries — Horton, Florence (Farr) Emery, and MacGregor Mathers, all of whom appear as images of the esoteric students Yeats imitated as Athanase. Since the mental action resembles that of the Gregory elegy,[13] we may focus on the meaning of "the dead." In the earlier poem, the figures were dead in a double sense: they had physically died, and they had become artistic images in the poem, part of the artifice of eternity opposed to time. This Shelleyan association of death with completion or fulfilment, which had informed Yeats's poems of the nineties, spills over into "All Souls' Night," where the ghostly (a deliberate Yeatsian pun) images become fit auditors for Yeats's "mummy truths," both of the poem and of *A Vision*. As creations of imagination they can share Yeats's own imaginative communications. As conclusion to the *Tower* volume, the poem neatly reverses the situation of the initial "Sailing to Byzantium," when Yeats had wanted to be instructed by the spirits; as a result of lessons learned in poems like "The Tower," he can now summon spirits to be instructed by him in imagination's truth. That is, the volume as a whole resurrects flagging passion and harnesses it to imaginative vision. A different kind of action informs the next pair of Yeats's Greater Romantic Lyrics.

Like "The Double Vision of Michael Robartes," Yeats's famous "The Second Coming" calls up impersonal images rather than those fashioned from the poet's past. Yeats ascribes their source to Spiritus Mundi, which in a note to another poem from *Michael Robartes and the Dancer* he defines as "a general storehouse of images which have ceased to be a property of any personality or spirit" (VP 822). The poem's brevity reveals its structure as a Greater Romantic Lyric clearly:

> Turning and turning in the widening gyre
> The falcon cannot hear the falconer;
> Things fall apart; the centre cannot hold;
> Mere anarchy is loosed upon the world,
> The blood-dimmed tide is loosened, and everywhere   5
> The ceremony of innocence is drowned;
> The best lack all conviction, while the worst
> Are full of passionate intensity.
> Surely some revelation is at hand;
> Surely the Second Coming is at hand.   10
> The Second Coming! Hardly are those words out
> When a vast image out of *Spiritus Mundi*
> Troubles my sight: somewhere in the sands of the desert
> A shape with lion body and the head of a man,
> A gaze blank and pitiless as the sun,   15
> Is moving its slow thighs, while all about it
> Reel shadows of the indignant desert birds.
> The darkness drops again; but now I know
> That twenty centuries of stony sleep
> Were vexed to nightmare by a rocking cradle,   20
> And what rough beast, its hour come round at last,
> Slouches towards Bethlehem to be born?   (VP 401–02)

The transition from description to vision comes midway in line 11, while that from vision to evaluation occurs immediately after line 17. But here Yeats prepares for vision not by passive revery or negative capability but by working himself into a prophetic frenzy. He adopts the stance of seer, and what he describes is not an actual landscape but a metaphoric one: we do not feel that a falcon flies off before his eyes any more than that he literally sees a blood-dimmed tide. Instead, he depicts the state of Europe as if from the top of a mile-high tower, from which he can see as far as the Germans in Russia—whom he mentioned in the original draft.[14] Scholarly quarrels about identity of falcon and falconer—whether Christ and man, nature and spirit, logic and mind—should not be allowed to obscure the emblem's significance, loss of control. It matches loss of rational control in the speaker's mental action as he moves to a rhetorical crescendo preparatory to vision.

Because the image seen in the mind's eye comes from Spiritus Mundi, Yeats does not have to recall it personally; consequently, he can increase urgency by writing the entire poem in the present tense. The vision section carries over the passionate tone of the quasi description to a displacement only in space and not in time. A here-there-here movement matches the familiar out-in-out structure. This vision of antithetical Egyptian Sphinx heralding the end of primary Christianity replaces the erratic falcon with birds once again wheeling in formation. Although Yeats often exults at the end of "scientific, democratic, fact-accumulating, heterogeneous civilization,"[15] commentators err in seeing that attitude in the poem. The vision "troubles" the speaker's sight; it is the sphinx whose eye is "blank and pitiless."

With the end of vision the speaker's return to himself completes the doubling action built into the poem by the paired birds, the title itself, and the repeated phrases "turning," "is loosed," "surely," "the Second Coming," and "is at hand." The change reminds us why the Greater Romantic Lyric attracted Yeats so much: its return upon itself suits his true subject, which is more his relation to his vision than the vision itself. Typically, the vision leaves the speaker in a state of partial illumination. Now he knows not only that a nightmarish coming is at hand, but also that it was caused by the rocking cradle of Jesus. This means, I think, not just that the gyres are reciprocal (living each other's life and dying each other's death), but that the new god appears savage because seen through the mental set of Christian civilization and its derivatives. The final question is genuine, not rhetorical; in Yeats's system we know that something is coming but we do not know precisely what, nor can we, for we are bound by the old civilization. Nor does the speaker rejoice, for his phrase "rough beast" suggests horror rather than delight.

"The Second Coming" is Romantic in more than form; it is shot through with Blakean and Shelleyan echoes in theme and diction. Behind the poem lurks "Ozymandias," with its picture of a monumental ruin in a desert, while Harold Bloom has identified the source of the center which cannot hold in the rejection of natural love by the Witch of Atlas.[16] Likewise, the phrase "stony sleep" comes from Blake's *Book of Urizen*, where it describes Urizen's transitional phase between his Eternal state and his rebirth as fallen man.[17] But reworking of the Last Fury's speech in act one of *Prometheus Unbound* dwarfs even those in significance:

> The good want power, but to weep barren tears.
> The powerful goodness want: worse need for them.
> The wise want love; and those who love want wisdom;
> And all best things are thus confused to ill.   (1.625–28)

> The best lack all conviction, while the worst
> Are full of passionate intensity.   (VP 402)

As many commentators, including the present one,[18] have pointed out, Yeats reverses the thrust of Shelley's apocalyptic lines by making them a prelude to another cycle rather than to (possibly temporary) transfiguration. Here, we may note the difference in mental action. Prometheus frustrates the Fury's plan to torture him with a vision of human suffering by unexpectedly drawing strength from it: "The sights with which thou torturest gird my soul / With new endurance, till the hour arrives / When they shall be no types of things which are." A vision of heroic and selfless virtues follows in the songs of the six spirits, preparatory to the poem's later apocalypse of love. In "The Second Coming," however, the comparable lines create a frenzy in the speaker which prepares him for a vision of the rough beast to come, after which he reverts to his original state, having grown in knowledge but not in power. There is a fatalism in the poem which Yeats's *Vision* system often prompted, in which the quest for Unity of Being turns into a quest for knowledge instead, whether "mummy truths" of "All Souls' Night" or half-knowledge of "The Second Coming." Against this, Yeats sets ironic self-criticism as in "The Phases of the Moon" or images of Unity of Being like the dancer in "Among School Children."

"The Double Vision of Michael Robartes" (VP 382) summons images from Spiritus Mundi or the Great Memory and returns us to Yeats's concern with the poet's relation to Unity of Being. In a Greater Romantic Lyric which begins and ends in the ruins of a chapel restored on the Rock of Cashel by Cormac MacCarthy in the twelfth century, Robartes sees "in the mind's eye" two visions—in terms of the system, the first of phase one and the second of phase fifteen. In the second, a girl emblematic of Unity of Being dances between Sphinx (this time a Grecian one, representing knowledge) and Buddha (love). Because all three have overthrown time, like other images in Yeats they seem both dead and alive. In the third movement of the lyric (out), Robartes's attention focuses on the girl who "outdanced" thought. He identifies her with a dream maiden forgotten when awake, one of the Shelleyan ideals of Yeats's youth, whom in later life he preferred to identify with Homer's Helen or Dante's Beatrice. Unlike her, he is caught not between perfect knowledge and perfect love but rather in the human tension between objective thought and subjective images. He faces this predicament both in life and in the two opposing states which form the poem. With vision fled, his gain is knowledge of a personal ideal, not of impersonal forces as in "The Second Coming." Development toward that ideal is the one freedom offered by Yeats's system, though he allows others outside of it. The lyric ends with his Romantic "moan" of recognition and equally Romantic resolve to render the experience artistically. Like a miniature *Prelude* or *Milton*, "The Double Vision of Michael Robartes" describes an action which is a prelude to poetry.

Yeats's next pair of Greater Romantic Lyrics, "The Tower, II" and "Meditations in Time of Civil War, VII," strike a middle ground between the personal images of dead friends in "In Memory of Major Robert Gregory" and "All Souls' Night" and the impersonal ones of inhuman extremes in "The Second Coming" and "The Double Vision of Michael Robartes." Both poems make the tower top into a symbolic outpost on the border between self and soul. Yet unlike "The Tower," discussed above, "Meditations"[19] draws its images not from past associations of the landscape but from an analogous event in history—the murder of Jacques

Molay, Grand Master of the Templars, which it counterpoints with figures derived from Gustave Moreau's visionary painting "Ladies and Unicorns." They become the ingredients of one of Yeats's most moving struggles against the hatred inherent in the age and in some of his own thought. As he stands upon the tower top, images of first the troop of murderers and then the procession of ladies swim "to the mind's eye." In terms of the poem's title, the first represent "Phantoms of Hatred" and the second those "Of the Heart's Fullness." The imagination tries to counter images of hatred with those of fullness, but as even they yield to "an indifferent multitude . . . brazen hawks . . . Nothing but grip of claws," the poem modulates out of vision into its third and final section. There Yeats descends from the tower top, regrets his separation from friends and public approval, but still resignedly affirms his continued allegiance to "the half-read wisdom of daemonic images." That moment becomes all the more poignant for its frank avowal of human cost.

Although Yeats paired "The Crazed Moon" with "Coole Park, 1929" in *The Winding Stair*, he had written it in 1923, shortly after the other Greater Romantic Lyrics on *Vision* themes. Like them, it can be read in terms of Yeats's system: in a late phase, the moon shines only on moonstruck, disorganized gropers, in contrast to her exuberant children of earlier phases, who danced in order. Further, the later children grow murderous as the gyre approaches conclusion, and they long maliciously to rend whatever comes in reach. But the poem can also be read more literally, as a Greater Romantic Lyric of mental action:

> Crazed through much child-bearing
> The moon is staggering in the sky;
> Moon-struck by the despairing
> Glances of her wandering eye
> We grope, and grope in vain,
> For children born of her pain.
>
> Children dazed or dead!
> When she in all her virginal pride
> First trod on the mountain's head
> What stir ran through the countryside
> Where every foot obeyed her glance!
> What manhood led the dance!
>
> Fly-catchers of the moon,
> Our hands are blenched, our fingers seem
> But slender needles of bone;
> Blenched by that malicious dream
> They are spread wide that each
> May rend what comes in reach.   (VP 487–88)

The three stanzas reenact the familiar triple pattern, matching out-in-out with present-past-present. The speaker first describes the current state of the old moon, then creates a vision of the moon in virginal pride inspiring both passion ("stir") and order ("dance"), and finally returns to the present with perceptions of our vain groping's goal—malicious destruction. The landscape here is remarkably insubstantial even for Yeats; one feels as though the speaker were charting a symbolic Romantic landscape rather than an actual scene. Polysemously, the moon can refer to a natural object, the twenty-eight phases of *A Vision*, historical development in clock time, or imagination withering from exultance to despair. In his current condition, the speaker's only triumph is to re-create past glory from memory.

Yeats transfers that theme to his favorite Irish setting in the following poem of *The Winding Stair*, "Coole Park, 1929." The poem contributes to the book's running modern adaptation of Romanticism, following the Shelleyan tower of "Blood and the Moon" and literary history of "The Nineteenth Century and After" and "Three Movements," picking up the Greater Romantic Lyric form of "The Crazed Moon," and anticipating Romantic self-avowal in "Coole Park and Ballylee, 1931" and Romantic artifice in "Byzantium." He returns to the Coole-Ballylee region for the national ballast with which he habitually sought to weight Romanticism. The landscape's significance derives neither from mere personal experience nor from the arbitrary mythology of *A Vision*, but from its importance to actual historical figures, albeit ones transformed by Yeats's imagination. These historical types, which include the younger Yeats himself, become quasi-objective analogues to Romantic symbols of passion and mood.

The poem opens with a conventional enough beginning for a Greater Romantic Lyric: in a specific landscape at nightfall, the speaker meditates on a bird's flight and even identifies the surrounding trees as a sycamore and a lime.[20] Although the swallow may pick up the Neoplatonic echoes[21] which Yeats associated with Romanticism in general and Shelley in particular, its overt development in the poem follows orthodox Romantic use of singing birds to symbolize artists and their works. The ensuing portions champion freedom from oppressive nature, which Yeats always commended in Romanticism, in explicating why the speaker fixes his eye on works constructed "in nature's spite."

With the vision of former glory in the second stanza, the speaker reverts to the past. Noble Hyde, meditative Synge, and impetuous Shawe-Taylor and Hugh Lane, with Yeats himself in ironic companionship, become heroic figures whose action indicates the poem's real symbol of passion and mood, Lady Gregory herself. Her character most rouses Yeats's intensity of vision as he moves in the third stanza from remembering the past to creating the powerful image of swallows whirling in formation around her true north. The concluding couplet, with its off-rhyme of "lines" and "withershins" and suggestion both of gyres and imaginative *kairos* replacing natural *chronos*, exhausts his imagination in a momentary blaze.

Superficially, the "here" of the final stanza seems to signal the close of a conventional Greater Romantic Lyric. We expect completion of normative here-there-here, out-in-out, and present-past-present movements. But Yeats plays against our vain anticipation, for "here" turns out to be placed in an imagined future. It is as if Wordsworth's "Tintern Abbey" or Coleridge's "Frost at Midnight" omitted their return to the present which separates their vision of the past from that of the future. Instead, Yeats moves directly from past to future in imagining later travelers, scholars, and poets (or perhaps the ghosts of those mentioned in stanza two) taking their stand at a ruined Coole and paying tribute to Lady Gregory. By replacing a return to self with a return to vision, Yeats shifts our attention away from the speaker and toward his overt subject. We end in contemplation of Coole rather than of Yeats's relation to it.

Yeats's adventures with the Greater Romantic Lyric show a sensibility with affinities to Shelley and Blake reworking a poetic form developed principally by Coleridge, Wordsworth, and Keats. The resultant collision exploded the original importance of nature to the form. For Yeats vision became the summoning of images and, in the highest case, active creation of them *de novo*. He pruned his natural descriptions radically, reducing them to a minimum and exploiting their national associations. This transformed his predecessors' concern with tension between mind and nature to tension between mind and images. That dialectic suited his antinomial correction of the emphasis on ideal beauty in his earlier works; through it, he could reach a poetry of insight and knowledge rather than of longing and complaint. The resultant Greater Romantic Lyrics of mental action form one branch of Yeats's mature and innovative Romanticism.

Notes

1. *The Variorum Edition of the Poems of W. B. Yeats*, ed. Peter Allt and Russell K. Alspach (New York: Macmillan, 1957), p. 480. Hereafter cited in the text as VP followed by page number. Cf. Yeats's note to *The Winding Stair*: "In this book and elsewhere I have used towers, and one tower in particular, as symbols and have compared their winding stairs to the philosophical gyres, but it is hardly necessary to interpret what comes from the main track of thought and expression. Shelley uses towers constantly as symbols" (VP 831). Yeats had traced Shelley's use of towers in "The Philosophy of Shelley's Poetry."

2. An abbreviated text of this essay was read at the Midwest Modern Language Association Meeting in Chicago, November 1975. A still longer version will form part of a larger study, *Transformations of Romanticism in Yeats, Eliot, and Stevens*. I am grateful to the American Council of Learned Societies for a fellowship in support of this work.

3. I have already given my views on Yeats's early romanticism in *Yeats and Shelley* (Chicago: University of Chicago Press, 1970); Harold Bloom uses a different approach to arrive at many similar and some quite different views in his *Yeats* (New York: Oxford University Press, 1970). The two books are in part complementary.

4. "Structure and Style in the Greater Romantic Lyric," in *From Sensibility to Romanticism: Essays Presented to Frederick A. Pottle*, ed. Frederick W. Hilles and Harold Bloom (New York: Oxford University Press, 1965). p. 528.

5. Cf. "pictures of the mind" in "In Memory of Eva Gore-Booth and Con Markiewicz" (VP 475).

6. "Structure and Style in the Greater Romantic Lyric," p. 532. Ellipses mine.

7. A. Norman Jeffares has even suggested a possible echo in "The Tower" of Blake on bodily decay; see his A Commentary on the Collected Poems of W. B. Yeats (Stanford: Stanford University Press, 1968), p. 258.

8. W. B. Yeats, Memoirs, ed. Denis Donoghue (London: Macmillan, 1972), p. 133. See pp. 33 and 84 for Yeats's conception of his youthful love as romantic.

9. Essays and Introductions (New York: Macmillan, 1961), p. 291.

10. Horton's contemplation of an image links this poem to the more recondite "Phases of the Moon" (1919), where the creatures of the full moon, or phase fifteen, fix the mind's eye "upon images that once were thought" (VP 375).

11. Mythologies (London: Macmillan, 1962), pp. 345–46.

12. In The English Review and The Little Review, 1918.

13. It moves out-in-out, with a parallel present-past-present pattern.

14. See Jon Stallworthy, Between the Lines: Yeats's Poetry in the Making (Oxford: The Clarendon Press, 1963), p. 17.

15. This phrase comes from Yeats's own note to "The Second Coming" (VP 825).

16. Yeats, p. 320.

17. Margaret Rudd first noticed this in her Divided Image: A Study of William Blake and W. B. Yeats (London: Routledge & Kegan Paul, 1953), p. 119. There is an interesting discussion in Bloom, Yeats, p. 319.

18. In Yeats and Shelley, pp. 195–98.

19. VP 425. See VP 827 for Yeats's note.

20. Yeats's prose draft for the poem began: "Describe house in first stanza." Parkinson has a valuable discussion of the evolution of the poem, in W. B. Yeats: The Later Poetry (Berkeley and Los Angeles: University of California Press, 1964), pp. 80–81, followed by a longer one of "Among School Children."

21. Jeffares compares Pythagoras' use of a swallow image; see A Commentary, p. 344.

Sex and the Dead: *Daimones* of
Yeats and Jung

James Olney*

My title I take from W. B. Yeats, and I claim his authority also in saying that it has to do with a very serious business. "Poems," that daimonic man wrote to his old friend Olivia Shakespear in 1927, "seem to disturb the spirits—once at Gogarty's when I was reading out my *Calvary* and came to the description of the entrance of Lazarus, the door burst open as if by the blast of wind where there could be no wind, and the family ghost had a night of great activity. From all which you will see that I am still of opinion that only two topics can be of the least interest to a serious and studious mind—sex and the dead."[1] Now, Yeats was a man of

*From Studies in the Literary Imagination 14, no. 1 (Spring 1981): 43–60.

considerable humor, and it may at first appear that he is merely indulging that humor in his remark to Mrs. Shakespear. However, while I would not claim that humor is entirely absent here, I would nevertheless make two observations: one, that Yeats is often most humorous when he is most serious (indeed, when most serious and studious); two, that there is scarcely a poem of his mature and late years that is not illuminated by an understanding of his notions about sex and the dead — or, to put it in other words, an understanding of what I shall term *daimones* and daimonism. In the 1925 version of *A Vision* Yeats wrote, "I could I daresay make the book richer, perhaps immeasurably so, if I were to keep it by me for another year, and I have not even dealt with the whole of my subject, perhaps not even with what is most important, writing nothing about the Beatific Vision, little of sexual love; but I am longing to put it out of reach that I may write the poetry it seems to have made possible."[2] There was no need really for Yeats to say much in *A Vision* about sexual love since the poetry said everything on that subject that Yeats had learned from those spirits of the dead that he called the Instructors. The dead taught him about sex; sex taught him about the dead; and there is hardly a poem from 1915 on that does not reveal the teaching of the one about the other — or, more often, of both about each other.

But Yeats's was not the only serious and studious mind being troubled, delighted, and enlightened by family ghosts and their activities during the first twenty-five or so years of this century. Consider the following account of some unruly spirits carrying on on a Sunday in 1916:

> It began with a restlessness, but I did not know what it meant or what "they" wanted of me. There was an ominous atmosphere all around me. I had the strange feeling that the air was filled with ghostly entities. Then it was as if my house began to be haunted. . . .
>
> Around five o'clock in the afternoon on Sunday the front doorbell began ringing frantically. . . . Everyone immediately looked to see who was there, but there was no one in sight. I was sitting near the doorbell, and not only heard it but saw it moving. We all simply stared at one another. The atmosphere was thick, believe me! Then I knew that something had to happen. The whole house was filled as if there were a crowd present, crammed full of spirits. They were packed deep right up to the door, and the air was so thick it was scarcely possible to breathe. As for myself, I was all a-quiver with the question: "For God's sake, what in the world is this?" Then they cried out in chorus, "We have come back from Jerusalem where we found not what we sought." That is the beginning of the *Septem Sermones*.[3]

Septem Sermones ad Mortuos, a little book that R. F. C. Hull describes as "a piece of automatic writing in the form of a Gnostic prose poem," bears on its title page the name "Basilides of Alexandria," but the foregoing account of ghostly spirits and the origins of the book is of course from C. G. Jung of Zurich. The first lines of the book are these: "The dead came back from Jerusalem, where they found not what they sought. They prayed me let them in and besought my word, and thus I began my teaching." While Jung claims to teach the dead rather than, as Yeats more modestly claims, to have been taught by the dead, there can be no question but that the lesson of the *Seven Sermons to the Dead* are remarkably similar to the revelations of *A Vision* and that the source of the lessons in both cases is the realm of the *daimones*: both books teach lessons of the *daimones*, from the daimones, about the nature of daimonism.

What, however, is a *daimōn* and what has it to do with either sex or the dead? Let us hear Basilides of Alexandria, *né* C.G. Jung, preaching sex to his congregation of the dead:

> The world of the gods is made manifest in spirituality and in sexuality. The celestial ones appear in spirituality, the earthly in sexuality.
>
> Spirituality conceiveth and embraceth. It is woman-like and therefore we call it MATER COELESTIS, the celestial mother. Sexuality engendereth and createth. It is man-like, and therefore we call it PHALLOS, the earthly father. . . . For the Mother and the Phallos are superhuman daemons which reveal the world of the gods. They are for us more effective than the gods, because they are closely akin to our own nature. . . . Spirituality and sexuality are not your qualities, not things which ye possess and contain. But they possess and contain you; for they are powerful daemons, manifestations of the gods, and are, therefore, things which reach beyond you, existing in themselves (*Memories*, pp. 386–87).

So according to the long-dead master of Gnostic obscurity — for Basilides was an historic figure of the second century A.D. as well as a mask for Jung — *daimones* are both celestial and earthly in nature; they are superhuman but are nevertheless subordinate to the gods proper; they are akin to our own nature but akin also to the dead; and while they are half human and closely tied to something within us, they yet seem to come upon us from without. Or as Yeats, in his essay on "Magic," put the same point, more elegantly and more succinctly (if less anciently) than Jung / Basilides, "Our most elaborate thoughts, elaborate purposes, precise emotions, are often, as I think, not really ours, but have of a sudden come up, as it were, out of Hell or down out of Heaven."[4] Those thoughts, purposes, and emotions that seem most a man's own and most characteristic of him individually, Yeats nevertheless, like Jung, understood to be of the realm of the *daimones* above us or below us and surrounding us all about.

When it comes to theurgy and the practice of magic, as it often does with Yeats, the *daimones* are naturally of crucial importance: the Adept obviously must have some awareness and some knowledge of the nature of those powerful spirits if he is going to evoke them successfully, if he is going to call them up or down and have them come, and if he is going to have something of their more-than-human power transferred into his human hands. It is not irrelevant that Yeats's motto—his secret name—in the Order of the Golden Dawn was "Demon est Deus Inversus." This motto, if I may translate loosely and somewhat irreverently, means "*Daimon* is God turned on his head"; which is much the same as saying, in the classic phrasing of the Hermetic texts, "As above, so below." The poet, too, as Yeats says in his essay on "Magic," is a kind of magician who evokes the spirits in his deployment of language—in sound, rhythm, image, and symbol. The favored phase on the Great Wheel in *A Vision* is undoubtedly phase seventeen—the phase of the poets (Dante, Shelley, Landor, and almost certainly Yeats himself)—and this is the phase that Yeats calls the phase of "The Daimonic Man." The vision is comprehensive, the plenum is full: daimonic spirits above, daimonic spirits below, and in between Daimonic Man, Poet and Magician. Jung was neither a poet nor a magician, and later in his life he half-disavowed the *Septem Sermones*, calling them a "youthful sin" and giving them, like his autobiography, no place in his *Collected Works*. Nevertheless, it is almost too easy to find parallels in Jung's *Collected Works*—i.e., in what he considered his scientific writings—for the Basilidean and Yeatsian vision of a universe filled top to bottom with spirits that possess us and live through us, that "come up, as it were, out of Hell or down out of Heaven" and make their purposes willy-nilly ours. "If we examine our lives," Jung says in volume IV of the *Collected Works*, "we . . . perceive how a mighty hand guides us without fail to our destiny, and not always is this hand a kindly one. Often we call it the hand of God or of the devil, thereby expressing, unconsciously but correctly, a highly important psychological fact: that the power which shapes the life of the psyche has the character of an autonomous personality. . . . [T]he source of any such destiny appears as a daemon, as a good or evil spirit."[5] And elsewhere in the *Collected Works* we are told that it is "more 'correct' psychologically" to use the words *daimōn* and *daimonion* "to explain . . . the natural forces that appear in us as instincts," for those two Greek words, as Jung goes on to say, "express a determining power which comes upon man from outside, like providence or fate" (CW, IX, part 2, pars 50–51). But when Jung says this in *Aion*, he is not saying anything new: he had himself said it all thirty-five years earlier in the guise of Basilides preaching sex to the clamorous dead.

The word *daimōn*, as Jung points out, is of course Greek in origin, and the concept of the *daimōn* received its original elaboration—and I should say really its full elaboration—from Greek poets and philosophers. With the *daimōn* as with so many things: the Greeks said it all first. We find *daimōnes* up to their characteristic activities as early as Homer, and even more interestingly in Hesiod; they turn up in the Presocratics— notably in Heraclitus and Empedocles—and are very prominent in Plato; from Plato, naturally, they were taken up by the Neoplatonists—Plotinus, Porphyry, Iamblichus—and by the Gnostics and Hermetists; and from all these they were handed on to St. Augustine and the Christian Middle Ages — where, however, the *daimones* were mistreated to an interpretation that was far too narrow and too exclusive, not to say grossly humiliating: the Christian interpretation in effect takes the God of Yeats's motto and turns him right side up again, declaring (as St. Augustine did in fact declare) that demons do indeed exist but are forces entirely of evil and are responsible for most or all of our woe. The point, perhaps, is made if we remark that sex is felt as a demon in St. Augustine — but not as a *daimōn*; and while fallen angels become demons operating out of Hell, the pious dead go to Heaven and neither descend nor condescend to exercise a daimonic influence in mortal affairs. Consequently, I shall disregard Christian demonism as being largely irrelevant — a simplification and perversion of a complex and noble doctrine — and shall also disregard for the most part Neoplatonic, Gnostic, and Hermetic developments as being mere supererogation and in the end more obscurantist than anything else. This leaves us with Hesiod, with Heraclitus and Empedocles, and with Plato who put together, singly and in concert, a concept of the *daimōn*, embracing both sex and the dead, that we find alive and very well indeed in Yeats and Jung.

In his *Works and Days* Hesiod provides us with a convenient point of departure in his mythic explanation of the origin of *daimones*. A *daimōn*, according to the *Works and Days*, is a guardian spirit, a spirit of one of the great dead now watching over mortal men. "First of all," Hesiod says, describing the generations of men, "the deathless gods who dwell on Olympus made a golden race of mortal men who lived in the time of Kronos." Though mortal, Hesiod goes on to say, their lives were easy, comfortable, and joyous, and their deaths were peaceful, "as though they were overcome with sleep." "But when the earth hid this race," Hesiod continues, and here he switches from the past tense of the golden race to the present tense of degraded man who has suffered a devolution from golden to silver to brazen to heroic to the ordinary race of humanity — "when the earth hid this race, they are noble daimons through the counsels of great Zeus, guardians on earth of mortal men" (11.109–123, tr. G. S. Kirk). We might remark first of all that it is only the great dead who become Hesiodic *daimones*: he does not mention any of the intervenient generations — silver, brazen, or heroic — as succeeding to that estate. It is not, in other words, the insipid, tepid life of the average man that is going to provide the passion and the spirituality necessary to the *daimōn*. Yeats and Jung unquestionably agreed with Hesiod's genealogy of daimonism, and they had reason to: their own Hesiodic *daimones* were the spirits of dead men who had been in their lives great in both passions and deeds. For Jung there was Basilides, there were the raucous spirits who crowded his house to the door, and there was most of all Philemon — for which we can fairly understand Goethe in medieval dress. For Yeats there were the Instructors who brought him an ancient system of philosophy as well as metaphors for his poetry, and there was Leo Africanus, explorer, geographer, and historian. Where these spirits of the great dead came from both Yeats and Jung well knew: they were agreed on the internal/external — that is, psychological but also historical — provenance of the spirits. "The unconscious," Jung remarks casually in his autobiography, feeling free to unbutton there in a way he might not do in his *Collected Works*, "corresponds to the mythic land of the dead, the land of the ancestors. If, therefore, one has a fantasy of the soul vanishing [as Jung had], this means that it has withdrawn into the unconscious or into the land of the dead. There it produces a mysterious animation and gives visible form to the ancestral traces, the collective contents. Like a medium, it gives the dead a chance to manifest themselves" (*Memories*, p. 191).

It was in fact a medium in Yeats's case who first gave the dead Leo Africanus a chance to manifest himself. What we learn, among other things, from Yeats's account of this manifestation is that not only do *daimones* come to us from outside, as external and objective beings, but they can also be quite abrupt with us if we fail to know them and to understand what they say. Writing in his journal in 1912, Yeats recorded his experience at the séance when he met his first, very own Hesiodic *daimōn*: "There was the usual trumpet," Yeats says, "and . . .

> there came a very loud voice through the trumpet. It had come for "Mr. Gates." Or so the medium heard the voice. I said that was me. Then the voice said, "I have been with you from childhood. We want to use your hand and brain." "You possess key," or, "you are a key mind", I forget which. "I am Leo the writer — writer and explorer." I tried by questions to get more. "When did he live; in eighteenth century?" He then said, "Why man," or such expression implying impatience, "I am Leo, the writer. You know, Leo the writer." When I said I did not, I thought he added, "You will hear of me at Rome." He then went. After him came a feeble voice of which we could get little that was clear. This voice was suddenly interrupted by the very loud voice again, telling me "to sit up straight in my chair." I was leaning forward. At this point the influence was broken. One terrified lady had already left, and now two left.[6]

In spite of this rather unpromising beginning, Leo stayed around for a period of time — giving Yeats a chance to check him out in *Chambers' Biographical Dictionary* — and he eventually proposed, through a medium, that the two of them, Leo and Yeats, enter into a correspondence, and suggested further that having written out any questions that bothered him, Yeats should proceed to write answers to his own questions but as if in the tone and style of Leo (the logic of this schizoid procedure being that Leo was apparently not altogether "other" or entirely independent of Yeats; and besides, being a spirit, Leo could not take physical pen in spiritual hand and write on physical paper: it was to be five years or so before he or other spirits and instructors could avail themselves of Mrs. Yeats's abilities in automatic writing). One question did bother Yeats; he asked it—"was Leo Africanus real, or only a phantom of the mind?"—and then he answered it: "He said he was part of the unconscious, but also, most certainly, Leo Africanus the geographer." Virginia Moore (who quotes the Leo Africanus/Yeats correspondence) calls this "straddling the issue," but it is not really—at least it is not if we accord to the Hesiodic *daimōn* the same subtlety and duality of explanation given to it by both Yeats and Jung. "Though grave-diggers' toil is long," as Yeats puts it in "Under Ben Bulben,"

> Sharp their spades, their muscles strong,
> They but thrust their buried men
> Back in the human mind again.

It was there—"Back in the human mind again"—that Leo Africanus went, and there also the dead in Jung's psychic/mythic language: "The unconscious corresponds to the . . . land of the dead, the land of the ancestors," and he continues (skipping over the passage previously quoted), "From that time on, the dead have become ever more distinct for me as the voices of the Unanswered, Unresolved, and Unredeemed; for since the questions and demands which my destiny required me to answer did not come to me from outside, they must have come from the inner world" (*Memories*, pp. 191–92). Thus too Leo Africanus came to Yeats, from the land of the dead and from the inner world, came as Yeats's *daimōn* and his destiny, an archetypal guardian spirit—in Jungian language, the archetype of the Wise Old Man—came, like the dead to whom Jung preached, to fulfill his own purposes in the living and through them to live once again.

Here, imperceptibly, we have crossed the thin but important line that separates Hesiod's grand and simple mythic formulation of the *daimōn* from Heraclitus' gnomic, complex, and immensely suggestive psychological/philosophical formulation of the same thing. The Heraclitean *daimōn* begins with Hesiod, as in Fr. 63: "they [i.e., the great dead] rise up and become guardians, wakefully, of living and dead." Already, however, there is here a slight variation on Hesiod, for Heraclitus, the great exponent of antinomies in perpetual opposition, cannot refrain from coupling the opposites, as he invariably does, in a single phrase: "living and dead." In Heraclitus—and this is as much a mark of his verbal genius as of his philosophic daring—the two become virtually a single, hyphenated entity: "living-and-dead." Heraclitus approaches the *daimōn* in two ways—both of them ways dear to the hearts of Yeats and Jung—and in so doing he provides the necessary bridge from Hesiodic myth to Platonic philosophy. The *daimon* in Heraclitus is a guardian spirit, but, in a refinement on Hesiod and in an extension of his idea that points the way forward to Plato, Yeats, and Jung, that *daimon* is not something external to ourselves: rather, it is our psychic heritage, our character—determined by our ancestral past and manifest in our moral beings. ἦθος ἀνθρώπῳ δαίμων: W. K. C. Guthrie says, the fragment (DK 119) is "scarcely translateable";

Guthrie's own translation is perhaps as good as any — "A man's individuality is his *daimōn*." With Heraclitus we are approaching — and with Empedocles we come closer until with Plato we finally achieve — formulation of what Jung called "the main archetype," for which there are so many specific images — the archetype, that is to say, of the self. "By fate and necessity . . ." Yeats explains in *A Vision*, "is understood that which comes from without, whereas the *Mask* is predestined, Destiny being that which comes to us from within."[7] But — to paraphrase Yeats himself — "If Fate and Destiny should meet/What a crop of mummy wheat!" And Fate and Destiny do indeed meet in the Heraclitean *daimon*, subjective and objective, creative force from within and creative force from without, the man himself and his antinomic other — the self a perpetual process, a continual exchange and interchange, very like reality in Michael Robartes' elegant analogy as reported by Owen Aherne: "I can remember Robartes saying in one of his paradoxical figurative moods that he pictured reality as a number of great eggs laid by the Phoenix and that these eggs turn inside out perpetually without breaking the shell" (1925 *Vision*, p. xxiii).

The second approach made by Heraclitus to the *daimōn* is to be found in Fr. 62: "Immortal mortals, mortal immortals, living the others' death, and dying the others' life." No other thought, it seems to me, and no other image teased and fascinated Yeats's mind so much as this one. The fragment is everywhere in Yeats — in poems, plays, essays, and letters — whether as allusion, as quotation, as misquotation, or as creative adaptation. While Jung was less devoted to this particular fragment than Yeats (he quotes it only once, in CW, VI), the idea behind it of mysteriously joined, interpenetrating, and self-reversing opposites is of the very essence of his theories of the psyche. Instead of simply referring to the great Ephesian ancestor, as Yeats does again and again, as authority on the profound and endless paradoxes of psyche, Jung concocts a series of fancy phrases to the same end: psyche is composed of complementary and compensatory opposites he tells us, and it enacts the universal psychological law of *enantiodromia;* or self is a *complexio oppositorum*, a *coniunctio oppositorum*, a *hieros gamos*, a *mysterium coniunctionis*. But all these expressions say the same thing, and Heraclitus, as Yeats knew, had said it all earlier and much better in his dark and riddling way: "Immortal mortals, mortal immortals, living the others' death, dying the others' life."

After Yeats had had the opportunity to check out his daimonic visitant in the biographical dictionary, he came to recognize that a personal *daimōn* is not only Hesiodic but is also and very importantly Heraclitean as well. For what he discovered about Leo Africanus was that he was his — Yeats's — own opposite, and that it was for this precise reason that he chose Yeats (or that Yeats's share in the collective unconscious chose Leo) for inter-daimonic communication. They were like reversed mirror images of one another, or like an image thrown from the convex mirror of the unconscious onto the concave mirror of consciousness and so, as Heraclitus always insisted, continually back and forth. "I know all or all but all you know," Leo wrote to his antinomic twin, "we have been over the same books, I have shared your joys and sorrows, and yet it is only because I am all things furthest from your intellect and your will that I alone am your interlocutor." Intellect and will, as Yeats of course recognized and as Jung could have confirmed, are functions of consciousness, so that we can see in Leo's words simple restatement of Jungian doctrine: the unconscious stands in a compensatory relationship to consciousness. In Heraclitus, the *daimōn* is for the first time, but will remain so hereafter right down to Yeats and Jung, a spirit of mediation in a world of opposites and of mediation between opposed worlds—immortal mortals, mortal immortals; it is a force that joins, with a powerful instress, all contraries and so prevents the psychic universe from flying into sexual and ethical fragments; for as Heraclitus insisted, we are always really one with our unconscious, opposite number. In *Per Amica Silentia Lunae* Yeats writes, "Plutarch's precepts and the experience of old women in Soho . . . will have it that a strange living man may win for Daimon an illustrious dead man," and how could Yeats disagree, for had not he—a sufficiently "strange living man"—won Leo Africanus for his *Daimōn?* "But now," Yeats continues, "I add another thought: the Daimon comes not as like to like but seeking its own opposite, for man and Daimon feed the hunger in one another's hearts."[8] What we see here as Plutarch and old women in Soho joining hands with Yeats was in the history of ancient Greek mythology and philosophy Hesiod shading off into Heraclitus.

Empedocles' contribution to the science of daimonism, though it comes in a single and somewhat obscure passage, is nevertheless of crucial importance in the concatenation of the entire theory. The man who could say of himself, "I go about among you an immortal god, no mortal now," was hardly likely to adopt the same humanity-centered perspective—a matter of natural processes and ethical conclusions—as Hesiod and Heraclitus. Empedocles, unlike his two predecessors, saw, or claimed to see, from beyond mortal experience, not from within. Whereas Hesiod—good husbandman poet that he was—viewed the *daimōn* in human, natural, and generational perspective, and Heraclitus—the original paradoxicalist—viewed it as a matter of perpetually interacting, conjoined opposites, Empedocles envisions a *daimōn* that is only incidentally and unfortunately implicated in time but whose true essence is supra-temporal and whose real abode is in eternity. Hesiod and Heraclitus see the *daimōn* as it were *sub specie temporis*, in the aspect of time; Empedocles sees it *sub specie aeternitatis*, in the aspect of eternity, and what he thereby introduces into the evolving theory of daimonism is the notion that the *daimōn* is immortal and is incarnated and reincarnated in a series of bodies. This doctrine of metempsychosis, which is of course central to Plato's vision, will become the archetype of rebirth for Jung, and for Yeats "the most plausible of the explanations of the world" (*Memoirs*, p. 48). Empedocles' *daimōn* is a fragment of undying Love imprisoned in a succession of dying bodies — an immortal soul, as Yeats puts it, "sick with desire/And fastened to a dying animal"; it is that part of man that is not subject to death and that is potentially divine, for it was of the gods in the past and, according to Empedocles, will be of the gods again, but is now an exile, doomed for a certain term to go the ways of mortality before it will be sufficiently purified to return to its divine and proper home. "There is an oracle of Necessity," Empedocles says in the relevant portion of Fr. 115, "an ancient decree of the gods . . . that whenever one of the *daimōnes*" sins by shedding blood or swearing false oaths, "he must wander for thrice ten thousand seasons away from the blessed ones, being born through time in all manners of mortal forms, changing one toilsome path of life for another. . . . One of these I now am, an exile and a wanderer from the gods. . . ." In the superbly confident statement of "Under Ben Bulben" — "Many times man lives and dies/Between his two eternities" — we can easily recognize the oracular and visionary spirit of Empedocles; and when Yeats says to himself in his Diary in 1930, "I have to face Berkeley's greatest difficulty: to account for the continuity of perception," we find him very shortly thereafter arriving at a solution which depends on the Empedoclean *daimōn* — on the indestructible and occult self: "That continuity," Yeats decides, "is in the Passionate Body of the permanent self or daimon."

So, by the circuitous route of Empedocles' *Purifications* and Yeats's *Vision*, we arrive back at Jung's main archetype, the self, a supratemporal, Jung would say, and virtually immortal experience of the psyche. There is no doubt but that Jung believed in a permanent, indestructible, occult, and ultimate self; did he, however, believe also in reincarnation? We would, I think, have to say that, typically enough, he did and he didn't: he believed sometimes but not other times; he believed in this way but not in that way; he gave with one hand and took away with the other; and he equivocated whenever he could. I am not going to go into all the evidence because it is too extensive and confusing, but it seems to me that Jung gives three different responses when asked about reincarnation: sometimes he evades the question by taking refuge in obscurity (and he was a past master of obscurantism when he chose to be); at other times he "psychologizes" reincarnation so that he can say that he believes in the psychological reality of reincarnation but can beg off expressing any opinion of it in philosophical, religious, or metaphysical terms; and finally, in old age, he hints that he believes after all in literal, personal reincarnation. The gist of the psychological explanation of reincarnation is that the collective unconscious is immortal — or as near immortal as to our minute, insect-eye's view makes no difference; therefore, since we share in the collective unconscious, and the collective unconscious forms a part of our being, when we live again those innate passions and perform once more those instinctive actions that have been the essential human experience from time immemorial—when we live out the archetypes of the collective unconscious and so take on the lineaments of what Jung liked to refer to as the two-million-year-old Man—we naturally have the sense that that part of us at least is immortal and that we have done this all before—as, collectively, we have done. Elsewhere, however (*Memories*, p. 317), Jung toyed with the notion that he personally—and presumably other men likewise—embodied a transmigratory *daimōn* in the full Empedoclean sense, a *daimōn* that had lived before in other bodies (in the body of Goethe he implies at one point). In any case, the *daimōn*, Empedoclean or Hesiodic/Heraclitean, is at the very heart of the matter: define your *daimōn* and you simultaneously define your mode of immortality.

I am of course aware that up to this point I have rather neglected one of the two subjects of interest to a serious and studious mind: the dead have doubtless received their due, but sex—except for the conflicting and complementary opposites of Heraclitus, which is a pretty thin and abstract variety of sex after all—sex has hardly come into the picture at all. It is only with Plato—or rather with Aristophanes and Socrates in Plato's *Symposium*—that sex at last rears its daimonic head. Moreover, besides discovering the *daimōn* engaged in erotic practises unrevealed to Hesiod, Heraclitus, and Empedocles, Plato also drew up behind him, as it were, the composite teachings of his three daimonic predecessors. To conserve space I shall merely cite the Platonic passages that elaborate on Hesiod, Heraclitus, and Empedocles. In the *Phaedo* (107e) a Hesiodic *daimōn* is allotted to the individual; in the *Republic* (617e) every individual *chooses* a Heraclitean *daimōn*; and in the *Timaeus* (90a) every soul is possessed of an Empedoclean transmigratory *daimon* which acts as a kind of individual over-soul impelling him towards God whence the *daimōn* itself originated. All these Platonic and pre-Platonic senses of the *daimōn* are present to Yeats when he says, "The Greeks . . . considered that myths are the activities of the Daimons, and that the Daimons shape our characters and our lives. I have often had the fancy that there is some one myth for every man, which, if we but knew it, would make us understand all he did and thought" (E & I, p. 107). Plotinus delighted Yeats's heart by declaring (or at least Yeats thought he declared) that there is a unique archetype for every human soul; but we need not involve ourselves in Plotinian mysticism to understand what Yeats means here for what he means is a composite of what Hesiod, Heraclitus, Empedocles, and Plato meant about *daimones*.

In the *Symposium* Socrates, the last of the revellers in that dialogue to give his views on Eros, says that he learned all he knows on the subject from Diotima, a woman of Mantinea who is also a prophetess and seer. When Diotima denies that Eros is a god, Socrates reports this ensuing exchange (202e):

> "What would Eros be then?" I said. "A mortal?"
> "Far from it."

"But what then?"

"Like the things earlier," she said; "midway between mortal and immortal."

"What is that, Diotima?"

"Δαίμων μέγας, a great *daimōn*, Socrates, for everything daimonic is midway between divine and mortal."

Daimones, as Diotima goes on to say — and Eros, sexual love, is a great *daimōn* — are responsible for making the universe what we call it — *a universe:* a single, unified, complete whole. Being half-divine and half-human, immortal mortals, they mediate between gods and men, and in thus filling up the gap between they bind everything into one great whole. "For God mingles not with man; but through Love all the intercourse and converse of gods with men, whether they be awake or asleep, is carried on" (203a, tr. Jowett). Just so, according to Jung who, in "Marriage as a Psychological Relationship," writes, "Normal sex life . . . is in truth, a genuine and incontestable experience of the Divine, whose transcendent force obliterates and consumes everything individual; a real communion with life and the impersonal power of fate" (CW, XVII, par. 330). We have only to recall that *daimōn* is in one sense fate or destiny and that Eros is a ἀαίμων μέζας to realize that what Jung is talking about here is nothing other than daimonism. Normal sex life — or, I suppose, abnormal for that matter — is a *daimōn* that possesses us, not we it. Leda's sex life would probably not qualify as altogether normal, but I think she, and her poet, would agree with Jung and Diotima on the daimonic nature of Eros as a spirit binding gods and mortals:

> How can those terrified vague fingers push
> The feathered glory from her loosening thighs?
> And how can body, laid in that white rush,
> But feel the strange heart beating where it lies?

Diotima's argument is that Eros of all kinds, or at all levels — whether sexual love; love of glory, fame, and wisdom; or love of absolute Beauty, absolute Truth, absolute Good — that all love is a desire for immortality which the various lovers achieve through procreation, through the works they leave behind them, and through a mystical union with that which is in itself and by its very nature immortal.

This desire for immortality on the lover's part, his yearning for wholeness, completion, perfection, recalls Aristophanes' excellent and witty tale about Eros earlier in the *Symposium*. Aristophanic lovers — at least those who were originally parts of a bisexual whole, the creature Aristophanes calls ἀνώρ ζυνον: man-woman — seek their other necessary half, their daimonic opposite or antinomy, so that, throwing their arms about themselves in that other, they may recover a lost happiness, wholeness, and immortality. "Passionate love," Yeats says in *A Vision*, "is from the *Daimon* which seeks by union with some other *Daimon* to reconstruct above the antinomies its own true nature" (p. 238). Its own true nature, above the antinomies, in the Thirteenth Cone or Leda's Egg, is the condition of the Sphere. Earlier in the same book Yeats writes, "The present Pope has said in his last Encyclical that the natural union of man and woman [equivalent of Jung's 'normal sex life'] has a kind of sacredness. He thought doubtless of the marriage of Christ and the Church, whereas I see in it a symbol of that eternal instant where the antinomy is resolved. It is not the resolution itself" (p. 214). Yeats means much the same thing here as he does when he says elsewhere that the Sphere is a symbol of that ultimate reality which — precisely — can be symbolized but cannot be known; much the same thing also as when he has Michael Robartes remark that "The marriage bed is the symbol of the solved antinomy, and were more than symbol could a man there lose and keep his identity . . ." (*Vision*, p. 52) — could he, that is, become his *daimōn* yet remain himself and so ascend into his own archetype. In a diary entry transferred into his *Autobiographies* Yeats writes of that great symbolic love of Solomon and Sheba that, in poetry, stood for his and George's own love: "It seems to me that true love is a discipline, and it needs so much wisdom that the love of Solomon and Sheba must have lasted, for all the silence of the Scriptures. Each divines the secret self of the other, and refusing to believe in the mere daily self, creates a mirror where the lover or the beloved sees an image to copy in daily life; for love also creates the Mask." What Yeats spiritualizes and even etherealizes here he brings back down to hard-core sexual earth in "Solomon and the Witch," a poem which is all yearning after sphericity, a condition to be achieved through the workings of Eros, that ἀίμυν μέζας. Solomon, after Sheba's questioning about some strange events of the preceding night, proceeds to enlighten her:

> "A cockerel
> Crew from a blossoming apple bough
> Three hundred years before the Fall,
> And never crew again till now. . . .
> He that crowed out eternity
> Thought to have crowed it in again."

"Yet," Sheba remarks, in apparent disappointment, "the world stays," and to this Solomon replies,

> "If that be so,
> Your cockerel found us in the wrong
> Although he thought it worth a crow."

But the last word goes to Sheba who, in the "forbidden sacred grove" where King and Queen, sun and moon — as Jung says in *Psychology and Alchemy*, "the primordial pair of opposites" — are joined, there she hopes that she and her lover may couple in daimonic union and so restore the universe to its spherical, prelapsarian condition of resolved antinomies and immortality. "The night has fallen," Sheba says to Solomon,

"not a sound
In the forbidden sacred grove
Unless a petal hit the ground . . .
And the moon is wilder every minute.
O! Solomon! let us try again."

I think that, in this discussion of Eros as a great *daimōn*—a discussion that intends to be rational after all—there is no point in trying to go beyond Sheba's ecstatic cry. Let us assume, as I think Yeats assumed, that Solomon and Sheba made it.

It only remains now to indicate how sex and the dead are really one according to Yeats and Jung—are one in such a way that Yeats might have written to Olivia Shakespear that there is only one subject of the least interest to a serious and studious mind: sex-and-the-dead; because the two do meet at a certain point, do join together like a hook fitted to its eye, and do become, if not identical, at least inter-determinative the one of the other. We might seem to have the answer to the question of the tie that binds sex and the dead when Yeats speaks of a transcendent beauty as "already visible to the dead and to souls in ecstasy, for ecstasy is a kind of death" (E & I, p. 71). But I think we should be mistaken to take this as the answer—that sexual "ecstasy is a kind of death"—for the connection we seek is not between sex and death—that connection is almost a cliché; it was Dylan Thomas, not W. B. Yeats, who worked that vein and exhausted it thoroughly. No, the vital connection (if "vital" be not too great a paradox here) is not between sex and death but between sex and the dead. Yeats brings us a little closer to the point when he says, in his essay on "The Body of Father Christian Rosencrux," "the great passions are angels of God"—and so, we might remark, are the dead as well—and it is our greatest obligation, as it is also our supreme consummation and ecstasy, Yeats continues, "to embody them [great passions/angels of God] 'uncurbed in their eternal glory' . . ." (E & I, p. 197). But where do these great passions—and sexual emotion is unquestionably one of them—where do they come from? Yeats provides a hint, and another piece to the puzzle, when he writes, in the 1925 *Vision*, "In our dreams we communicate with the dead in their *Waking State*, and these dreams never come to an end though they are only known to us while we sleep" (p. 246). Jung said the same thing point for point, though in psychological/mystical language rather than poetic/mystical language, when he maintained that we dream all the time—and so mingle with the dead, i.e., figures of the collective unconscious—"only our consciousness makes such a noise in the waking state that we no longer hear it" (CW, XVIII, par. 162). The dead dream us and we dream the dead, according to Yeats's imagination; or in Jung's terminology, we are the consciousness of the dead and they our great unconscious. Thus we give waking life to the dead and they animate our sleeping life for us, but both lives are going on all the time, continuous and unbroken, the living and dead toe to heel, heel to toe, as Yeats one place puts it, reversed mirror images the one of the other.

Spirits of the intense, passionate dead—whether the intensity be of thought or of feeling—"seem to live backward through time," Yeats tells us in his introduction to *Words upon the Window-pane*[9]; and according to Yeats's vision, which he presents not only in *A Vision* but also in poems, plays, and essays, the purpose of this living backward in time—which is for us a living forward in time—is that they, the passionate dead, may thereby embrace the *daimōn*, be reduced with it to ashes in the conflagration (like Swedenborg's angels in sexual union), and be phoenix-like reborn a Jungian third out of the conflicting two but much more than either of the opposites and on another level of being altogether from the mere sum of those opposites. Speaking of the lover who yearns for the deadly embrace of his own antinomy, Yeats says in *On the Boiler*, "It is as though he wanted to take his own death into his arms and beget a stronger life upon that death" (Ex., p. 430). This is what, in *The Rhizome and the Flower*, I have called the daimonic progression: a sort of Platonic ladder made up of resolutions, integrations, and creations at successively higher levels of reality, freedom, and perfection. Daimonic opposites join to produce a third, which unites with its daimonic opposite to produce another third, which . . . and so on until there is a symbolic resolution of all antinomies in the symbolic Sphere. "Their aim," Yeats says, "is to enter at last into their own archetype, or into all being: into that which is there always" (Ex., p. 366). This is nothing less than Jung's *mysterium coniunctionis*, and it may be remarked that Yeats, developing ideas that are strikingly Jungian, adopts a terminology of archetypes for which Jung has become so famous—or so infamous depending on one's point of view; it should also be remarked, however, that Yeats was talking about archetypes, and knew a great deal about them from his own connections with *Anima Mundi*, well before Jung discovered the collective unconscious, took up the archetypes, and gave them their psychological currency.

It is in the essay called "Anima Mundi" that Yeats at last provides us with the clew we seek, the missing link that connects sex with the dead: "The dead living in their memories are, I am persuaded, the source of all that we call instinct, and it is their love and their desire, all unknowing, that make us drive beyond our reason, or in defiance of our interest it may be; and it is the dream martens [sic] that, all unknowing, are mastermasons to the living martens building about church windows their elaborate nests . . ." (Myth., p. 359). Instinct—there, of course, and at last, is the connection: patterns of instinct—those channels and forms according to which it is possible and necessary for us to perceive as we do, to understand as we are able, and so to live as we must—are inherited, and are to be traced to their source in the living dead—or to "the dead living in their memories"—who dream us into passionate life. At the joined apices of the two cones, where the living backward of the dead becomes our living forward—living the others' death, dying the others' life—there we find instinct, there we find the *daimōn* of sexual passion whose other face is the *daimōn* of the great dead. It is "the dead living in their memories" who are "the source of all that we call instinct"; just so, Jung would say, for the unconscious—which equals the "land of the dead"—"is the deposit of all human experience right back to its remotest beginnings . . .; it is also the source of the instincts, for the archetypes are simply the forms which the instincts assume. From the living fountain of instinct flows everything that is creative; hence the unconscious is not merely conditioned by history, but is the very source of the creative impulse" (CW, VIII, par. 339). *Daimones* are forces that come upon us from without and well up in us from within, forces of nature that seize on the individual and his life for their fulfillment; and they are also the residue of experience—hence instincts in either way, the dead (which could be our own past lives) living in their memorial wisdom and passion. "The collective unconscious," according to Jung, "consists of the sum of the instincts and their correlates, the archetypes," and an archetype, as he has already pointed out in the same essay, "might . . . be described as the *instinct's perception of itself*, or as the self-portrait of the instinct . . ." (CW, VIII, pars. 277–80). When an archetype takes hold of us (nor can we avoid possession by them since we are human and possessed of all the instincts specific to humans), then—as Yeats and Jung jointly maintain— events of the day do not (as in Freud) determine the images of our dreams nor does experience in the world determine our vision; rather our vision breaks the world and reforms it according to an image that comes from deep within and from far in the past. An instinct insistently forces its own self-portrait on us, and it is not—nor will it ever be—the portrait of anyone in the world; so that all our Freudian incestuous desires—Yeats and Jung agree—are deeper and other than the son's desire for his mother or the brother's for his sister. They are nothing less than the serpent's closing on his own tail, Antaeus returning to the earth, the self wedding the anti-self in a *hieros gamos*, Narcissus joined to his daimonic image, Leda's Egg turning inside out and outside in without ever breaking the shell. The figures of such visions and dreams, Yeats one place declares, are "shadows of the impulses that have made them, messages . . . out of the ancestral being of the questioner" (E & I, p. 36). Another way—less poetic but more psychological—of saying this is that such visionary and dream figures are self-portraits of specifically human instincts which are them- selves the inherited product of the accumulated experience of the race. In yet other words, they are archetypal images from the collective uncon- scious, symbolic figures from *Anima Mundi, daimones* reflecting the cumulative experience and psychic possibilities of humankind and, at the same time, shaping that experience and those possibilities.

I am going to give Yeats the final word on sex and the dead as I also gave him the first; and fittingly enough, the last word, like the first, is to be found in a letter to Olivia Shakespear. In that letter Yeats describes to Mrs. Shakespear a bizarre and (to him) very convincing occult experience—an experience with a medium who revealed some astounding and verifiable knowledge that the medium could not possibly have possessed except it came from a Great Mind and Great Memory—and then Yeats says: "After this and all that has gone before I must capitulate if the dark mind lets me. Certainly we suck at the eternal dugs. How well too it puts my own mood between spiritual excitement, and the sexual torture and the knowledge that they are somehow inseparable!" (*Letters*, p. 731). Jung, I should think, was unquestionably sucking the same daimonic nourishment—"spiritual excitement, and the sexual torture and the knowledge that they are somehow inseparable"—sucking it just as passionately as Yeats, and at the same time as he, from another teat on those same eternal dugs.

Notes

1. *The Letters of W. B. Yeats*, ed. Allan Wade (New York: The Macmillan Company, 1955), pp. 729–30; hereafter cited in the text as *Letters*.

2. *A Vision: An explanation of life founded upon the writings of Giraldus and upon certain doctrines attributed to Kusta Ben Luka* (London: privately printed by T. Werner Laurie, 1925), p. xliii; hereafter cited in the text as 1925 *Vision*.

3. *Memories, Dreams, Reflections*, recorded & ed. by Aniela Jaffé, trans. Richard and Clara Winston (New York: Pantheon Books, 1963), pp. 190–91; hereafter cited in the text as *Memories*.

4. *Essays and Introductions* (New York: Macmillan & Co., 1961), p. 40; hereafter cited in the text as E & I.

5. *Freud and Psychoanalysis*, in *The Collected Works of C. G. Jung*, trans. R. F. C. Hull (Princeton Univ. Press, 1961) IV, par. 727. Jung's *Collected Works* will hereafter be cited in the text as CW with references given by volume and paragraph number.

6. *Memoirs*, ed. Denis Donoghue (New York: The Macmillan Company, 1973), pp. 264–65.

7. *A Vision* (London & New York: Macmillan & Co., 1037), p. 86; hereafter cited in the text as *Vision*.

8. *Mythologies* (New York: The Macmillan Company, 1959), p. 335; hereafter cited in the text as Myth.

9. *Explorations*, selected by Mrs. W. B. Yeats (New York: The Macmillan Company, 1962), p. 366; hereafter cited in the text as Ex.

The Evolution of
William Butler Yeats's
Sequences II (1929–38)   M. L. Rosenthal and Sally M. Gall*

1. *Words for Music Perhaps*

The twenty-five poems of *Words for Music Perhaps*, with the exception of the opening seven Crazy Jane poems, were written in two separate batches: Poems VIII–XX in 1929 and perhaps early 1930, and XXI–XXV in the latter half of 1931. The Crazy Jane poems span these years, three dating from March 1929 (I, VII, II), one from October 1930 (III), one from July 1931 (V), and two from November 1931 (IV, VI). They contain the heart of the sequence and make up a smaller sequence of their own whose essential preoccupation—like that of the volume as a whole—is the true nature of love. Yeats's exploration, however, moves forward by juxtaposition of highly agitated or otherwise intense states of awareness, not by the more logical development of, say, Plato's *Symposium*. Yeats uses to the hilt the opportunities provided by a cast of characters and by various refrains to play off a number of passionate beliefs and experiences against each other. Crazy Jane, all by herself, serves as a mouthpiece for quite a number of moods and perceptions. Indeed she, of all Yeats's characters or personae, approaches most closely the complex sensibility that informs the more directly personal great poems like "Byzantium," "Among School Children," The Circus Animals' Desertion," and "The Man and the Echo."

However, despite the variety, from the opening defiant imprecations of "Crazy Jane and the Bishop" to the exultant torment of "Crazy Jane Grown Old Looks at the Dancers" the shaping force is the same: a driven vision of enrapturing love that can fulfill both body and soul. Concomitant notes of pain, loss, and frustration—inescapable aspects of the mortal, human condition—punctuate the fundamentally ecstatic set of the group.

"Crazy Jane and the Bishop," the opening poem of the sequence, presents Jane's sensibility at its most exacerbated and sets certain key axes of thought and feeling that the rest of the sequence explores:

> Bring me to the blasted oak
> That I, midnight upon the stroke,
> (*All find safety in the tomb.*)
> May call down curses on his head
> Because of my dear Jack that's dead.
> Coxcomb was the least he said:
> *The solid man and the coxcomb.*

*From *The Modern Poetic Sequence: The Genius of Modern Poetry* (New York and Oxford: Oxford University Press, 1983), 122–45.

With typical economy, Yeats plunges us into the middle of an emotional
storm. The speaker here (and throughout the sequence) is identified as
Crazy Jane only by the title; no time is wasted introducing a cast of
characters or describing a dramatic situation. But by the end of the second
stanza we know all we need to of the external events that have brought
Jane to such a pitch:

> Nor was he Bishop when his ban
> Banished Jack the Journeyman,
> (*All find safety in the tomb.*)
> Nor so much as parish priest,
> Yet he, an old book in his fist,
> Cried that we lived like beast and beast:
> *The solid man and the coxcomb.*

Here are the raw materials for a ballad or other melancholy narrative
of lovers' separation and the death of the beloved wandering somewhere in
foreign lands, but Yeats is after a different effect entirely. The plot is
subordinated to a succession of lyric intensities; Jane is hardly a stock
figure from romantic balladry; and the main drive of the sequence is
towards an understanding, in emotional, intellectual, and sensuous terms,
of the highest possibilities of love and its connection with artistic creation.

The emotional assault of the opening poem — dominated by rage —
establishes immediately the enduring nature of the bond between Jack and
Jane. Interference with their passion by the narrowly moralistic has been
neither forgotten nor forgiven with the years; nor, seemingly, could the
gap between two such antagonistic ways of life be bridged in any rational
way. What can Jane do except "spit" at the distorted being who subverts
love in the name of arid spirituality? And what could a man dominated by
such a vision have to say to a woman who exemplifies, for him, sin and
beastliness — except to continue railing? Yeats starts us off on Jane's side in
this debate between orthodox religion and sexual passion — sexual passion
that has endured beyond the grave.

With the second poem, "Crazy Jane Reproved," the hyper-aesthetic
joins the moral-religious and sexual pagan views on love:

> I care not what the sailors say:
> All those dreadful thunder-stones,
> All that storm that blots the day
> Can but show that Heaven yawns;
> Great Europa played the fool
> That changed a lover for a bull.
> *Fol de rol, fol de rol.*
>
> To round that shell's elaborate whorl,
> Adorning every secret track
> With the delicate mother-of-pearl,
> Made the joints of Heaven crack:

> So never hang your heart upon
> A roaring, ranting journeyman.
> *Fol de rol, fol de rol.*

The reproving speaker here is neither the Jane of the first poem, nor the Bishop, nor Yeats exactly. Rather, the voice is that of an artist who perceives that divinity manifests itself in the difficult creation of beautiful form divorced from human turbulence and sexual passion. This speaker would discard Zeus with the bull and would deny the violent energy associated with artistic transcendence. Jane and Yeats would reply *"Fol de rol, fol de rol,"* for this truth is only partial. (The artistically ritualized violence and brutality of the dance in the seventh poem are more to the point, — and poems I, II, and VII, remember, were the original starting points of the sequence.)

The next three poems, "Crazy Jane on the Day of Judgment," "Crazy Jane and Jack the Journeyman," and "Crazy Jane on God" explicitly introduce the supernatural. The Judgment Day in the first of these, if the "he" in that poem is God, is interestingly idiosyncratic. Jane does most of the talking, with God limited to sympathetic-sardonic agreement: *" 'That's certainly the case,' said he."* Also, the small *h* in *"he"* suggests that this is not the final Judgment of traditional Christianity, and obviously Jane is still caught in her obsession with profane rather than divine love. The preposition "on" in the title may of course mean "about" rather than "at," in which case one must read the poem as an intimately relaxed, half-bitter exchange between Jane and her lover — and the "judgment day" of the title simply indicates some ultimate point in time from whose perspective all the implications of love (and life itself) will at last become clear. In any case, this remarkably vivid poem centers on the evocation of extreme states of feeling hardly containable within any boundaries of rational thematic statement. It is clear, though, that Jane's concept of human love involves soul as well as body, and that the first stanza is close to a key perspective already seen in "A Woman Young and Old" and developed with great economy and saving humor in the later "The Three Bushes." Yet the assertion is more a note of yearning than a point of argument:

> "Love is all
> Unsatisfied
> That cannot take the whole
> Body and soul";
> *And that is what Jane said.*

The stanza implicitly synthesizes the opposing positions expressed in the opening poems: Jane's and the Bishop's, the sailor's and the aesthete's. In addition, it sets the scene for the next poem, "Crazy Jane and Jack the Journeyman," where the effects of love satisfied and unsatisfied are juxtaposed and the very nature of love is seen as unfathomable. But it is the simplicities of "Crazy Jane on the Day of Judgment" that are so ambiguously suggestive: the almost delphic opening proclamation we have quoted, the clever self-characterizing of an intense and articulate woman in the second stanza, the description of a day of black desolation (but without explanatory context) in the third, and the return to questions of love's mystery in the fourth. The tonal shifts, together with the alternating ironic refrains — *"And that is what Jane said"* and *" 'That's certainly the case,' said he"* — make for a remarkable play of cosmic bemusement, earthy realism, shivering despair and abandonment, and self-ironic deflation.

If one responds to this tonal mixture primarily, rather than attempting intellectual translation, the poem is perfectly attuned to the passionate opening of "Crazy Jane and Jack the Journeyman," which follows it.

> I know, although when looks meet
> I tremble to the bone,
> The more I leave the door unlatched
> The sooner love is gone,
> For love is but a skein unwound
> Between the dark and dawn.

This first stanza could almost be an embittered woman's worldly comment on the inevitable results of giving oneself to a man. Its tone radiates a mystical desolation (despite an attempt at rational control) encompassing both sexual excitement and its transitoriness. Then, in a characteristically Yeatsian abrupt turn, the second stanza sustains this affect at first — repeating the mystical love-skein image and suggesting that the spirit must shed it in sadness — and then takes an entirely new tack of bright exultation:

> A lonely ghost the ghost is
> That to God shall come;
> I — love's skein upon the ground,
> My body in the tomb —
> Shall leap into the light lost
> In my mother's womb.

The leap after death into the immortal "light lost / In my mother's womb" is impossible — in Jane's passionate, pagan "theology" — without one's having thoroughly explored and exhausted mortal love in one's lifetime. Otherwise, the spirit cannot free itself for that leap into transcendent joy:

> But were I left to lie alone
> In an empty bed,
> The skein so bound us ghost to ghost
> When he turned his head
> Passing on the road that night,
> Mine must walk when dead.

We have here the philosophical center of the Crazy Jane sequence, and the best gloss on the poem is Plato's *The Symposium*. Jane is in some senses a modern version of Socrates' far calmer instructress, Diotima, who (in Benjamin Jowett's translation) tells the world's aptest male pupil:

> For he who has been instructed thus far in the things of love, and he who has learned to see the beautiful in due order and succession, when he comes toward the end will suddenly perceive a nature of wondrous beauty . . . not growing and decaying, or waxing and waning . . . not fair in one point of view and foul in another . . . And the true order of going or being led by another to the things of love, is to use the beauties of earth as steps along which he mounts upwards for the sake of that other beauty . . .

For the reader of Yeats, incidentally, the relation between this passage and the "fair" and "foul" lines in "Crazy Jane Talks with the Bishop" is striking. But our immediate concern is Diotima's idea of using the "things of love" — the "beauties of earth" — to mount upwards toward that "wondrous beauty." (We may well recall the shell imagery in "Crazy Jane Reproved," and the birch tree of "Crazy Jane and the Bishop.") Diotima's vision of transforming delight in eternally beautiful forms is close, of course, to Jane's blissful certainty that she will "leap into the light lost / In my mother's womb." This leap may be contrasted with the difficulty of reaching celestial love while still under the spell of the physical evoked in "The Delphic Oracle upon Plotinus," the closing poem of *Words for Music Perhaps*. "Salt blood blocks his eyes" — that is the predicament of Plotinus, and the usual human predicament when love has not been fully experienced and so we are blocked off forever from ultimate transcendent vision. It would probably be forcing the poem to suggest that Plotinus' purely abstract thought will never enable him to live fully enough to be readied for the higher phase — but Yeats *was* capable of just this kind of paradoxical reversal, giving spiritual priority to the supposedly wanton: Jane over the Bishop.

To return to the poem at hand, we are not talking about impatiently sloughing off obstacles to higher things, but rather of experiencing the "things of love" fully so that the higher beauty will be reached in the only possible way: through "due order and succession." If the process is cut short (a violence symbolized in the Bishop's banishment of Jack), then the situation of the first four poems in the sequence must obtain. In the first, Jack's ghost walks. In the second passion is inadequately valued. In the third Jane is still chained to the things of earthly love. And in the fourth she predicts similar results from being "left to lie alone / In an empty bed." No wonder the curses of the first poem are so violent.

The fifth poem, "Crazy Jane on God," has something of the distancing of "Crazy Jane Reproved," but with its deep, visionary purity prefigures the rich but wryly acquiescent tones of Poems XIV–XX. The God of the title and refrain — *"All things remain in God"* — is like the beautifully creative Heaven of "Crazy Jane Reproved," except that here all the violence of historical and personal change is transmuted into song — "My body makes no moan / But sings on." The next poem, "Crazy Jane Talks with the Bishop," holds the same place in this sequence that "Meeting" does in "A Woman Young and Old." Again we have two furious old people confronting each other, bound together in the one case by their former love, in this case by their passionate commitment to their respective ideas of love. This sixth poem dramatizes the conflict alluded to in "Crazy Jane and the Bishop," but now we have a dialogue at once stinging and exuberant, rather than frenzied raging. And this time Jane has the last word. In the first poem she could only react passionately to being accused of living with her lover like "beast and beast." Here she preempts the Bishop's Christian authority itself. She overrides his arid conception that Love prevails only in a "heavenly mansion, / Not in some foul sty" with her own earthy version, in which "Fair and foul are near of kin, / And fair needs foul." Her own boldly sexual reading of the meaning of Christ's conception and birth ends the dialogue triumphantly:

> "A woman can be proud and stiff
> When on love intent;
> But Love has pitched his mansion in
> The place of excrement;
> For nothing can be sole or whole
> That has not been rent."

We have already noted Diotima's paradoxical comment on fair and foul in *The Symposium*. Beneath the violence of the stanza just quoted, so different in tone from Plato despite its philosophical cast, lurk certain similarities. Part of Diotima's discourse on love touches precisely on the aspect shared by man and beast, the "bodily lowliness" that goes along with the "heart's pride":

> "For love, Socrates, is not, as you imagine, the love of the beautiful only." "What then?" "The love of generation and birth in beauty."

For Crazy Jane, then, being "rent" is necessary for both physical and spiritual (including creative) generation and wholeness. As the refrain has it in "Crazy Jane Grown Old Looks at the Dancers," love is "like the lion's tooth." In this seventh poem, all the more savage intensities of the sequence are aesthetically converted into passionate, murderous dance-movements that powerfully counterbalance hatred and love. The word "love" appears in the refrain only, but the whole implication is that great hatred springs from but one source: equally great love. Even if one disagrees with this interpretation, it is still undeniable that the poem exudes the excitement of artistically controlling a ferocious energy. Here we have the artistic analogue to the creation of the shell's "elaborate whorl," and indeed the human blazes with emotional and sensuous awareness far beyond the creation that "Made the joints of Heaven crack."

Words for Music Perhaps opens with its strongest poems, the "Crazy Jane" group we have just discussed. We shall not go into the others in such detail. Of the next thirteen poems (VIII–XX), "Her Anxiety" (Poem X) and "Three Things" (Poem XV) are probably the most successful. Again, in this 1929 group, we have a movement from youth to old age. "Her Anxiety" focuses the youthful concerns in its two stanzas and refrain:

> Earth in beauty dressed
> Awaits returning spring.
> All true love must die,
> Alter at the best
> Into some lesser thing.
> *Prove that I lie.*
>
> Such body lovers have,
> Such exacting breath,
> That they touch or sigh.
> Every touch they give,
> Love is nearer death.
> *Prove that I lie.*

Yeats catches both the mutual absorption of lovers and its supposed inevitable lessening with the passage of time brilliantly in the second stanza. Yet one might almost wish he had contented himself with his crisply superb opening stanza, whose lyrical start softens the epigrammatic, staccato quality of what follows. At their simplest, the first two lines merely observe that wintry beauty will give way to the even greater beauty of spring. Or perhaps these lines annihilate the succession of seasons of growth and decay between one spring and another. After all, earth dressed in the beauty of one spring can look forward to renewal with absolute certainty, whatever wintry death may intervene. If we favor the first reading, however, "Earth in beauty dressed" provides a curiously erotic image for the bare winter landscape awaiting the spring, analogous to the relationship of human lovers in the next stanza.

In either case, the certainty of spring's return goes counter to the course of love, which — since it resides in mortal, aging bodies — must with equal certainty "alter . . . into some lesser thing." But there is also a resonance (reinforced by the ambiguity we have mentioned) in the first two lines that gives the poem an added poignancy; the spring and rebirth that winter awaits are unavailable to the old. The refrain's demand has been satisfied time and again, incidentally, in "A Man Young and Old," "A Woman Young and Old," the Crazy Jane poems, and here in such poems as "Young Man's Song (IX), "His Confidence" (XI), and "His Bargain (XIV). The "proof" has been furnished in many different ways, all powerfully moving because, despite all the dauntless giving of the lie to time's destructiveness, the poignancy of empirical experience remains undiminished and is powerfully expressed in the very language of the counter-assertions. The heart remains "offended" even as it insists on the immortality of a loved woman's true beauty, as we are shown in "Young Man's Song":

> "She will change," I cried,
> "Into a withered crone."
> The heart in my side,
> That so still had lain,
> In noble rage replied
> And beat upon the bone:
>
> "Uplift those eyes and throw
> Those glances unafraid:
> She would as bravely show
> Did all the fabric fade;
> No withered crone I saw
> Before the world was made."
>
> Abashed by that report,
> For the heart cannot lie,
> I knelt in the dirt.
> And all shall bend the knee
> To my offended heart
> Until it pardon me.

Platonic vision (recalled in words taken from the higher-spirited earlier poem, "Before the World Was Made," in "A Woman Young and Old") transcends earthly ruefulness but does not banish it. The point is made as beautifully but more bluntly in the closing lines of "His Confidence" ("Out of a desolate source, / Love leaps upon its course"). "His Bargain" goes further than all of these poems in its defiance of fatality. Or, at any rate, we are shown how seriously we are to take the earlier allusions to a time "before the world was made." The commitment to unchanging love antedates even "Plato's spindle" and eternity itself — and yet, subtly, the poem's brave show is belied by its tone:

> Who talks of Plato's spindle;
> What set it whirling round?
> Eternity may dwindle,
> Time is unwound,
> Dan and Jerry Lout
> Change their loves about.
>
> However they may take it,
> Before the thread began
> I made, and may not break it
> When the last thread has run,

> A bargain with that hair
> And all the windings there.

"His Bargain" has, with a combined gentle dignity and romantic intensity, brought the spheres of spiritual and profane love together — an acceptance and affirmation of the wildly symbolic offering of the woman who speaks in the preceding poem, "Her Dream." She had dreamed that she had "shorn [her] locks away" and "laid them on Love's lettered tomb" — a surrender to the inevitable death of love, and a mourning sacrifice of her sense of her own womanly beauty. But the cosmos has other plans:

> But something bore them out of sight
> In a great tumult of the air,
> And after nailed upon the night
> Berenice's burning hair.

In both poems love dies but its death is not accepted. Together "Her Dream" and "His Bargain" introduce a reprise, in a less violently passionate key, of the exaltation of love that reached its height earlier on in this sequence with "Crazy Jane Talks with the Bishop" and "Crazy Jane on God." It is the key of mellowed reconciliation.

The new, gentler synthesis can be clearly seen in "Three Things." Here the singing, wave-whitened bone of a woman is like Jane's body singing of past glory in "Crazy Jane on God." The bone celebrates life's sensuous pleasures as if they were the true source of all joy, worldly or otherwise. The three-fold pleasure involves that of her child, men she has gratified, and her own total fulfillment — sexual and spiritual — with her "rightful man." A similar zest for life informs "Lullaby" (XVI), "Those Dancing Days are Gone" (XIX), and the folk refrain of "I am of Ireland" (XX):

> *"I am of Ireland,*
> *And the Holy Land of Ireland,*
> *And time runs on," cried she.*
> *"Come out of charity.*
> *Come dance with me in Ireland."*

The dancing motif is picked up in the first of the closing group of five poems ("The Dancer at Cruachan and Cro-Patrick"), all written in the last half of 1931 and employing a male complement to Crazy Jane, Tom the Lunatic, in all but the twenty-fifth poem. Tom celebrates the sexual principle seen as the vital center of deity and artistic creativity. His last song, "Old Tom Again," is a magnificently paradoxical prophecy of the creative imagination's triumphing over the temporal:

> Things out of perfection sail,
> And all their swelling canvas wear,
> Nor shall the self-begotten fail
> Though fantastic men suppose

> Building-yard and stormy shore,
> Winding-sheet and swaddling-clothes.

Following this incantatory echo of Jane's envisioned leap into the light lost in her mother's womb, comes "The Delphic Oracle upon Plotinus." Just as "A Woman Young and Old," "A Man Young and Old," and the seven Crazy Jane poems end with poems involving a certain amount of aesthetic distancing, so now ends *Words for Music Perhaps*. The Old Tom poems have moved rather far from the personal into epigram and visionary statement; the struggle to realize the ideal through the flesh becomes almost pure symbol in the closing poem:

> Behold that great Plotinus swim,
> Buffeted by such seas;
> Bland Rhadamanthus beckons him,
> But the Golden Race looks dim,
> Salt blood blocks his eyes.

> Scattered on the level grass
> Or winding through the grove
> Plato there and Minos pass,
> There stately Pythagoras
> And all the choir of Love.

2. Between *Words for Music Perhaps* and *Last Poems and Two Plays*

Placed near the end of *The Winding Stair and Other Poems*, "Vacillation" (1931–32) is on the border between long poem and sequence. Mostly it seems a meditation centered on a series of images in poems of varied form, its tonalities ranging from musing to self-exhortation to humble gratitude to remorse to powerful conjuration of the past to self-affirmation: stages of thought as Yeats worries at the proper way to conduct a heroically artistic life. Beyond the personal, however, complex moments of realization are flung into this progression that stab into awareness of the mystery of human existence: the compressed vision, almost abstract, of man's whole condition in Poem I; the strange sexual-sacred images that glisten in Poem II; the moment of pure, blazing bliss reported in IV; the refrain "Let all things pass away" counterpoised to fresh images and violent ones of sheer life-experience in VI; the teasing quarrel with a theologian in VIII. Poem III, a clarion call to artists, ends on a note we remember from "Upon a Dying Lady" and foreshadows "Under Ben Bulben":

> Test every work of intellect or faith,
> And everything that your own hands have wrought,
> And call those works extravagance of breath
> That are not suited for such men as come
> Proud, open-eyed and laughing to the tomb.

Other such foreshadowings of *Last Poems* are of interest here—for instance, the remorseful fifth poem anticipates the powerful "The Man and the Echo." Only Poem IV, however, approaches Yeats at his best, and "Vacillation" as a whole seems mainly a preliminary structuring on its way to *Last Poems*.

The twelve "Supernatural Songs" (c. 1934) are more successful, mainly because they include "What Magic Drum?" (VII), "Meru" (XII), and the fairly successful epigrammatic poem "The Four Ages of Man" (IX). The first seven poems, in the visionary mode, introduce a new character, the mystic Ribh. He adds a more religious-philosophical-historical dimension to Crazy Jane's and Tom the Lunatic's preoccupations with love and the nature of God. Unlike the Bishop, who used an "old book" to destroy Jack's and Jane's love-making, Ribh at the opening of the sequence is reading his "holy book" in the light provided by the celestial love-making of Baile and Aillinn. (This is an expanded and reoriented version of the cleaving of souls in the closing stanzas of "A Last Confession," in "A Woman Young and Old.") Ribh stresses the sexual nature of Divine creation even more vigorously than Tom and denounces "every thought of God mankind has had" (V). (Notice how the line "Hatred of God may bring the soul to God" will be transmuted in "Under Ben Bulben," in Yeats's exhortation to artists to "bring the soul of man to God. / Make him fill the cradles right.") Then, in "What Magic Drum?" Ribh-Yeats fuses male and female, bestial and human, into a wondering, gently awestruck vision of the Godhead utterly in contrast to the imagined violent rough beast slouching "towards Bethlehem to be born" in "The Second Coming":

> He holds him from desire, all but stops his breathing lest
> Primordial Motherhood forsake his limbs, the child no longer rest,
> Drinking joy as it were milk upon his breast.
> Through light-obliterating garden foliage what magic drum?
> Down limb and breast or down that glimmering belly move his mouth
>   and sinewy tongue.
> What from the forest came? What beast has licked its young?

"What Magic Drum?" ushers in a series of poems closely linked to historical cycles (compare "Leda and the Swan" at the opening of the "Dove or Swan" chapter of *A Vision*). In this concern "Supernatural Songs" resembles the civil-war sequences and "Vacillation" more than the love sequences, but with the sexual basis an integral part of historical concern—especially in "Whence Had They Come?" and "Conjunctions." Of the epigrammatic poems in "Supernatural Songs"—"There" (IV), "The Four Ages of Man" (IX), "Conjunctions" (X), and "A Needle's Eye" (XI), the ninth is most successful in its cumulative power, as body, then heart, then mind win, until the final blow falls:

> Now his wars on God begin;
> At stroke of midnight God shall win.

This poem and too many others in "Supernatural Songs" gain much of their interest from the reader's familiarity with Yeats's theories of history and personality as presented in *A Vision*. The sonnet "Meru," like "What Magic Drum?," is enriched by but not dependent on such knowledge. The basic conception is close to that of the sixth section of "Vacillation," with its refrain "Let all things pass away," and to "The Gyres" and "Lapis Lazuli," but the emphasis in "Meru," as in the civil-war sequences, is more on desolate awareness—the "desolation of reality"—than on the tragic joy such awareness may bring:

> Hermits upon Mount Meru or Everest,
> Caverned in night under the drifted snow,
> Or where that snow and winter's dreadful blast
> Beat down upon their naked bodies, know
> That day brings round the night, that before dawn
> His glory and his monuments are gone.

After "Supernatural Songs," the only sequence Yeats published before *Last Poems and Two Plays* was the unique ballad-and-song cluster centered on "The Three Bushes," in the 1938 volume *New Poems*. Written in 1936, it is a small planetary system: a fast-paced ballad about a lady, a lover, and a chambermaid with small units of subjectively concentrated feeling whirling about it, as it were. The ballad is followed by "songs" of the individual characters: three by the lady, one by the lover (hardly the "laughing, crying, sacred song, / A leching song" his hearers ask him to sing in the ballad), and two by the chambermaid.

The six songs dwell on the central sexual experience, the substitution at night of chambermaid for lady, from the three perspectives. Poetically, this structure is an intriguing device for affective exploration, sorting out as it does the essential lyrical elements from their surface ordering in the tale and allowing them to take over from any priorities of suspense or "interpretation" the ballad itself might suggest. The affective exploration also engages with old preoccupations of the poet having to do with body and soul, both in the meaning of love and in the priorities of the artist. The lover, a maker of songs, needs both kinds of love—spiritual and physical—to create. And the lady's deception of him partially resolves the dilemma of "A Last Confession" (Poem IX in "A Woman Young and Old"), in which the woman gives her soul and loves "in misery" but has "great pleasure with a lad" she loves "bodily." It is only partially resolved for her, obviously, since she must wait for death to have complete union—her success symbolized by three bushes on the three graves, growing inextricably together:

> And now none living can,
> When they have plucked a rose there,
> Know where its roots began.
>   *O my dear, O my dear.*

This little sequence is a beautiful reduction of emotional motifs to their essentials before the great final effort in *Last Poems*.

3. *Last Poems and Two Plays*

Thus far we have been discussing Yeats's sequences in their final form. We have not concerned ourselves with earlier printed arrangements or paid any attention to Yeats's various working versions. But it might be useful to remind ourselves that there may be a good deal of shuffling of poems before the final order, or at least the provisionally final order, takes shape. At this stage, new poems or sections may well arrive: here a strengthening of intensity, there a muting contrast, or, very possibly, some further poetic exploration of the implications of two newly juxtaposed poems. One crucial decision may imply a whole flotilla of smaller ones, so that deciding to place a poem exactly *there*, or discard this one entirely, means that something must be dropped or rewritten, or a cluster of poems shifted in position. To hark back for a moment to an earlier chapter, we should note here that — given the special circumstances of Emily Dickinson's life as an essentially unpublished poet — it is more than remarkable that she should have carried the process as far as she did.

Often this process goes on after the first publication. Whitman is only the first in a very long line of sequence shufflers. And to take one small instance in Yeats's work: he made changes in the Crazy Jane grouping between the 1932 Cuala edition of *Words for Music Perhaps* and the 1933 edition of *The Winding Stair and Other Poems*, reversing the order of "Crazy Jane and Jack the Journeyman" and "Crazy Jane on the Day of Judgment" and adding "Crazy Jane Talks with the Bishop" between "Crazy Jane on God" and "Crazy Jane Grown Old Looks at the Dancers." Eventually, however, the original pressure that brought the sequence into being exhausts itself; and even poems resulting from a similar pressure but, say, five years along in the poet's career, will just have to form their own constellation. *This* one is finally filled, although the poet probably seldom feels it is more than a tentative approximation of the best of several possibilities.

When we come to someone's last poems (Sylvia Plath's and Anne Sexton's are cases in point), we are extraordinarily lucky if the poet has had the time or forethought to arrange them for us. True, if he or she had lived just a few days or weeks longer a different order might have emerged; but that contingency, in turn, would demand decisions similar to those we have been discussing. All this is, naturally, by way of preamble to a consideration of *Last Poems and Two Plays* (1939), Yeats's hidden lyric sequence with dramatic complement. It has been very well hidden indeed since 1940, when Macmillan brought out *Last Poems and Plays*, garbling the sequence (originally published in Dublin by the Cuala Press) and reversing the plays' order as well.

The garbling was as follows. First, the nineteen "last" poems were tacked onto the earlier *New Poems* (Cuala Press, 1938). Second, their proper order was disregarded. Three of the opening four poems were shifted to the end *and* rearranged. They include the crucial *opening* poem, "Under Ben Bulben," which was made to *close* both the sequence and the "Lyrical" section of *The Collected Poems*. The original fifth poem, "Three Marching Songs," was dumped, with remarkable insensitivity, further on between "News for the Delphic Oracle" and "Long-Legged Fly." "Hound Voice" and "John Kinsella's Lament for Mrs. Mary Moore" were gratuitously reversed. "The Man and the Echo" leap-frogged over two poems to introduce the new closing group ("Cuchulain Comforted," "The Black Tower," and "Under Ben Bulben"), effectively burying "Politics," Yeats's original choice for the last poem in his last sequence. And third, three poems from *On the Boiler* (Cuala Press, 1939) were inserted: "Why Should Not Old Men Be Mad?," "The Statesman's Holiday," and "Crazy Jane on the Mountain." That the order of the 1939 *Last Poems and Two Plays*, though published six months after Yeats's death, was indeed Yeats's own has been demonstrated conclusively by Curtis Bradford, who located a table of contents in Yeats's handwriting.[1] There is no indication at all that Yeats would have agreed to the 1940 version.

The order of the sequence under discussion, then, is (1) "Under Ben Bulben," (2) "Three Songs to the One Burden," (3) "The Black Tower," (4) "Cuchulain Comforted," (5) "Three Marching Songs," (6) "In Tara's Halls," (7) "The Statues," (8) "News for the Delphic Oracle," (9) "Long-Legged Fly," (10) "A Bronze Head," (11) "A Stick of Incense," (12) "Hound Voice," (13) "John Kinsella's Lament for Mrs. Mary Moore," (14) "High Talk," (15) "The Apparitions," (16) "A Nativity," (17) "The Man and the Echo," (18) "The Circus Animals' Desertion," and (19) "Politics." The lyric section of the book is followed by two plays: *The Death of Cuchulain* and *Purgatory*.

Yeats's sequence, as opposed to Macmillan's nonsequence, moves not toward but away from the prophetic, exhortatory, heroically Irish grappling with death in "Under Ben Bulben" and the poems through "In Tara's Halls." After these it shifts to the heroic, sexual, artistic, classical transcendence of "The Statues," "News for the Delphic Oracle," and "Long-Legged Fly"; to the more personal sexual flaunting and heroic memories of poems 10–14; and to the closing group, in which the poet, under pressure of the terrifying unknown, struggles with some ultimate definitions of his life and art. Eschewing heroics and "high talk" at the last, the poems from "The Apparitions" through "Politics" have their own bravery, dignity, and powerful affirmation of passionate intensity. Here also a rigorous and somewhat appalled self-appraisal balances a touching desire for communion between one human being and another, no matter what the cost to one's pride. This overall progression was of course nullified by the Macmillan editors' apparent desire to give a coolly upbeat heroic ending to Yeats's *oeuvre*. Although we know the last poems he wrote were "Cuchulain Comforted" and "The Black Tower," his aesthetic decisions about where to place them in his sequence are another matter entirely. So was his decision *not* to round off his work with the stoically distanced epitaph closing "Under Ben Bulben"—"*Cast a cold eye / On life, on death! / Horseman, pass by*"—but rather with a passion for life still flaming from his page: "But O that I were young again / And held her in my arms!" (Few life-delirious poets, who hope as well that their art will not perish with them, really favor snapping it shut with an epitaph.)

We are thrown abruptly into Yeats's last sequence, somewhat in the manner of the opening of "A Woman Young and Old" ("She hears me strike the board and say"). The title of that poem, "Father and Child," establishes the dramatic situation. However sudden and striking its first impact, "Under Ben Bulben" is not as specific, so that we are not sure initially who is being asked by whom to swear to what:

> Swear by what the sages spoke
> Round the Mareotic Lake
> That the Witch of Atlas knew,
> Spoke and set the cocks a-crow.
>
> Swear by those horsemen, by those women
> Complexion and form prove superhuman . . .

The cluster of mystifying allusions in these lines contributes to their assault on our capacity for awe and unreasoning response to a challenge. The audience being asked to take the oath turns out, further on, to be a sophisticated modern one that needs to summon up primitive energies: "You that Mitchel's prayer have heard, / 'Send war in our time, O Lord!' " It contains "poet and sculptor," "Irish poets"—in fact all the "indomitable Irishry" willing to preserve heroic and artistic values fast vanishing from Ireland and the world:

> Irish poets, learn your trade,
> Sing whatever is well made,
> Scorn the sort now growing up
> All out of shape from toe to top,
> Their unremembering hearts and heads
> Base-born products of base beds.
> Sing the peasantry, and then
> Hard-riding country gentlemen,
> The holiness of monks, and after
> Porter-drinkers' randy laughter;
> Sing the lords and ladies gay
> That were beaten into the clay
> Through seven heroic centuries;
> Cast your mind on other days
> That we in coming days may be
> Still the indomitable Irishry.

By singing "whatever is well made," poets will be fulfilling the commands given in the preceding section:

> Poet and sculptor, do the work,
> Nor let the modish painter shirk
> What his great forefathers did,
> Bring the soul of man to God.
> Make him fill the cradles right.

The key to spiritual and physical renewal lies in the "other days," in the artists' preservation of the heroic Irish legends and myths and celebration of the intensely alive peasants and aristocrats, with proper attention as well to both "holiness" and randiness. Presumably what the artists are to swear to is that they will follow this artistic program with its social and political and spiritual implications: seek to implement the "profane perfection of mankind" that is the "purpose set / Before the secret working mind." The jaunty rhythms and randiness of some of the language in "Under Ben Bulben" are far in tone from "Her Vision in the Wood" (the eighth poem in "A Woman Young and Old"), where the wounded man is her "heart's victim and its torturer," but the artist's role in providing images of perfection is the same:

> Michael Angelo left a proof
> On the Sistine Chapel roof,
> Where but half-awakened Adam
> Can disturb globe-trotting Madam
> Till her bowels are in heat . . .

The majority of the poems in this sequence are fueled by Yeats's conviction that it is up to the artists following him to continue to provide symbols from the "other days" to counter modern degeneracy. (See also *The Death of Cuchulain* and *Purgatory*, and the very explicit *On the Boiler* for other versions of this preoccupation.) Fortunately the poems are poems, not political rhetoric, and this pragmatic program is rarely as intrusive as it is in "Under Ben Bulben." True, one can find it easily in the lusty swashbuckling of "Three Songs to the One Burden" and "Three Marching Songs." But it is completely subsumed in the two excellent poems sandwiched between the sets of three: "The Black Tower" and "Cuchulain Comforted."

Of course, "The Black Tower" concerns "oath-bound men" waiting for their own "right king" to reappear, but the poem's archetypal evocativeness and complexity involve far more than a staunch holding against modern political and social barbarity. The "burden" of the immediately preceding songs is the heroic refrain "*From mountain to mountain ride the fierce horsemen*," and the last of the three "Songs" is of the 1916 Easter uprising, cast in heroic terms. (The first song celebrates the lusty sexuality of Crazy Jane and her ilk; the second projects a spiritual oasis in the midst of a people given over to the "devil's trade"—a center of power essentialized in the refrain.) The ancient men of the old black tower follow right on the heels of the modern heroes who had "gone out to die / That Ireland's mind be greater, / Her heart mount up on high." The suggestion is strong that men such as Pearse and Connolly were inspired by the enduring image of the oath-bound men of the black tower, those who wait patiently but probably in vain to hear the "king's great horn" again. The poem is a brilliant portrayal of one aspect of a mentality in communion with the past and the great dead. In that sense it projects a fundamental human predicament: of dedication in the face of intolerable odds. The essential hopelessness of the situation comes through in the heroes' response to the excitable, unheroic old cook's naive optimism ("But he's a lying hound") and in the impotence of the dead in the final refrain. Yet the refrain has an exultantly ominous note of reawakening as well:

> There in the tomb the dark grows blacker,
> But wind comes up from the shore:
> They shake when the winds roar,
> Old bones upon the mountain shake.

"Cuchulain Comforted" moves further into a realm of the dead where neither heroic action nor despicable inaction any longer has meaning. A community of cowards teach the individualistic hero to become one of them; all will have become singing birds together. The scene is an unearthly counterpart to "The Black Tower." In both the heroic spirit exists in a kind of Limbo. In the first, its external emblems are strongly asserted, as though enduring in the minds of men of succeeding generations. In the second, it would seem that only art (the "singing" of the birds) preserves faint traces of the memory. (The two poems together bring Pound's "The Return" irresistibly to mind.) In contrast, "Three Marching Songs" militaristically hurtle back to the present and its call for fanatical political action. "In Tara's Halls" presents us with an awkward little parable of the ruler who knows when it is time to abdicate.

Yeats is at his best again in the next three poems: "The Statues," "News for the Delphic Oracle," and "Long-Legged Fly." Passages in *On the Boiler* throw an interesting light on the first of these. Yeats frequently wrote prose drafts of poems but rarely printed them, and so "The Statues" is unusual in its close correspondence to these scattered passages:

> The old Irish poets lay in a formless matrix; the Greek poets kept the richness of those dreams and yet were completely awake. Sleep has no bottom waking on top. Irish can give our children love of the soil underfoot; but only Greek, co-ordination or intensity.

> . . . civilization rose to its high tide mark in Greece, fell, rose again in the Renaissance but not to the same level. But we may, if we choose, not now or soon but at the next turn of the wheel, push ourselves up, being ourselves the tide, beyond that first mark. But no, these things are fated; we may be pushed up.

There are moments when I am certain that art must once again accept those Greek proportions which carry into plastic art the Pythagorean numbers, those faces which are divine become all there is empty and measured. Europe was not born when Greek galleys defeated the Persian hordes at Salamis, but when the Doric studios sent out those broadbacked marble statues against the multiform, vague, expressive Asiatic sea, they gave to the sexual instinct of Europe its goal, its fixed type.[2]

"The Statues" fleshes out this meditation on modern Irish and Classical Greek cross-fertilization superbly, celebrating the artist who carried into "plastic art the Pythagorean numbers" by describing the effect of such statues on the living:

> But boys and girls, pale from the imagined love
> Of solitary beds, knew what they were,
> That passion could bring character enough,
> And pressed at midnight in some public place
> Live lips upon a plummet-measured face.

Nothing else in the poem quite measures up to the shock here of the coming together of flesh and ideal in the superb line "live lips upon a plummet-measured face." The rest of the poem supplies the historical and political justification for this erotic center. "News for the Delphic Oracle" has a similar erotic center, but this time placed at the end rather than the beginning. The poem's movement is from the humorously "sighing" Pythagoras, Plotinus, Irish heroes, and that familiar "choir of love" from "The Delphic Oracle upon Plotinus" (the closing poem of *Words for Music Perhaps*), to the intolerable yearning of these soulful characters for the delights of brawny, earthy sex:

> Foul goat-head, brutal arm appear,
> Belly, shoulder, bum,
> Flash fishlike; nymphs and satyrs
> Copulate in the foam.

"Long-Legged Fly," the best poem in the sequence, touches the heroic, sexual, and artistic centers we have been discussing, but does so purely presentatively and lyrically. In it the meditating mind so strongly present in "The Statues" is relegated to the first line of each stanza and to the haunting refrain, *"Like a long-legged fly upon the stream / His [Her] mind moves upon silence."* Similarly, the lengthy description of the Isles of the Blest and their denizens in "News for the Delphic Oracle" is not as sharply effective as the placing here of three historical figures—Caesar, Helen, and Michelangelo—in concrete, intense vignettes that present them at the height of their own forms of inspiration. The "Caesar" of the first stanza, cast as the preserver of civilization, is caught not in the midst of slaughter but meditating his strategy of conquest. Helen, Yeats's symbol of the sexual force in action in history and art, is glimpsed at the onset of puberty—"part woman, three parts a child"—practicing a dance straight out of the lusty Irish countryside. Finally, Michelangelo is described in the midst of that creative act which will, in the words of "Under Ben Bulben," "disturb globetrotting Madam / Till her bowels are in heat":

> That girls at puberty may find
> The first Adam in their thought,
> Shut the door of the Pope's chapel,
> Keep those children out.
> There on that scaffolding reclines
> Michael Angelo.
> With no more sound than the mice make
> His hand moves to and fro.
> *Like a long-legged fly upon the stream*
> *His mind moves upon silence.*

All three figures are in utterly self-absorbed reverie, silently concentrating all their energies toward whatever form of creation is their *métier*—military action, physical beauty, art. Whatever the violent and generative impact of the results of such thought, the act of creation itself belongs to another realm, on which the outside world—soldiers, barking dogs, neighing ponies, the young girl's companions, noisy children—must not be allowed to intrude. *Yeats* may speculate on the results of Caesar's plans, Helen's perfection of her beauty, Michelangelo's painting, and all their analogues in every generation—as he does in the first line of each stanza. But he has depicted the creative figures themselves as yielding totally to the act, not to its results. Hence the singular purity of effect compared with the exhortations in "Under Ben Bulben."

"A Bronze Head," the next poem, introduces personal reminiscence into this sequence for the first time. Yeats is meditating on what is probably a representation of Maud Gonne but could be that of any woman who gave herself to some form of extremism, destroying imaginative possibility and wholeness of being. In the first stanza he contemplates the contrast between the work of art and the terrifying emptiness of the old woman who, like "man" in "Meru," has evidently ravened, raged, and uprooted until she has achieved a similar "desolation of reality"—"*Hysterica passio* of its own emptiness." From there Yeats slides into a consideration of which stage of the woman's life was the "real" one, and of his own prescience in youth of what she would become. In the final stanza he endows her with his hatred of modern degeneracy. The images are variations on ones familiar from the earlier sequences and from "Under Ben Bulben," the six songs, and "The Statues":

> Or else I thought her supernatural
> As though a sterner eye looked through her eye
> On this foul world in its decline and fall;
> On gangling stocks grown great, great stocks run dry,
> Ancestral pearls all pitched into a sty,

Heroic reverie mocked by clown and knave
And wondered what was left for massacre to save.

Fortunately, this is the end of the relatively unalloyed eugenics theme in
the lyrics, although in *Last Poems and Two Plays* one encounters strong
statements of it in the old man's prologue to *The Death of Cuchulain* and
in *Purgatory* as well. And with "A Stick of Incense," a candidate for one of
Yeats's worst poems, unalloyed sniggering crudeness exits as well.

Of the next five poems—"Hound Voice," "John Kinsella's Lament for
Mrs. Mary Moore," "High Talk," "The Apparitions," and "A Nativity"—the
fourth and fifth most effectively sound the notes that will dominate the
end of the sequence. "Hound Voice" is a personalized, not very effective
draft, in a sense, of "The Black Tower"; and the "Lament" is a small
vaudevillian masterpiece whose bawdy surface comedy barely conceals its
far-reaching elegiac strain. "High Talk" starts with a flamboyant bit of
boasting—"no modern stalks" upon stilts higher than the poet's—but at
the same time there are several disquieting elements. These are, first,
failure to match the accomplishment of one's forebears; second, the
necessity to start all over again—to "take to chisel and plane"—and
finally, the closing passage that recalls, although it does not match, the
image of the swan leaping into the desolate heaven in the third section of
"Nineteen Hundred and Nineteen." Once again we have the heroic spirit
braving death:

Malachi Stilt-Jack am I, whatever I learned has run wild,
From collar to collar, from stilt to stilt, from father to child.
All metaphor, Malachi, stilts and all. A barnacle goose
Far up in the stretches of night; night splits and the dawn breaks loose;
I, through the terrible novelty of light, stalk on, stalk on;
Those great sea-horses bare their teeth and laugh at the dawn.

In contrast, "The Apparitions" mocks such fantasizing, projecting an
aging figure desperately assuring himself that he has a "full" heart and the
strength to bear the "increasing Night / That opens her mystery and
fright." His appalled awareness of oncoming death is carried by the
refrain, *"Fifteen apparitions have I seen; / The worst a coat upon a
coathanger."* Personal fear is touched on here, as it is to some extent in the
the closing couplet of "A Nativity":

Why is the woman terror-struck?
Can there be mercy in that look?

"The Man and the Echo," the first of the powerful closing triad, limns
the struggle of the "old and ill" poet to put his actions "in one clear view"
and stand in "judgment on his soul." The result is terror, not peace. The
"echo" has no message except death and mystery; and instead of the
"terrible novelty of light" in "High Talk," the final image is of the poet
deep in the dark cleft, listening to a death cry:

> Up there some hawk or owl has struck,
> Dropping out of sky or rock,
> A stricken rabbit is crying out,
> And its cry distracts my thought.

This darkest moment in the sequence is followed by a strenuous consideration of the sources of Yeats's art—as "The Man and the Echo" is concerned to some extent with the disastrous effect of his art and actions on certain individuals. Throwing aside the symbols and "stilted boys" of his earlier work, the poet returns to the "heart" that had originally provided the impetus for his work until his creations took all his love, "and not those things that they were emblems of." The staggering difference between then and now is conveyed by the contrast between the dream-images that once grew out of a heart "embittered" by need and the squalid reality that is the heart's ultimate, "foul" workshop:

> Those masterful images because complete
> Grew in pure mind but out of what began?
> A mound of refuse or the sweepings of the street,
> Old kettles, old bottles, and a broken can,
> Old iron, old bones, old rags, that raving slut
> Who keeps the till. Now that my ladder's gone,
> I must lie down where all the ladders start,
> In the foul rag-and-bone shop of the heart.

The pure mind—like that conveyed so powerfully in "Long-Legged Fly"—is only half the creative process. At the end of his life, Yeats savagely sums up the leavings of a lifetime, which are now only the contents of his heart. The closing stanza, especially, points up the infuriating dichotomy between the enduring art images and the all-too-mortal flesh and leads brilliantly into the last poem, "Politics," with its poignant focusing on the dominating desire of the old man—not for political or artistic achievement, but for youth and love:

> And maybe what they say is true
> Of war and war's alarms,
> But O that I were young again
> And held her in my arms!

This heart's truth, affirmed in the midst of impending war, involves only the individual: *his* anguish; *his* longing; *his* affirmation of love. Here is the kind of intensity of feeling on which Yeats's art has been based throughout. No *artist* can both "cast a cold eye / On life, on death" and create "masterful images" that outlive the poet and affect the future.

Notes

1. "Yeats's *Last Poems* Again," in *Yeats Centenary Papers*, ed. Liam Miller (Dublin: Dolmen Press, 1966), pp. 259–88. *The Poems of W. B. Yeats: A New Edition*, ed. Richard J.

Finneran (New York: Macmillan, 1983; London: Macmillan, 1984), separates *New Poems* and *Last Poems* and orders them properly at long last.

2. William Butler Yeats, *On the Boiler* (Dublin: The Cuala Press, 1939), pp. 28, 29, and 37 respectively.

BIBLIOGRAPHY

The annotated list below includes only collections of previously published material, not gatherings of original scholarship. With the exception of the first, all of the volumes offer introductions by their editors. They are listed in chronological order of publication.

Some Critical Appreciations of William Butler Yeats as Poet, Orator, and Dramatist. New York: n.p., 1903. Perhaps the rarest item in Yeats criticism, this pamphlet was prepared by John Quinn in conjunction with Yeats's first American lecture tour. It offers sixteen brief selections, including a letter from Robert Louis Stevenson praising "The Lake Isle of Innisfree."

The Permanence of Yeats. Edited by James Hall and Martin Steinmann. New York: Macmillan, 1950. The seminal collection of early criticism, this volume contains work from as early as 1919, J. Middleton Murry's notorious review of *The Wild Swans at Coole* ("a swan song"), through 1948. Most of the leading New Critics are represented, as are W. H. Auden and T. S. Eliot, the latter with his landmark 1940 lecture on "The Poetry of W. B. Yeats." Useful in its time, the "Select Bibliography" has been superseded by K. P. S. Jochum's massive *W. B. Yeats: A Classified Bibliography of Criticism* (Urbana, Chicago, and London: University of Illinois Press, 1978).

Yeats. Edited by B. R. Mullik. Delhi: Chand, 1961. Of little interest, this volume reprints selections from seven books, 1934–58.

Yeats: A Collection of Critical Essays. Edited by John Unterecker. Engelwood Cliffs, N.J.: Prentice-Hall, 1963. A useful collection of work published from the 1940s through the early 1960s. Of particular note is the only printing of the revised version of Curtis Bradford's important essay on "Yeats's Byzantium Poems: A Study of Their Development."

Yeats: Last Poems. A Casebook. Edited by Jon Stallworthy. London: Macmillan, 1968. Includes criticism of both *New Poems* (1938) and *Last Poems and Two Plays* (1939). The volume offers material from the 1930s, both critical comment and a selection from the correspondence of Yeats and Dorothy Wellesley, as well as from later scholarship, mainly of the 1960s. Of special interest in Curtis Bradford's essay on the proper order of *Last Poems*.

William Butler Yeats: The Byzantium Poems. Edited by Richard J. Finneran. Columbus, Ohio: Charles E. Merrill, 1969. A casebook on "Sailing to Byzantium" and "Byzantium," including some relevant selections from Yeats's prose.

W. B. Yeats: A Critical Anthology. Edited by William H. Pritchard. Harmondsworth, England: Penguin, 1972. The fullest and the best gathering since *The Permanence of Yeats*, this volume contains commentary from as early as 1886 (Gerard Manley Hopkins) through 1971 (essays by Helen Vendler and the editor). Some excerpts by Yeats are also provided. Yvor Winters's unsympathetic *The Poetry of W. B. Yeats* (1960) is included in full.

Critics on Yeats. Edited by Raymond Cowell. London: George Allen and Unwin, 1971. An unimaginative collection, with brief excerpts from some contemporary accounts followed by equally brief selections from later critics.

William Butler Yeats: A Collection of Criticism. Edited by Patrick J. Keane. New York: McGraw Hill, 1973. A solid collection of criticism of the 1950s and the 1960s, including such important essays as Northrop Frye's "The Top of the Tower: A Study of the Imagery of Yeats" (1970). The "Selected Bibliography" is particularly useful, though some of the works cited as "soon-to-be published" never appeared.

W. B. Yeats: The Critical Heritage. Edited by A. Norman Jeffares. London, Henley, and Boston: Routledge and Kegan Paul, 1977. This volume contains 155 selections, dating from 1884 to 1939, most of them reviews. Although some valuable material is offered, the editing of the collection is quite inadequate, as demonstrated in "W. B. Yeats: Some Recent Bibliographical and Editorial Work," *Review*, 1 (1979): 233–49.

Yeats: Poems, 1919–1935. Edited by Elizabeth Cullingford. London: Macmillan, 1984. This volume covers the poems from the expanded edition of *The Wild Swans at Coole* (1919) through *A Full Moon in March* (1935). It includes substantial excerpts from Yeats's own writings as well as contemporary comments and criticism from 1949 to 1974.

INDEX